The Reconstruction
of Disturbed Arid Lands

AAAS Selected Symposia Series

Published by Westview Press, Inc.
5500 Central Avenue, Boulder, Colorado

for the

American Association for the Advancement of Science
1333 H Street, N.W., Washington, D.C.

The Reconstruction of Disturbed Arid Lands

An Ecological Approach

Edited by Edith B. Allen

AAAS Selected Symposium **109**

AAAS Selected Symposia Series

This Westview softcover edition is printed on acid-free paper and bound in softcovers that carry the highest rating of the National Association of State Textbook Administrators, in consultation with the Association of American Publishers and the Book Manufacturers' Institute.

Published in 1988 in the United States of America by Westview Press, Inc., 5500 Central Avenue, Boulder, Colorado 80301, and in the United Kingdom by Westview Press, Inc., 13 Brunswick Centre, London WC1N 1AF, England

Library of Congress Cataloging-in-Publication Data
The Reconstruction of disturbed arid lands: an ecological approach/
  edited by Edith B. Allen.
      p. cm. -- (AAAS selected symposium; #109)
  Includes bibliographies.
  ISBN 0-8133-7716-1
  1. Reclamation of land. 2. Arid regions ecology.
3. Revegetation. I. Allen, Edith B. II. Series: AAAS selected
symposium; 109.
S613.R42 1988   88-28687
631.6'4--dc19   CIP

Printed and bound in the United States of America

The paper used in this publication meets the requirements of the American National Standard for Permanence of Paper for Printed Library Materials Z39.48-1984.

10   9   8   7   6   5   4   3   2   1

About the Series

The AAAS Selected Symposia Series was begun in 1977 to provide a means for more permanently recording and more widely disseminating some of the valuable material that is discussed at the AAAS Annual National Meetings. The volumes in this series are based on symposia held at the Meetings that address topics of current and continuing significance, both within and among the sciences, and in the areas in which science and technology have an impact on public policy. The series format is designed to provide for rapid dissemination of information, so the papers are reproduced directly from camera-ready copy. The papers published in the series are organized and edited by the symposium organizers, who then become the editors of the various volumes. Most papers published in the series are original contributions that have not been previously published, although in some cases additional papers from other sources have been added by an editor to provide a more comprehensive view of a particular topic. Symposia may be reports of new research or reviews of established work, particularly work of an interdisciplinary nature, since the AAAS Annual Meetings typically embrace the full range of the sciences and their societal implications.

ARTHUR HERSCHMAN
Head, Meetings and Publications
American Association for the
Advancement of Science

Contents

vii

Acknowledgments

This volume contains the proceedings of a symposium sponsored by the American Association for the Advancement of Science in May 1986, plus some invited chapter contributors. I thank the Institute for Land Rehabilitation, Utah State University, Logan, and the AAAS for their financial support of the international contributors. The Department of Range Science, Utah State University, provided support in the preparation of this volume, and special thanks go to Roma Henderson for her time and patience. Chapters in this volume were externally reviewed, and I thank the reviewers for their useful suggestions.

Edith B. Allen

1. Introduction

The desertification of arid and semi-arid lands is proceeding at a rapid rate worldwide. Over 9 million km^2 are severely disturbed by soil erosion and salinization (Dregne 1983), and are in need of reconstruction to return them to their former or some other useful state. Most of the attempts to reconstruct these lands are based on agronomic, rather than ecological, concepts to reintroduce native or other non-crop species. An agronomic approach is appropriate for high-yield crop or pasture lands, but where the goal is to establish a stable, self-sustaining ecosystem that requires minimal additional resources from man, an ecological approach is needed. For example, seeding or planting in rows, fertilization, and irrigation are currently practiced to reestablish native ecosystems, but these practices bear little relationship to natural processes of establishment, are expensive to maintain, and can be inhibitory to successful establishment of desirable arid plants. Each of the chapters in this volume emphasizes an understanding and application of the basic ecological relationships among plants, animals, microorganisms, the physical environment and man to reconstruct useful, primarily wildland ecosystems.

Several terms are used to describe the return of disturbed lands to a useful state. Three of them, restoration, reclamation, and rehabilitation, were defined by a National Academy of Sciences committee concerned with surface coal mining in the western United States (NAS 1974). According to the committee, restoration implies that the exact conditions before

1

mining will be replicated afterwards. Reclamation was
defined to mean that the site will be similar in
ecological functioning after disturbance, and will be
habitable for similar but not necessarily the same
organisms. Rehabilitation means that the land will be
made useful, but with a different land use and usually
different species. Since all three revegetation goals,
especially the former two, are represented in this book,
clearly none of these three terms alone would be
appropriate. Reconstruction is used as a compromise
term; the dictionary definition is to build an image of
what something was in its original form. Thus it covers
most of the efforts described in the chapters of this
volume.

The range of precipitation zones covered in this
volume is actually broader than the ecological definition
of aridity. Arid and semi-arid lands are of primary
concern, but two of the chapters discuss subhumid lands,
one including open _Eucalyptus_ forest (chapter by Bell)
and one on tall grass prairie (Burton et al.). Since
periodic drought is a problem in plant establishment in
subhumid lands, these chapters are relevant to true arid
lands. Hyperarid environments are not included here
because their productivity is so low that they are seldom
subject to disturbance by man (Dregne 1983). Because of
low post-reconstruction economic returns, most
reconstruction is limited to semiarid or moister
ecosystems (e.g., Naveh and Lieberman 1984). Exceptions
to this are on arid mined lands where revenues generated
from the mineral extracted are mandated for the cost of
reconstruction (chapters by Depuit and Redente,
Whitford), and on sites where natural or man-induced
water harvesting occurs for increased productivity (Yair
and Shachak 1982). An ecological approach that enhances
the processes of natural succession may also make
reconstruction of more arid lands economically feasible.

This volume examines a variety of disturbances.
Agriculture and domestic grazing are by far the greatest
causes of desertification, and are the subject for
reconstruction in the chapters by Burton et al., Naveh,
E. Allen, Whitford, and Greenwood. Fire is treated as a
disturbance primarily in the chapter by Oechel. Mining
figures importantly in four of the chapters (Bell, Depuit
and Redente, E. Allen, M. Allen) even though the land
area disturbed by mining is minuscule compared to the

worldwide problem of desertification. For instance, some 930,000 ha have been surface mined for coal in the United States (U.S.DOE 1984). However, mining is often a more severe disturbance than others. It has received much public attention and, in response to public pressure, is subject to reclamation laws in many nations. The importance of mining disturbances is thus not related to the land area disturbed, but rather to the amount of funded research and the number of hectares that consequently have been reclaimed. These efforts represent a unique ecological data base to be used to reconstruct many other kinds of arid and semiarid disturbances.

The ecosystems discussed are as diverse as the kinds of disturbances. They include semiarid Mediterranean ecosystems (Oechel, Naveh), arid and semiarid shrub-grasslands (Depuit and Redente, Whitford, Greenwood, E. Allen, M. Allen), tall grass prairie (Burton et al.), and open forest (Bell).

Basic questions about reconstruction of the structure and functioning of ecosystems are addressed from different disciplinary viewpoints. The first two chapters largely take an autecological approach. Residual and colonizing seeds after disturbance may dictate plant community composition during later succession (Bell), and seedling tolerance to drought stress in part determines the initial composition after fire (Oechel).

The remaining chapters are synecological in approach. Burton et al. take the restoration ecologist's view of recreating a predisturbance community to discuss how an understanding of resource partitioning in undisturbed communities will aid in restoring those communities. The next chapter (E. Allen), focuses on different initial conditions that may dictate the subsequent trajectory of succession. The chapter by M. Allen is concerned with plant architecture and dispersion, where the pattern in which plants are introduced into a disturbed site specifically determines the microorganisms as well as hastening the rate of succession of the ecosystem as a whole. The relationships between plants and microorganisms, and the decomposition and mineralization functions the microorganisms should carry out in reconstructed land, are explored by Whitford. Depuit and Redente examine the

3

effects that different reconstruction techniques have on ecosystem development.

Greenwood and Naveh take a landscape scale approach. Disruption of the hydrologic cycle and its reconstruction by reintroduction of appropropriate plant species is Greenwood's theme. Naveh discusses the importance of understanding the entire landscape before making decisions on reconstruction, as there are interactions among the landscape elements that will affect the outcome of any reconstruction process.

While the authors take different approaches to reconstruction ranging from population to physiological, community, ecosystem and landscape ecology, there is a central theme that appears in each of the chapters. Each of the authors asks whether restoration to a predisturbance state is possible, or whether we must settle for reclamation or rehabilitation. The different viewpoints are compared in the concluding chapter.

LITERATURE CITED

Dregne, H.E. 1983. Desertification of Arid Lands. Advances in Desert and Arid Land Technology and Development. Volume 3. Harwood Academic Publishers, Chur, Switzerland.

National Academy of Sciences. 1974. Rehabilitation Potential of Western Coal Lands. Ballinger Publishing Company, Cambridge, Massachusetts.

Naveh, Z. and A.S. Lieberman. 1984. Landscape Ecology. Theory and Application. Springer-Verlag, New York.

United States Department of Energy. 1984. Ecological Studies of Disturbed Landscapes. A Compendium of the Results of Five Years of Research Aimed at the Restoration of Disturbed Ecosystems. Office of Scientific and Technical Information DOE/NBM-5009372.

Yair, A. and M. Shachak. 1982. A case study of energy, water and soil flow chains in an arid ecosystem. Oecologia 54: 389-397.

2. Seed-related Autecology in Restoration of Mined Jarrah Forest in Western Australia

ABSTRACT

A basic understanding of the autecology of native species is essential to restoration of mine sites. The soil seed bank of the jarrah (<u>Eucalyptus</u> <u>marginata</u>) forest of Western Australia provides sufficient seed ($101-1,579$ seeds m^{-2}), but the floristic composition was found to be inappropriate to reconstruct the species-rich, shrub-dominated understorey of the native ecosystem. A phenology of seed availability facilitated efficient collection of appropriate seed and experiments on viability and germination stimuli ensured maximization of the re-establishment phase in bauxite and coal mining restoration. Characteristics of the native habitat (e.g. fire and soil pH) provided clues to expected tolerance of species to the post-mining environment. Knowledge that the 'initial floristic composition' model of forest succession best described the jarrah forest succession pattern lead to the realization of the importance of <u>initially</u> providing as many of the species of the native forest ecosystem as possible since plant establishment is limited to the first year following disturbance. Use of seed bearing topsoil, pre-treated understorey species seed, and nursery-stock tree seedlings ensures the most economical method to rapidly reconstruct damaged regions of the jarrah forest following bauxite and coal mining.

INTRODUCTION

How to Select and Plant Pumpkin Seeds
by W.H. Blackwell, Jr.

Use atomic hybrid golden X sexy
Gynomorphic variety only of course but
Don't neglect to nick the rims
And then
Flat side down and
Not too deep you know
About 6-8 per hill and
Hills not too high (avoids runoff) and
About 6 feet apart or
8 if there's room and
By all means
Put some potash in your hole
Or else 10-5-5 or
5-5-10 and
Crumble the dirt in
Preferably friable (good crumb structure) and
Humic (plenty of cow shit) and
Good sand content for workability.

Or else

Just stick the suckers in the ground.

Blackwell (1978) provides a somewhat whimsical recipe for the successful establishment of pumpkin. Most weekend gardeners opt for a strategy lying somewhere between the two implied endpoints in this continuum. Their plans and desires will usually lie further up the continuum of complexity than the ultimate standard of field activity. The realities of time, money and energy are the most common causes of reduced level of accomplishment.

The continuum of accomplishment for the reconstruction of disturbed ecosystems is even wider than those between Blackwell's pumpkin establishment techniques. I would hope that the goal of every applied ecologist working in the reconstruction of disturbed lands would be to establish an ecosystem which provides all the structural and functional attributes of the pre-disturbance ecosystem in their region of concern. Legal requirements for restoration rarely consider functional ecosystem goals. In many countries of the world, governmental requirements for reconstruction of disturbed lands often read something like Blackwell's first technique - a combination of individually reasonable and tested assumptions which, when added together, cannot be accomplished under the existing technical and economic realities of the day. The "ability to pay" generally also comes into the continuum of accomplishment. Large multinational mining companies are generally expected to reconstruct their minesites to a far greater extent than small local companies. Individual small claim owners are not pressured to do any reconstruction at all in all but the most progressive countries. The "do nothing" end of the reconstruction continuum would therefore lie beyond that of Blackwell's second technique in the establishment of pumpkin plants.

The Darling Range of Western Australia provides the people of Western Australia with major economic resources in timber, minerals, fresh water and recreation. Management and control of land use in this region lies with the State Government of Western Australia primarily through the Department of Conservation and Land Management. Mining of bauxite and coal are major mineral extraction activities in this region of native forest vegetation. As with other lands, managers generally seek to maximize output and to minimize costs (Bormann and Likens 1969). They also have the added responsibility of protecting the producing capital of their land for future generations. The re-establishment of a species-rich forest ecosystem with its unique characteristics of ecosystem structure and function is the challenge of mining rehabilitation in the Darling Range. This chapter outlines some of the research carried out in cooperation with the Department of Conservation and Land Management, Alcoa of Australia Ltd. and Western Collieries Ltd. on aspects of rehabilitation of mined land in the Darling Range. The emphasis will be on seed-related autecology beginning with a characterization of the soil seed bank, its component inputs and outputs, and the ultimate influence of this bank of propagules on the achievement of the ultimate goal of re-establishing this species-rich forest ecosystem.

7

EXISTING FOREST ECOSYSTEMS

The jarrah (<u>Eucalyptus</u> <u>marginata</u> Donn ex Sm.) forest of south-west Western Australia lies predominantly in the Darling Range just east and then extending to the south of Perth, the capital city. Physiographically the "Darling Range" is merely the south-western margin of the Great Plateau of Western Australia (Mulcahy et al. 1972). The dominant granites of the plateau have weathered primarily to the ferruginous and aluminous gravels characterized now as sandy, nutrient-poor, red and yellow laterites (Smith 1952). The sedimentary strata in the rift valley, Collie Basin region weather to beached sandy soils with compacted pan-like layers below. The climate is a typical Mediterranean one, oceanic with winter rain (Koeppen's classification Csb), except that it is somewhat more equitable than the other Mediterranean regions such as California, Chile, South Africa and Morocco. Rainfall in the region of the jarrah forest ranges from approximately 600 mm per annum on the eastern boundary to nearly 1,400 near the town of Dwellingup with the majority falling between May and October. The comparative equitability is attributed by Gentilli (1948) to warm ocean currents along the coast. The native vegetation structure is an open forest with a generally depauperate overstorey dominated by jarrah with marri (<u>Eucalyptus</u> <u>calophylla</u> Lindle) the major associate (Havel 1975). The understorey of sclerophyllous shrubs can be extremely rich (Havel 1975, Bell and Koch 1980) with members of the Papillionaceae, Proteaceae and Myrtaceae the most common families. Herbaceous perennial herbs are scattered throughout the understorey but annuals are somewhat uncommon in mature forest areas.

MINING REHABILITATION

Alcoa of Australia Ltd. mines bauxite in the Darling Range. Each year about 300 ha of mined land are reconstructed. This involves landscaping the mined area, returning fresh topsoil, deep ripping, sowing seed of native understorey species (mainly legumes), planting eucalypt seedlings and fertilizing (Tacey 1979).

Western Collieries Ltd. mine bituminous coal in the Collie Basin in the southern part of the Darling Range.

Following open-cut coal extraction, the pits are refilled with overburden, contoured and spread with topsoil. Native seed mixes are spread, Eucalyptus and other seedlings planted and fertilizer added. A range of ameliorating agents are currently being tested to reduce soil acidity of raw overburden when insufficient fresh topsoil is available. Western Collieries rehabilitates about 30 ha per year.

Both mining companies respread topsoil as part of the rehabilitation process. The topsoil provides organic matter, soil-stored seed and vegetative propagules, and the soil organisms essential for the rapid establishment of mycorrhizal and symbiotic nitrogen-fixation associations with establishing seedlings. The seed mixes contain primarily jarrah forest legumes and other easily collected native species. The native legumes are predominantly species which appear early in the natural sequence of succession following fire in the jarrah forest (Bell and Koch 1980). During reconstruction they are expected to supplement the poor nitrogen regime of the disturbed ecosystems early in the revegetation process and to help establish a nutrient cycling pattern more rapidly as they tend to be much shorter-lived than most other shrubs of the jarrah forest understorey (Ward et al. 1985).

SOIL SEED BANK

In most habitats occupied by higher plants, the number of individuals present as seeds greatly exceeds the number present as growing plants. This reserve of seeds present in the soil and on its surface has been termed the 'soil seed bank' (Harper 1977). The seed bank is supplemented by additions following each reproductive event (seed rain) and diminished through seed predation, seed loss through decay and senescence and due to germination of viable seed (Fig. 1).

In the context of the reconstruction of mine sites in the jarrah forest, particular information concerning the seed bank is essential. Seed quantities and the species composition of the bank of propagules are important as the topsoil transfer step in the rehabilitation is partly designed to provide a source of seed to the newly

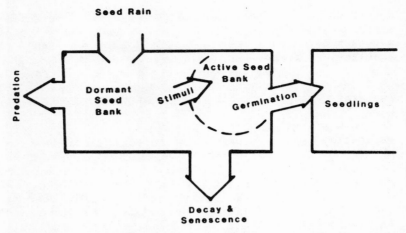

Fig. 1. Theoretical diagram of the events affecting the soil seed bank (after Harper 1977).

revegetated mine regions. In order to maximize the transfer from the seed bank to the seedling stage in revegetation, a number of ecologically important questions must be raised. Among these are: (1) Do we know all there is to know about the seed bank of the jarrah forest? (2) Are we sufficiently knowledgeable about the stimuli which change dormant seed into seed which will germinate with available winter rains? (3) Are we sufficiently aware of the process of germination for all jarrah forest species to optimize this transfer step? and (4) Do we know all there is to know about the type, quantity and periodicity of input of seeds to the seed bank?

SEED BANK RESEARCH

Past research on soil seed banks from a range of habitats provides some expectations concerning the numbers of seed to expect in topsoils of the jarrah forest (Table 1). Grasslands and marshes tend to have greater stores of viable seeds in the soil seed bank than shrublands or forests. Severe habitats such as the saline marsh, high altitude or latitude forests tend to have relatively few seeds in the soil seed bank. Tilled arable soils have a wide range of seed numbers. Of significance is that the soil seed banks would seem to contain sufficient numbers of seed to provide the reconstruction needs of establishing seedling numbers for most regions of the world.

Table 1. Quantities of viable seed in the soil seed store of a range of habitat soils and regions.

Vegetation Type	Seeds per m^2 Minimum	Source
Tilled Agricultural Soils		
Arable Fields - England	28,700	Benchley and Warrington 1930
Arable Fields - Canada	5,000	Bodd et al. 1954
Arable Fields - U.S.A.	1,000	Robinson 1949
Arable Fields - Honduras	7,620	Kellmann 1974a
Grasslands and Marshes		
Freshwater Marsh - U.S.A.	6,405	Leck and Graveline 1979
Saltwater Marsh - U.S.A.	31	Milton 1939
Perennial Meadow - Wales	38,000	Chippendale 1934
Meadow Steppe - U.S.S.R.	18,875	Golubeva 1962
Annual Grassland - U.S.A.	29,000	Major and Pyott 1966
Shrublands and Heaths		
Heath - Wales	17,500	Chippendale 1934
Forests		
Fir Forest - U.S.S.R.	12,000	Karpov 1960
Secondary Forest - U.S.A.	12,000	Oosting and Humphries 1940
Subalpine Forest - U.S.A.	3	Whipple 1978
Subartic Forest - Canada	0	Johnson 1975
Conifer Forest - Canada	1,000	Kellman 1970
Primary Forest - Canada	206	Kellman 1974b

For the jarrah forest of Western Australia, recent data indicate that the soil seed bank contains numbers of seed which would rank it somewhere near the low end of forest sites around the world (Table 2) (Vlahos and Bell 1986). Densities of the jarrah forest seed bank ranged from 388 to 1579 seeds m^{-2} in natural forest regions. Estimates from the available seed bank in a sample of the soils being transported to bauxite reconstruction sites were lower (101-167 seeds m^{-2}) but this may be due to the dilution effect of incorporating a deeper cut of soil in the reconstructed topsoils compared to the samples taken for the study of the jarrah forest seed store components. As the general aim of bauxite reconstruction is to achieve a density of at least one plant per m^2 after the first year of establishment, the total of more than 100 per m^2, assuming viability, seems sufficient for these quantitative purposes.

Table 2. Quantities of viable seed germinated under glasshouse conditions from field collected soil.

Jarrah Forest	Seeds per m^2	Source
Site 1	876	Vlahos and Bell 1986
Site 2	1,579	"
Site 3	743	"
Site 4	468	"
Site 5	558	"
Site 6	388	"
Transported Topsoil		
Lot 1	101	This paper
Lot 2	167	"

Species composition of the reconstruction of Darling Range sites is also an important criterion of revegetation success. The shrub-dominated understorey of the jarrah forest can be very rich, with 40 m plots usually containing more than 30 species (Bell and Koch 1980). If the reconstructed regions are to function as the original forest ecosystem, as many of the original species as possible should be established in the reconstructed ecosystems.

Literature sources on species composition of the seed bank indicate that the prominent species existing as seed in the soil can often be very different from the living vegetatative flora (Table 3). This appears very true of the ecologically more complex ecosystems of forests where the soil seed store usually harbors seeds of earlier successional periods. The soil seed store of the jarrah forest is also dominated by seed of species not commonly found in the existing vegetation (Vlahos and Bell 1986). Density estimates of the jarrah forest soil seed bank reveal that the vast majority of seeds are from annual and subshrub species despite the predominance of shrubs in the existing vegetation (Fig. 2). From these data it is apparent that greater numbers of species of shrub seed must be supplemented to successfully return the currently dominant species to the reconstructed ecosystems.

In an attempt to determine the proportion of species in the native forest to the reconstructed mine sites, a series of comparisons were made using plots from areas in the forest remaining near the source of topsoil and in the reconstructed mine sites where this topsoil was spread. Because the mine sites also received the mix of legumes it was impossible to tell whether these particular legume species were also transported as components of the soil seed bank. The data on percentage of species successfully returned by topsoil transfer shows the percentage calculated both with and without the seed-mix legume species to indicate the maximum and minimum percentages of species transport (Table 4). The maximum value of 41% of species indicates that the reconstructed minesite ecosystem will have to be supplemented to achieve a more representative total of species found in the native forest ecosystem. Of the native perennial species occurring in the existing above-ground flora in the six jarrah forest sites, less than a third of these species also occurred in samples of the soil seed bank from these sites (Table 4).

Table 3. Predominant species in the soil seed bank
of selected vegetation types of the world.

Vegetation Type	Predominant Species in the Soil	Source
Tilled Agricultural Soils		
Arable Fields - England	Weedy annuals	Benchley and Warrington 1940
Arable Fields - Canada	Weedy annuals	Budd et al. 1954
Arable Fields - U.S.A.	Weedy annuals	Robinson 1949
Arable Fields - Honduras	Weedy annuals	Kellman 1974a
Grasslands and Marshes		
Fresh water Marsh - U.S.A.	Annuals and perennials of the surface vegetation	Leck and Graveline 1979
Perennial Hay Meadow - Wales	Dicotyledons	Chippendale and Milton 1934
Meadow Steppe - U.S.S.R.	Minor species of the vegetation	Golubeva 1962
Perennial Grassland - U.S.A.	Minor species of the flora, many annuals	Lippert and Hopkins 1950
Perennial Pasture - England	Annuals and species of the vegetation	Champness and Morris 1948

14

Table 3. Predominant species in the soil seed bank continued.

Vegetation Type	Predominant Species in the Soil	Source
Grasslands and Marshes continued		
Annual Grassland	Annual grasses	Major and Pyott 1966
Shrublands and Heaths		
Heath - Wales	Major species of the vegetation	Chippendale and Milton 1934
Forests		
Fir Forest - U.S.S.R.	All earlier successional species	Karpov 1960
Secondary Forest - U.S.A.	Arable weeds of early succession	Oosting and Humphries 1940
Subalpine Forest - U.S.A.	Herbaceous species	Whipple 1978
Primary Conifer Forest - Canada	Shrubs and herbs	Kellman 1974b
Coniferous Forest - Canada	Alder	Kellman 1970

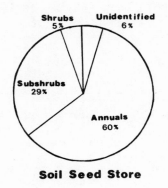

Soil Seed Store

Fig. 2. Proportions of total seed density in the jarrah forest soil seed bank separated according to life form class (after Vlahos and Bell 1986).

Principal Components Analysis was used determine the overall floristic similarity between the existing flora of native jarrah forest sites, the seed banks of these native jarrah forest sites, the existing vegetative flora of a range of reconstructed bauxite mine sites and the seed bank stores of these rehabilitated sites. The sample ordination from the centered form of Principal Components Analysis ordination again showed that the floristic composition of the existing native jarrah forest sites was, indeed, very different from the floristic composition of the soil seed bank at those sites (Fig. 3). The residual soil seed bank found in reconstruction sites was very similar to the soil seed bank of native forest sites. The distribution of sites along the major axis of floristic similarity (axis 1) indicates that the floristic composition of existing bauxite minesites probably includes more species common to the mature forest than components of the soil seed bank would provide. This "movement" in the ordination hyperspace is due to the influence of the species added by seed mix spreading and planting. It also indicates that there is still a large number of species to return to the bauxite mine reconstruction sites to have comparable floras to the native forest.

Table 4. Percentage of all jarrah forest species originally growing in top soil collection area successfully returned by topsoil transfer to mined sites and the percentage of only the perennial species in the vegetation occurring as seed in the soil. The range in first column is due to the difficulty of identifying whether particular species were supplied by the topsoil or by the seed mix additions.

Forest Site	Percentage of All Species Successfully Returned by Topsoil Transfer	Percentage of Perennial Species in the Vegetation Occurring as Seed in the Soil
1	-	29
2	13 - 28	25
3	13 - 28	25
4	35 - 41	17
5	32 - 41	26
6	20 - 31	11

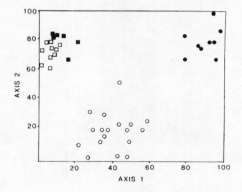

Fig. 3. Centered Principal Components Analysis stand ordination for presence and absence data from the native jarrah forest vegetation sites (●), the soil seed store (■), the existing components of rehabilitated bauxite mine sites (O), and the soil seed bank components of the rehabilitation sites (□).

17

Records of the reproductive phenology for 101 jarrah forest understorey species indicate that late spring and early summer is the period when seed additions to the seed bank would be greatest (Fig. 4). Observations in the forest reveal, however, that the seed set can be very sporadic in most of the species of the jarrah forest understorey with only a few individuals producing seed during any single year. Because more than 70% of the species resprout vegetatively following fire, continued survival of individuals of a species generally

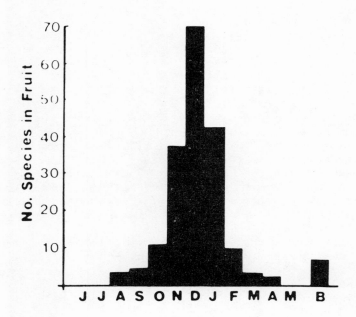

Fig. 4. Jarrah forest seed availability phenology. Numbers of species with seed for each calendar month and the number of species with bradysporous (seed continuously carried in protective follicles) fruits (B).

does not require seed production, dispersal and establishment (Christensen and Kimber 1975, Bell and Koch 1980). Obligatory reseeding species, however, are killed outright by fires and must re-establish in the post-fire habitat from seed stored in protective fruits on the parent plant which open following fire (bradyspory) or from soil-stored seed which are generally stimulated by heat to germinate. A number of species in the Proteaceae and Myrtaceae have this bradysporous (or plant-stored seed) fire response mechanism. Many jarrah forest members of the Mimosaceae and Papillionaceae have soil-borne seed which are stimulated to germinate by high temperatures (Shea et al. 1979). The legume seed spread onto rehabilitated mine sites is pre-treated by boiling (Glossop 1980). Little prior work, however, has been done on the germination characteristics of many jarrah forest understorey species.

VIABILITY AND GERMINATION

The viability of seed produced in the forest environment and the capacity of these seeds to germinate are factors playing a major role in the understanding of the regenerative abilities of native plants. Because the seed bank studies revealed a paucity of understorey shrub seed in the topsoil, collection and treatment of a greater array of shrub seed seems essential to further supplement the seed mix currently spread into rehabilitated minesites.

Seeds from a range of shrub species were collected during the summer of 1983-84. Viability was tested using a 1% aqueous solution of 2,3,5-triphenyl tetrazolium chloride (Lakon 1949). Germination percentage was determined in triplicate samples of seed placed in jarrah forest topsoil under glasshouse conditions. A second series using a wide range of native legume species was established following a 2 min. boiling pre-treatment. The data on the legume species acquired in this study and results previously reported by Glossop (1980) are shown in Table 5. The results of the viability and germination tests on the non-legume species from the jarrah forest are included in Table 6.

Table 5. Jarrah forest legume seed viability and germination percentage data. Viability was tested by tetrazolium chloride. Germination mean of three trials after 80 days in this study. Germination percentages of Glossop (1980) recorded after 35 days and indicated (+). This study source indicated (*).

Species	Viability %	Germination No Treatment	2 Min. Boiling	Source
Acacia alata	76	6	9	*
Acacia lateriticola	--	0	0	+
Acacia cyclops	--	13	27	+
Acacia decurrens	--	6	93	+
Acacia extensa	--	8	61	+
Acacia graffiana	--	10	69	+
Acacia podalyrifolia	--	5	45	+
Acacia pulchella	--	7	36	+
Acacia saligna	--	6	34	+
Acacia urophylla	--	0	0	+
Albizzia lophantha	80	0	64	*
Bossiaea aquifolium	--	0	0	+
Chorizema dicksonii	70	0	84	*
Chorizema ilicifolium	92	6	76	*
Chorizema rhombeum	78	3	78	*
Gompholobium capitatum	80	2	24	*
Gompholobium knightianum	90	2	68	*
Gompholobium polymorphum	66	0	42	*
Hardenbergia comptoniana	--	3	20	+
Hovea chorizemifolia	--	-	10	*
Kennedia coccinea	--	5	42	+
Kennedia prostrata	--	5	21	+
Labichea punctata	90	0	58	*
Mirbelia dilatata	32	0	36	*
Oxylobium lanceolatum	86	3	16	*
Oxylobium linearifolium	82	33	34	*

Table 6. Jarrah forest non-legume species seed viability by tetrazolium chloride test and topsoil germination following 80 days under glasshouse conditions.

Species	Viability (%)	Germination (%)
Agrostocrinum scabrum	52	4
Boronia spathulatum	30	2
Clematis pubescens	10	0
Dianella revoluta	-	0
Eriostemon spicatus	8	0
Glischrocaryon aureum	0	0
Grevillea quercifolia	95	4
Grevillea wilsonii	-	2
Hakea undulata	44	68
Hibbertia hypericoides	28	0
Hybanthus floribundus	6	10
Leptomeria cunninghamii	0	0
Lomandra sonderi	56	2
Opercularia echinocephala	10	0
Phyllanthus calycinus	6	7
Pimelia suaveolens	0	0
Platysace tenuissima	2	0
Tetratheca hirsuta	52	2
Thomasia pauciflora	13	8
Trymalium ledifolium	-	0
Trymalium spathulatum	4	8

The jarrah forest legume species generally produced a high proportion of viable seeds but heat stimulus was generally required to achieve germination (Table 5). The legume species tested here are predominantly polycarpic obligate reseeding species (see Bell et al. 1984) with life spans usually less than 15 years. The generally longer-lived non-leguminous species showed a wide range of seed viabilities but generally very poor rates of germination without pre-treatment. There were, however, numerous non-legume shrub species showing poor viability percentages.

The two groupings of jarrah forest understorey species seem to represent two different regions of the selection continuum (r- and K-) advanced for biological systems by MacArthur and Wilson (1967) and Pianka (1979) or the life form strategies (R-, C-, & S-) of Grime (1979). The obligate reseeding legumes represent the embodiment of r- (or R-) selection, involving maximum productivity and sexual reproduction in non-limiting, density-independent situations. The longer-lived resprouting species exemplify K- (or C- or S-) selection where these slow growing species with more conservative reproductive effort are adapted to utilizing limiting environmental resources with high efficiency in high density situations. The low reproductive output of the long-lived resprouting species of the jarrah forest will present a major obstacle in attempts to reseed these species into rehabilitated mine sites. Finding sufficient, viable seed on an annual basis could prove prohibitively expensive. Further efforts to determine the stimuli responsible for the germination inducement of viable, but dormant, seed of the non-leguminous species also seems warranted.

HABITAT TOLERANCE OF GERMINATING SEEDS

Establishment of seedlings in coal mining overburden can be difficult due to the very low pH values of the planting medium (Koch and Bell 1983). Soil pH values as low as 2.8 and many areas below 4.0 make rehabilitation of coal mine sites which cannot be topsoiled the major environmental difficulty to overcome in the Collie Basin region of the Darling Range (Bell 1984). Some natural tolerance to low pH might be expected as native community soils sometimes measure as low as 4.6. Formerly abandoned coal mine sites in the Collie Basin show some natural plant establishment and provided the opportunity to determine the natural tolerance of jarrah forest species to acidic soil conditions. Plants were identified on orphaned mining areas and a sample of the adjacent rooting medium was collected. Fig. 5 has listed the species identified from these coal mine overburden sites in relation to the order of acid soil tolerance. Species found near the top of the list would be expected to be better choices for seed mix species in the inhospitable regions of coal mine reconstruction which do not receive a covering of topsoil. The residual acidity in Collie Basin overburden is sufficient to require years of weathering to ameliorate the severely acid soil condition on these areas (Koch and Bell 1983). For this reason, the lowest pH overburden is usually buried deepest in the expended mine pits. Careful refilling of the pits ensures that the surface layers will have materials with inherently better pH and residual acidity conditions. Heavy seeding and interplanting of low pH tolerant plants ensures soil stabilization and cover. Problems still remain, however, in achieving species richness values approaching those in the pre-mining native forest regions in the Collie Basin.

FLORISTIC CHANGE WITH TIME

The classical view of ecological succession which developed in north temperate climates is that, following a disturbance, a series of plant species assemblages progressively occupy a site, each being replaced by a successor until a final assemblage (the 'climax community') develops which is capable of self-maintenance (Odum 1969). Egler (1969) was among the first to recognize that under certain circumstances the vegetation developing on disturbed sites early in a successional sequence was not eventually replaced and that the initial floristic composition of a site already contained the majority of species which would ultimately dominate the climax community. The succession of plant assemblages following fire in south-eastern Australian forests has been recognized to closely resemble this 'initial floristic composition' model of ecological succession (Purdie and Slatyer 1976). With a predominance of resprouting shrub and tree species in the jarrah forest ecosystem, it would be expected that the initial composition model would apply in Western Australia as well. Australian research on the pattern of species change following disturbances more severe than fire, however, has not been published.

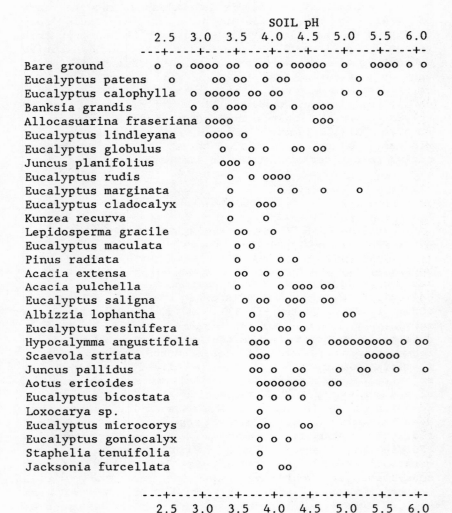

Fig. 5. Soil pH levels and pH conditions from the rhizosphere of plants growing in overburden from coal mining in the Collie Basin of Western Australia (from Bell 1984).

```
                          SOIL pH
        ---+----+----+----+----+----+----+----+----+-
           2.5  3.0  3.5  4.0  4.5  5.0  5.5  6.0

Briza maxima                    o    o    o
Oxylobium capitatum             o
Daviesia cordata                oo   o    ooo
Agonis linearifolia             oo o ooo
Pinus pinaster                  o o o
Sollya heterophylla             o    o
Pteridium exculentum              oo  o
Viminaria juncea                 o   oo
Lotus angustissimus               o
Euchilopsis linearis              o              o
Trifolium spp.                    o              o
Dasypogon bromeliifolius          o
Conostylis setigera               o
Chamaecytisus proliferus          o    o
Hakea prostrata                   o
Pultenaea ochreata                   o
Hemiandra pungens                    o    o
Hypochoeris radicata                 o
Phlebocarya ciliata                  o
Lechenaultia biloba                  o    o
Aira caryphyllea                   ooo
Xanthosia candida                    o
Xanthosia huegelii                   o
Bossiaea eriocarpa                   o
Kunzea ericifolia                    o o

        ---+----+----+----+----+----+----+----+----+-
           2.5  3.0  3.5  4.0  4.5  5.0  5.5  6.0
                          SOIL pH
```

Fig. 5. continued.

The implications for rehabilitation of mine sites in Western Australia of the initial floristic composition model are that one should not expect the native species composition of revegetation sites to change markedly in the coming years and, therefore, it is very important to maximize the establishment of species in the first years following disturbance. "Who got there first" is very important in the distribution of species in Western Australia, as the majority of species resprout from protected buds under bark or from bulbs, corms or lignotubers buried in the soil (Christensen and Kimber 1975, Bell and Koch 1980). Minor disturbances, such as fire, insect defoliation or drought, have little effect on the vegetation of an area once established. In the time sequence following fire, the jarrah forest is floristically the most diverse at approximately 5-7 years following a burn (Bell and Koch 1980). At this time the flora still contains the short-lived 'fire ephemerals' stimulated to germinate by the fire, the resprouting species which recovered from underground lignotuber tissues and the few species which require seed dispersal into disturbed site from the adjacent regions of the flora. Areas of the jarrah forest which have been protected from fire for long periods have fewer species than younger sites because of the loss of the fire ephemeral species (Bell and Koch 1980).

CONSEQUENCE TO RESTORATION

A forest ecosystem which provides all the structural and functional aspects of the natural jarrah forest is the goal of restoration of mine sites in the Darling Range of Western Australia (Fig. 6). The transfer of topsoil to the disturbed areas is the first step. Research on the seed store of the jarrah forest indicates that the seed supply of the topsoil is numerically sufficient to expect adequate ground coverage in the first years following disturbance, but the species composition needs supplementation. The long-lived species capable of resprouting following fire are the species primarily required in the restoration areas and are the species currently under-represented. Although heat is clearly a requirement for most jarrah forest legumes in the stimulation of dormant soil-borne seeds, the appropriate stimulus or the sequence of several stimuli to induce the germination of numerous other native forest species is still to be found. Alcoa of Australia Ltd. is presently establishing an understorey species orchard to supply seeds. Supplemental water and

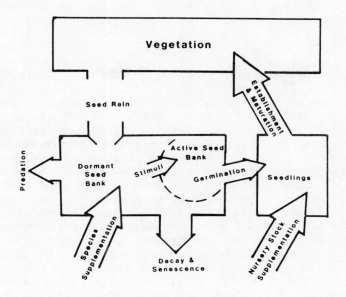

Fig. 6. Diagramatic representation of state variables and transfers in reconstructed ecosystems (adapted from Harper 1977).

nutrients should provide conditions for these plants which are more conducive to the production of viable seed than currently exist under natural forest conditions. Seed will continue to be collected in the native forest regions for the seed mix spread at the time the sites are prepared for tree planting. In addition to using the topsoil and a seed mix to enrich the seedling flora on restored minesites, understorey species nursery stock is now also being planted at the same time as the six-month old nursery stock of *Eucalyptus* species are being planted. Supplementation of viable, germinable seed to the reconstruction site seed store and of nursery stock seedlings to the first year seedling class of reconstructed sites will ensure an enhanced flora upon maturation of these sites. Some migration of species might be expected with time but in general the initial floristic composition of the site will determine the

27

major constitutents of the ecosystem for the foreseeable future.

CONCLUSIONS

In this chapter I have highlighted some of the problems in providing ecologically appropriate reconstructed ecosystems in the jarrah forest region of Western Australia. Due to the nature of the extreme richness of understorey species which are capable of resprouting following the natural and man-managed burns which occur in this fire-prone ecosystem, it is important to provide as many of these species to the initial floristic composition of the reclaimed area as possible. Studies on the soil seed bank have shown that soil under mature jarrah forest has a soil seed store which is depauperate in viable, germinable seeds of the major shrub species of the understorey. The paucity in the topsoil of species appropriate to quickly re-establish a forest with premining ecosystem attributes means that mine site environmental managers must supplement the seed bank and seedling classes of reclamation sites. Alcoa of Australia Ltd. is currently establishing a seed orchard to provide viable seed and a shrub nursery to provide native species container stock to improve the quality of reconstruction of areas they mine for bauxite. Reconstruction of coal mine spoils by Western Collieries Ltd. is more difficult due to the requirement of acid soil tolerance for species of seed and container stock. Seed is now collected from forest regions showing naturally low soil pH conditions. Continued efforts to determine the stimuli required to induce the germination of non-legume species are now in progress. These techniques will supplement the boiling pre-treatment currently used to enhance germination of the jarrah forest legume species. The jarrah forest of Western Australia is a multi-use forested ecosystem which is very important to the continued existence of modern man in Western Australia. It provides vital watershed protection for the drinking water reservoirs of the state, a timber source worth millions of dollars in domestic and export trade and a recreation resource valued by many of the more than one million people who live in the south-west of Western Australia. Although mining of bauxite and coal in the forested regions only affects about 300-400 ha per year it is important to ensure that these restored forest regions will provide future generations with the potential for future exploitation or conservation. Reconstruction sites may also provide special, high density recreation sites, thus protecting more sensitive regions of the native forest. A thorough working knowledge of the ecology of the region will provide the foundation for establishing a self-sustaining forest ecosystem in regions of mineral extraction which will provide all the structural and functional attributes required of the natural jarrah forest ecosystem.

ACKNOWLEDGMENTS

Numerous people within the Western Australian Department of Conservation and Land Management, Alcoa of Australia Ltd. and Western Collieries Ltd. have provided assistance and support. Of special significance have been Mr. David Fell and Mr. Steven Vlahos for aspects of the germination and soil seed store research, respectively, and Dr. John M. Koch for aspects of the Collie Basin research. Comments on the manuscript by Mr. Denis Brooks and Mr. Harry Butler were especially helpful. Funds for the position of Senior Lecturer in Plant Ecology in the Department of Botany were provided by Alcoa of Australia Ltd. and Western Collieries Ltd. The manuscript was first initiated while on sabbatical leave at the University of California, Davis, to whom I would like to acknowledge the provision of research space.

LITERATURE CITED

Bell, D.T., and J.M. Koch. 1980. Post-fire succession in the northern jarrah forest of Western Australia. Australian Journal of Ecology 5:9-14.

Bell, D.T., A.J.M. Hopkins, and J.S. Pate. 1984. Fire in the kwongan. Pages 178-204 in: J.S. Pate, and J.S. Beard, editors. Kwongan - plant life of the sandplain. University of Western Australia Press, Perth.

Bell, D.T. 1984. The flora of rehabilitated areas.
Pages 25-39 in B.G. Collins, B.G. editors. Mined
land rehabilitation - is it sustainable? Western
Australian Institute of Technology, School of Biology,
Bulletin No. 7, Bentley, Western Australia.

Benchley, W.E., and K. Warrington. 1930. The weed seed
population of arable soil. I. Numerical estimation of
viable seeds and observations on their natural
dormancy. Journal of Ecology 18:235-272.

Blackwell, W.H. Jr. 1978. How to select and plant
pumpkin seeds. Journal of Irreproducible Results
23:28.

Bormann, F.H., and G.E. Likens. 1969. The watershed
ecosystem concept and studies of nutrient cycles.
Pages 49-76 in G.M. Van Dyne, editor. The Ecosystem
Concept in Natural Resource Management. Academic
Press, New York.

Budd, A.C., W.S. Chepil, and V.L. Doughty. 1954.
Germination of weed seeds. III. The influence of crops
and fallow on the weed seed population of the soil.
Canadian Journal of Agricultural Science 34:18-27.

Champness, S.S. and K. Morris. 1948. The population of
buried viable seeds in relation to contrasting pasture
and soil types. Journal of Ecology 36:149-173.

Chippendale, H.G., and W.E. Milton. 1934. On the viable
seeds present in the soil beneath pastures. Journal
of Ecology 22:508-531.

Christensen, P.E., and P.C. Kimber. 1975. Effect of
prescribed burning on the flora and fauna of south-
west Australian forests. Pages 85-106 in J. Kikkawa
and H.A. Nix, editors. Managing terrestrial
ecosystems. Proceedings of the Ecological Society of
Australia Vol. 9.

Egler, F.E. 1969. Vegetation science concepts. I.
Initial floristic composition - a factor in old-field
vegetation development. Vegetatio 4:412-417.

Gentilli, J. 1948, Australian climates and resources.
Whitcombe and Tombs, Melbourne.

Glossop, B.L. 1980. Germination response of thirteen
legume species to boiling. Alcoa of Australia Limited
Environmental Research Bulletin Number 5.

Golubeva, L.V. 1962. (Data on the reserves of living
seeds in the soil under steppe vegetation). Biull.
Moskov. Obshch. Isp. Pirirody Otd. Biol. 67(5):76-89
(Cited in Major and Pyott (1966).)

Grime, J.P. 1979. Plant strategies and vegetation processes. Wiley, New York.

Harper, J.L. 1977. Population biology of plants. Academic Press, New York.

Havel, J.J. 1975. Site-vegetation mapping in the northern jarrah forest (Darling Range). I. Definition of site-vegetation types. Forests Department Bulletin 86, Perth, Western Australia.

Johnson, E.A. 1975. Buried seed populations in the subartic forest east of Great Slave Lake, Northwest Territories. Canadian Journal of Botany 53:2933-2941.

Karpov, V.G. 1960. (On the species composition of the viable seed supply in the soil of spruce - Vaccinium myrtillus - vegetation). Trudy Moskov. Obshch. Isp. Priod. 3:131-140.

Kellman, M.C. 1970. The viable seed content of some forest soil in coastal British Columbia. Canadian Journal of Botany 48:1383-1385.

Kellman, M.C. 1974a. The viable weed seed content of tropical agricultural soils. Journal of Applied Ecology 11:664-677.

Kellman, M.C. 1974b. Preliminary seed budgets for two plant communities on the coast of British Columbia. Journal of Biogeography 1:123-133.

Koch, J.M., and D.T. Bell. 1983. Amelioration of acidic coal mine overburden from Collie, Western Australia. Reclamation and Revegetation Research 2:155-165.

Lakon, G. 1949. The topographical tetrazolium method for determining the germinating capacity of seeds. Plant Physiology 24:389-394.

Leck, M.A., and K.J. Graveline. 1979. The seed bank of a freshwater tidal marsh. American Journal of Botany 66:1006-1015.

Lippert, R.D. and H.H. Hopkins. 1950. Study of viable seeds in various habitats in mixed prairie. Transactions of the Kansas Academy of Science 53:355-364.

MacArthur, R.H., and E.O. Wilson. 1967. The theory of island biogeography. Princeton University Press, Princeton, New Jersey.

Major, J., and W.T. Pyott. 1966. Buried, viable seeds in two Californian bunchgrass sites and their bearing on the definition of a flora. Vegetatio 13:253-282.

Milton, W.E.S. 1939. The occurrence of buried viable seed in soils at different elevations in a salt marsh. Journal of Ecology 27:149-159.

Mulcahy, M.J., H.M. Churchward, and G.M. Dimmock. 1972. Landforms and soils on an uplifted peneplain in the Darling Range, Western Australia. Australian Journal of Soil Research 10:1-14.

Odum, E.P. 1969. The strategy of ecosystem development. Science 164:262-270.

Oosting, H.J., and M.E. Humphries. 1940. Buried viable seeds in a successional series of old-field and forest soils. Bulletin of the Torrey Botanical Club 67:253-273.

Pianka, E.R. 1979. On r- and K-Selection. American Naturalist 104:592-597.

Purdie, R.W., and R.O. Slatyer. 1976. Vegetation succession after fire in sclerophyll woodland communities in south-eastern Australia. Australian Journal of Ecology 1:223-236.

Robinson, R.G. 1949. Annual weeds, their viable seed populations in the soil, and their effect on yields of oats, wheat, and flax. Agronomy Journal 41:513-518.

Shea, S.R., J. McCormick, and C.C. Portlock. 1979. The effect of fires on regeneration of leguminous species in the northern jarrah (Eucalyptus marginata Sm.) forest of Western Australia. Australian Journal of Ecology 4:195-205.

Smith, R. 1952. The soils of the south-west Australian agricultural region. Ph.D. Thesis, University of Western Australia.

Tacey, W. 1979. Landscaping and revegetation practices used in rehabilitation after bauxite mining in Western Australia. Reclamation Reviews 2:123-132.

Vlahos, S. and D.T. Bell. 1986. Soil seed bank components of the northern jarrah forest of Western Australia. Australian Journal of Ecology 11:171-179.

Ward, S.C., G.E.P. Pickersgill, D.V. Michaelsen, and D.T. Bell. 1985. Responses to factorial combinations of nitrogen, phosphorus and potassium fertilizers by saplings of Eucalyptus saligna Sm., and the prediction of the responses by DRIS Indices. Australian Forest Research 15:27-32.

Whipple, S.A.   1978.   The relationship of buried germinating seeds to vegetation in an old-growth Colorado subalpine forest. Canadian Journal of Botany 56:1505-1509.

Walter C. Oechel

3. Seedling Establishment and Water Relations After Fire in a Mediterranean Ecosystem

INTRODUCTION

Chaparral and other Mediterranean-type ecosystems occur in semiarid areas of cool wet winters and hot dry summers. These ecosystems are frequently characterized by periodic disturbance by fire. This is certainly true of chaparral. Chaparral in southern California burns every 20 to 40 years (Muller et al. 1968, Hanes 1971, Byrne 1978, Minnich 1983) with an average interval between fire of about 35 years. It is fairly rare for a stand to be more than 50 to 55 years old and it is difficult to find stands more than 100 years old. These periodic fires occur in unmanaged rural and urban areas and can occur in chaparral stands within the city, as did the San Diego Mission Hills fire which burned chaparral covered canyon walls and adjacent houses within the city limits in the late summer of 1986.

Since the chaparral is so frequently burned, it is a good system in which to observe adaptations to disturbance and patterns of recovery from disturbance. Recently we have been concentrating on the way that chaparral develops between fires and on the controls on establishment after a fire. The establishment period is very important because almost all of the recruitment into the stand occurs at the time of disturbance, and changes in the shrub community between fires occur primarily by attrition (Zedler 1981). Establishment is largely determined by conditions surrounding the fire event. This includes the soil seed bank established before the fire, the composition of the vegetation at the time of the fire, and the environmental conditions at the time of the fire and for several years after fire.

The intensity of the fire affects seed survival. We believe that fires can be too cool to stimulate germination or so hot that massive seed mortality occurs and the seed bank is depleted (Moreno and Oechel, unpublished, Jacks et al. in press). A cool fire may provide insufficient heat to stimulate germination and consequently a whole group of species may not regenerate. The amount of moisture in the soil coupled with the heat released in the fire is important. As is the case for microorganisms (Dunn and DeBano 1977), wet heat may result in considerable seed mortality due to the lethal effects of steaming and the greater lethality caused by the combination of moisture and heat. The moisture conditions for one or two years after the fire can be important in affecting seedling survival.

Excessive post-fire drought can result in major failure in germination and/or establishment of a previously major element in the vegetation (Jacks et al. in press). Under normal years, the extent of drought-induced mortality is somewhat unclear. Irrigation during the spring and summer period of establishment showed no positive effect on establishment, and the major mortality in control plots occurred before the onset of the maximum summer drought (Moreno and Oechel, unpublished).

Similarly, the role of competition is unclear. Removal of competing resprouts and herbaceous vegetation showed little enhancement of seedling survivorship. To the contrary, there was a tendency for seedlings of <u>Adenostoma</u> <u>fasciculatum</u> to do better in the presence of herbaceous vegetation (Moreno and Oechel unpublished data, Moreno and Oechel 1987).

In the first drought season following fire, seedlings face a very rapid drying front in the soil. To a great extent, survival appears to be a race between the rate of root system growth and development and the rate of development of the drying front. Seedlings respond with rapid root development. Roots exceed a depth of 35 cm a few months after germination and prior to development of the full summer drought. Parameters necessary to predict and control the establishment of chaparral seedlings after fire include stand composition, the physiological state of the resprouters at the time of fire (especially carbohydrate reserves), the soil seed bank before the fire, the fire intensity, the moisture content of the soil at the time of the fire, and, following fire, through the seedling establishment phase.

Of particular interest in predicting chaparral composition are dynamics of ecosystem development that occur between fire events and the role water availability plays in establishment after fire. The chaparral is comprised mainly of evergreen, sclerophyllous shrub species which are either resprouters (which may or may not also establish by seed after fire) or are obligate seeders which do not resprout. Immediately after the fire, resprouters appear to have an advantage. They have an extensive root system that can utilize the abundant soil water which is present after the fire due to the decreased transpiring canopy area and the improved nutrient status following fire. Burls of resprouters generally have a large carbohydrate reserve with which to support resprouting (Jones and Laude 1960, Oechel and Hastings, 1983 Moreno et al. unpublished). The conditions for resprouters appear very good following a fire. The seeders on the other hand don't have this established root system and are exposed to considerable water stress. One objective of our research has been to define the lethal plant water potentials for seedlings of the important chaparral species. Our goal is to use this information to predict the conditions and the microsites promoting establishment of the various species. This information will be used to help predict the new species composition following fire. This composition will set the potential resource use between the fire events, since ecosystem performance after a fire is thought to be strongly dependent on the composition of the vegetation. This resultant composition depends in part on the moisture conditions following fire and the species water relations characteristics.

The specific objective of the research reported here was to determine the plant water potential which is lethal to 50% of the seedling population, the LD_{50}, and to compare these data to water potentials observed for adults and seedlings in the field. Future research will concentrate on gathering the necessary additional information to predict post-fire seedling survival and population densities from information on the prefire vegetation and soil seedbank, fire conditions, soil conditions, and the post-fire environment.

FIELD SITES AND EXPERIMENTAL METHODS

Field Sites--San Diego State University has two field stations, each larger than one thousand hectares. One, Sky Oaks Biological Field Station, is north of Warner Springs, 1300 to 2000 m elevation with about 1100 mm of precipitation (Fig. 1). This site is where most of our recent field work has been carried out. The other field station, Santa Margarita Biological Reserve, is near the coast just east of the town of Temecula at about 300 - 700 m elevation. The Santa Margarita Biological Reserve is drier than the Sky Oaks Biological Field Station, and the precipitation is about 400 mm.

Field Seedling Water Potentials--To determine plant water potentials experienced in the field, the water potentials of 9-month old seedlings were measured at the site of a recent burn on Jamul Mountain, in East San Diego County near Proctor Valley Road. Predawn plant water potential was measured using a Scholander-type pressure device on June 9, 10, and 14, 1985 coinciding with the period of the greenhouse experiment.

LD_{50} Experiments--Plants were grown from seed or field transplants in PVC pipes, 10 cm in diameter and 200 cm tall that contain screened bottoms for drainage. The containers were filled with washed river sand with a bulk density of 1.51 g cm^{-3}, particle density of 2.25 g cm-3, and a pore space of 49%. Tall containers were selected to allow roots to grow deeply in the soil and to subject seedlings to a gradual development of water stress, thus mimicking natural development of drought as closely as possible. Among the species selected for study were the chaparral species Ceanothus greggii Gray, Adenostoma fasciculatum H & A, and Quercus dumosa Nutt.

One hundred seedlings of each species were established (one plant in each container) and were grown in a greenhouse. During establishment, irrigation was performed daily with 0.3 strength Hoagland's solution in the morning and distilled water in the evening. The period of water stress was initiated about 6 months after

37

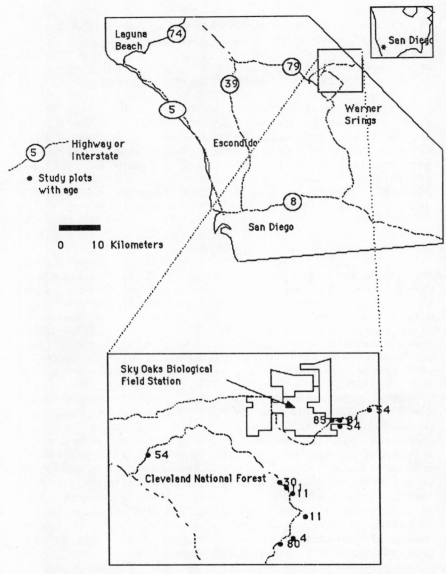

Fig. 1. Location of the SDSU Sky Oaks Biological Field Station in North San Diego County. Numbers represent the age of chaparral stands used in senescence studies.

establishment. The water stress period was affected by completely withholding water. Periodically throughout the drying cycle, 10 individual seedlings of each species were randomly selected and the plant water potentials determined with a Scholander presure chamber. These plants were then rewatered. Survival was assessed 15 days after rewatering by determining the number of plants which survived the drought treatment.

Polynomial regressions of measured water potential vs. survival were constructed for the laboratory data for each species separately. The resultant curves were used to estimate the plant water potential at which 50% of the population within each species died - the LD_{50}.

RESULTS

Field Plant Water Potentials of Seedlings--Water potentials of seedlings measured in the field varied widely with plant size, with intermediate-sized plants showing the greatest water stress. While the mean predawn water potential was -5.1 MPa, the most frequent water potential was between -12.5 and -15.0 MPa (Fig. 2). These water potentials are substantially lower than those which have generally been reported for mature individuals of the same species growing in the same general areas in southern Californian chaparral. Typical minimum water potentials for mature A. fasciculatum are about -6.5 MPa, about half the value observed for seedlings (Table 1 Poole et al. 1981, Reid 1985, Reid and Oechel, unpublished, Reid and Oechel 1984). We have no way of knowing what the fate of the individual seedlings with the lowest water potentials would have been had they not been sampled for water potential determination.

Following fire, reduced transpiring leaf area results in greater soil water potential and enhanced plant water status of resprouters (Oechel and Hastings 1983). The low plant water potentials of seedlings presumably occurs as a result of the limited seedling root system and the high evaporative demand of the post fire site.

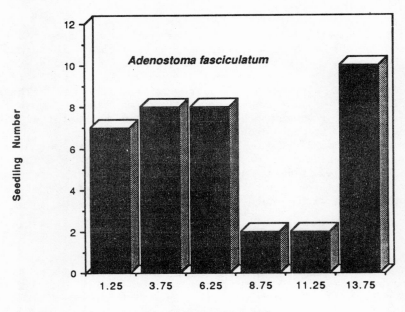

Fig. 2. Water potential of field seedlings of
Adenostoma fasciculatum on Jamul Mountain on June 9, 10,
and 14, 1985, about 9 months after a wildfire burned the
area.

LD_{50}--The results of the LD_{50} experiments indicate a
differential sensitivity among species to low plant water
or xylem potentials (Table 2). The ability of the
seedlings to survive severe water stress reflects the
field plant water stress experienced by mature
individuals of the same species (Table 1). The relative
sensitivity to water stress of these chaparral seedlings
is similar to the pattern of stomatal sensitivity to
drought reported previously for established plants (Poole
et al. 1981).
There was no mortality in A. fasciculatum at a water
potential of -11.2 MPa, but survival decreased to 38% at
potentials of -13.8 MPa. In C. greggii there was no
mortality at -10.0 MPa, but survival decreased to 48% of
the population when plant water potential reached -11.6
MPa. Drought induced mortality in seedlings of Q. dumosa
was initiated at a higher value of plant water potential
than in the other species. Q. dumosa seedlings tolerated

40

Table 1. Typical field water potentials of mature chaparral species used in these experiments.

Origin and Species	Typical Minimum Predawn Water Potentials (MPa)	Reference:	Rooting Depth:
California:			
Adenostoma fasciculatum	-6.5	Reid and Oechel, 1984	Deep
Ceanothus greggii	-5.5	Reid and Oechel, 1984	Shallow
Quercus dumosa	-5.5	Poole et al., 1981	Very Deep

Table 2. Minimum observed values of plant water potential (MPa) at zero mortality and established water potential at 50% mortality as determined in greenhouse experiments.

Species	LD_0	LD_{50}
Quercus dumosa	-6.0	-9.5
Ceanothus greggii	-10.0	-12.5
Adenostom fasciculatum	-11.2	-13.0

41

a water potential of -6.2 MPa, but survival decreased to 67% at a plant water potential of -8.7 MPa.

The LD_{50} values obtained in our study are lower than generally reported water potentials for mature plants of the same species (Table 1). This suggests that seedlings may be less conservative in water use than are mature plants or their roots are in dryer surface soil layers. As a result they experience lower water potentials. This pattern may be driven by seedling requirements for sufficient carbon uptake to establish root systems in advance of the summer soil drying front. This carbon uptake must result in water loss by the plant and may explain the potentially dangerously low plant water potentials experienced by chaparral seedlings. Failure to move roots into deeper soil layers with adequate soil moisture would definitely result in seedling death, and expenditure of water for sufficient carbon uptake to support adequate root growth is a necessary risk.

Resprouters are much better able to utilize the post-fire conditions than are the seedlings. With their extensive root system, they can tap water at depths where it has become more abundant due to reduction in leaf area following fire (Oechel and Hastings 1983). Many resprouters can reestablish after a fire by way of seedlings as well as from their lignotubers. Given this, it is not understood why the obligate seeding strategy in general or specifically species such as C. greggii are so successful in competition with resprouts.

CONCLUSIONS

One goal of this research is to accurately predict necessary conditions for successful seedling establishment and to evaluate the impacts on ecosystem resource use and production of differential establishment resulting in shifts in vegetation composition. Future research will be directed towards developing the ability to predict safe microsites for establishment. It should be possible to calculate the quantity of water required to produce the photosynthate needed to grow roots to a particular depth. Seedlings can only establish where there is sufficient moisture to support the photosynthesis and growth needed to establish roots beyond the summer drying front.

The ability of the seedlings to survive low plant water potentials is much higher than originally predicted. At the initiation of the research, it was expected that seedlings, not being hardened to the drought environment, would be quite sensitive to drought. It was also expected that the relative ranking of drought sensitivity would reflect the drought stress and stomatal sensitivities to plant water stress observed in adults in the field. As it turns out, while the latter prediction is certainly true, seedlings experience and can tolerate plant water potentials much lower than those normally experienced by adult shrubs.

It appears that adults are very conservative with respect to water use. They basically close stomates and severely restrict transpiration at about 1/2 to 1/3 of the plant water potential that seedlings (and presumably adults) can tolerate. This characteristic should provide a wide margin for error between the water potential at which transpiration is limited, and the water potentials that would be lethal.

The seedling stage is obviously very important in the life cycle of chaparral plants. Despite this fact, compared to the information available for the adult stage, there is relatively little information on the controls on the germination, physiology and growth of seedlings. Much of the water potential work that has been carried out in adults really does not help much in predicting changes in population size and dynamics. There is often little evidence of death in adults by causes other than old age. The water relations of adults is most likely of interest in predicting productivity rather than in predicting stand composition or survival. While the adults that are drought tolerant are those which most often appear on south facing slopes in the more arid habitats in the chaparral, it may be the physiology and tolerances of the seedlings which influence this observed pattern of distribution, rather than any extraordinary adaptations on the part of the adults.

To understand the controls on reestablishment of vegetation following natural and human caused disturbance in many systems, it is necessary to understand the controls on establishment and growth of the seedling stage. Work on naturally disturbed systems can provide insight into desirable characteristics of plants to be used in reclamation efforts. It would seem appropriate to screen potential candidates for use in reclamation efforts for the resistance of seedlings to water stress and for rates of seedling root development, water use efficiency, and overall water relations. Also, this work is important in helping predict the success of reclamation under variable precipitation regimes.

ACKNOWLEDGMENTS

The author wishes to acknowledge support from a grant from the National Science Foundation (BSR 8507699).

LITERATURE CITED

Byrne, R. 1978. California brushlands. Fossil record discloses wildlife history. California Agricultural Experiment Station, California Agriculture 32:13-14.

Dunn, P.H. and L.F. DeBano. 1977. Fire's effect on biological and chemical properties of chaparral soils. In H.A. Mooney and C.E. Conrad, editors. Proceedings of the Symposium on the Environmental Consequences of Fire and Fuel Management in Mediterranean Ecosystems. USDA Forest Service General Technical Report WO-3.

Hanes, T.L. 1971. Succession after fire in the chaparral of southern California. Ecological Monographs 41:27-52.

Jacks, P.M. P.J. Riggan, and P.H. Zedler. In press. Drought tolerance and the dynamics of community composition in chamise-Ceanothus chaparral. Ecological Monographs.

Jones, M.B. and H.M. Laude. 1960. Relationships between sprouting in chamise and the physiological condition of the plant. Journal of Range Management 13:210-214.

Minnich, R.A. 1983. Fire mosaics in southern California and northern Baja California. Science 219:1287-1294.

Moreno, J.M. and W.C. Oechel. 1987. Post-fire establishment of Adenostoma fasciculatum and Ceanothus greggii in a Southern California Chaparral: Influence of herbs and increased soil-nutrients and water. In Proceedings of the Vth International Conference on Mediterranean-Climate Ecosystems, Montpellier, France, July 15-21, 1987.

Muller, C.H., R.B. Henewalt, and J.K. McPherson. 1968. Allelopathic control of herb growth in the fire cycle of California chaparral. Bulletin of the Torrey Botanical Club 95:225-231.

Oechel, W.C. and S.J. Hastings. 1983. The effects of fire on photosynthesis in chaparral resprouts. Pages 274-285 in F.J. Kruger, D.T. Mitchell, and J.U.M. Jarvis, editors. Mediterranean-type Ecosystems. The Role of Nutrients. Springer-Verlag, New York, Heidelberg, Berlin.

Poole, D.K., S.W. Roberts, and P.C. Miller. 1981. Water utilization. Pages 123-149 in P.C. Miller, editor. Resource Use by Chaparral and Matorral. Springer-Verlag, New York.

Reid, C.D. 1985. Physiological indicators of senescence in two chaparral shrub species along a fire-induced age sequence. Masters Thesis, San Diego State University.

Reid, C. D. and W.C. Oechel. 1984. Bulletin de la Societé Botanique Francaise 131:399-409.

Zedler, P. H. 1981. Vegetation change in chaparral and desert communities in San Diego County, California. Pages 406-424 in D. C. West, H. H. Shugart, and D. B. Botkin, editors. Forest Succession: Concepts and Application. Springer-Verlag, Heidelberg.

Philip J. Burton, Kenneth R. Robertson,
Louis R. Iverson, Paul G. Risser

4. Use of Resource Partitioning and Disturbance Regimes in the Design and Management of Restored Prairies

ABSTRACT

The natural processes responsible for the origin and maintenance of native grasslands must be understood in order to restore North American prairies effectively. Grasslands historically have predominated where the climate ranged from semiarid to mesic but with periodic droughts, and where fires repeatedly removed dead above-ground biomass and retarded encroachment of woody invaders. As in most North American ecosystems, however, the particular assemblage of species naturally found at a site is frequently of recent origin and is not necessarily a stable combination.

The establishment and persistence of many mature prairie species may depend on specific soil moisture conditions that facilitate their localized competitive superiority. Both successional and climax prairie species may depend on some sort of general or local disturbances to free space for seedling establishment. Frequent disturbance in the form of fire, grazing or mowing is needed to remove standing dead plants and accumulated litter but this can cause varying effects on community composition. Established perennials are difficult to displace. Poor establishment from seed and constant invasion by exotic C_3 grasses, forbs and woody plants are the most common problems in prairie restoration efforts. Successful restoration methods emphasize the use of local genotypes, transplanting to enhance floristic diversity, and the use of manual weeding and fire to control exotic species.

Niche quantification may provide a means to match species more accurately to prevailing site conditions and to each other, in order to completely utilize the "resource space" so that invasion by exotics becomes less likely. The use of native C_3 grasses may also reduce invasion by such exotic cool season species as <u>Poa pratensis</u> and <u>Bromus inermis</u>. Native annuals may likewise form a more acceptable cover crop than exotic weeds or cereals. Ecosystem reconstruction provides many opportunities for testing fundamental theories of community ecology, which, in turn, could further enhance future restoration efforts.

INTRODUCTION

This chapter addresses problems associated with the restoration of a high level of species diversity in a comparatively mesic climate. We discuss the grasslands of the Central Plains of North America, with emphasis on the tallgrass prairie. Grasslands are supposedly restricted to semiarid zones (Holdridge 1947), but they achieve their richest development in terms of productivity and diversity of species in areas that receive 750 to 1000 mm of annual precipitation (Oosting 1956). Prairie plants must cope with intense biotic pressure from competition and grazing as well as the abiotic stresses of periodic drought, extreme temperatures and fire.

Natural grasslands once occupied one-quarter of the Earth's land area and 3.5 to 4.0 million km^2 (19.2%) of continental North America (Lemon 1970, Stevenson 1972, Risser et al. 1981, Singh et al. 1983). Generally characterized by level or gently rolling terrain, deep soils, low-to-moderate rainfall, and a moderately long growing season, North American grasslands have been largely converted to agriculture. The extent of destruction has often been proportional to native productivity and diversity: much shortgrass prairie remains in native pasture, while mixed-grass prairie is now predominated by wheat fields, and tallgrass prairie

47

has been almost totally replaced by maize and soybean row crops. Klopatek et al. (1979) estimate that 92% of the original <u>Bouteloua</u>-<u>Buchloe</u> (shortgrass) grasslands, 36% of the <u>Agropyron</u>-<u>Stipa</u> (mixed-grass) grasslands, and only 15% of the <u>Andropogon</u>-<u>Panicum</u>-<u>Sorghastrum</u> (tallgrass) prairies of the United States remain.

The productivity of these prairies and their soils has been responsible for their demise, and hence the impetus for their restoration. Other aspects of their ecology, namely the maintenance of their diversity and their adaptation to aboveground stress (drought, grazing and fire) can provide us with some useful guidelines for the most effective design and management of restored prairies.

<u>The Concept of Restoration</u>--Ecosystem restoration is a powerful concept in land management and in the testing of ecological theory (Aber and Jordan 1986). It is a central policy of many national park services around the world and of conservation organizations such as The Nature Conservancy (Jenkins 1973). The idea of restoring wildlands in addition to preserving them was a direct consequence of the nearly total destruction of tallgrass prairies by the 1930s. Local representatives of this ecosystem had become so scarce (especially northeast of the Missouri River and east of the Mississippi River) that reconstruction of the system <u>de novo</u> was virtually essential if prairie biota and processes were to be studied. The University of Wisconsin pioneered these efforts with the dedicated work of H. C. Greene and J. T. Curtis in establishing a diverse prairie landscape at the University of Wisconsin Arboretum beginning in 1936. Although similar efforts were initiated simultaneously elsewhere (e.g., the Trelease Grassland at the University of Illinois [Kendeigh unpublished]), the Wisconsin work is widely recognized as having laid the foundations of prairie restoration science. Such projects continue to be undertaken by universities as well as by state agencies, county and municipal park districts, and by conservation-minded landscapers and private landowners.

Despite the guidelines of the Surface Mining Reclamation and Control Act of 1977, efforts to restore natural vegetation in the United States are more prevalent in the tallgrass prairie region than in more arid grassland and desert regions, again because intact tallgrass prairie is so rare. Examples of restoration methods in this chapter, therefore, are drawn only from the tallgrass region; however, the principles should be generally applicable.

Objectives of Restoration--The ultimate objective of restoration is to create a stable ecosystem that is compositionally and functionally similar to that which existed prior to human disturbance. This ideal goal can never be completely attained (due to the dynamics of biogeography, local extirpations, difficulties in reestablishing native invertebrates, microflora and large carnivores, and the importance of innumerable chance events during community development), but it remains a reasonable and worthwhile objective. Whether restoration is economically feasible or whether it represents an appropriate use for a designated parcel of land are questions not addressed in this discussion. Nevertheless, the ultimate land use envisioned (e.g., preservation of genetic diversity, education, recreation, soil and water conservation, wildlife habitat) and the role of that parcel of land in the regional landscape (Risser et al. 1984) must be carefully considered. Restoration efforts can be time consuming, expensive, and subject to uncertainties, so the decision to undertake them should be weighed carefully. Prairie reconstruction should not be considered an alternative to the preservation or ecological enhancement of existing prairie remnants, since these latter efforts are more cost-effective and more likely to succeed.

Case studies and practical guidelines for prairie restoration (e.g., proceedings of the biennial Midwest or North American Prairie Conferences, and Reclamation and Management Notes) indicate that success depends as much on personal dedication and perseverance as on the application of scientific principles. The commitment to undertake years of manual seeding, transplanting, and weeding is laudatory but represents tremendous inputs of time and energy. As a consequence, successful prairie restoration projects tend to be few, small, and often private. Forty years of restoration efforts have developed many practical and effective "rules of thumb" but have not necessarily been guided by controlled experimentation and the systematic application of ecological theory. This chapter, therefore, attempts to bridge mainstream ecological research and mainstream restoration practice. Case studies of successful restoration efforts are provided and experimental methods for undertaking ecologically stable restoration are proposed. The theme we wish to emphasize is that a thorough understanding of the processes controlling the composition and maintenance of natural grasslands could result in more effective restoration efforts than can the simple mimicry of the floristics of prairie remnants. The more imaginative restoration efforts which result can, in turn, bring data to bear on many questions of community ecology theory.

WHAT MAKES A PRAIRIE?

Factors responsible for the origin and maintenance of North American grasslands have been debated for over a century. Ecosystems are a function not only of their abiotic environment and the properties of the species present but also of their history. Before attempting to reconstruct a prairie community, it is necessary to understand the factors responsible for the natural distribution, composition, and dynamics of native grasslands.

Phytogeography and Paleohistory--The major grasslands of North America (Fig. 1) are typically found in regions where patterns of summer precipitation and/or soils result in droughty conditions. Grasslands occur throughout a wide range of climatic zones and geological substrates. They exhibit local differences in topography and drainage as well as significant floristic differences. To infer a single explanation for the origin and natural maintenance of the physiognomic category we call "grassland" would be misleading. Principles of prairie restoration, therefore, are likely to be regionally specific.

The great continuous grasslands of the Central Plains stretch 1600 km from east to west and 3000 km from north to south (Fig. 1). They are typically divided into shortgrass, mixed-grass, and tallgrass zones, which follow a gradient of decreasing aridity from west to east in the rain shadow of the Rocky Mountains (Allen 1967, Sprague 1974). The dominant grass genera vary from

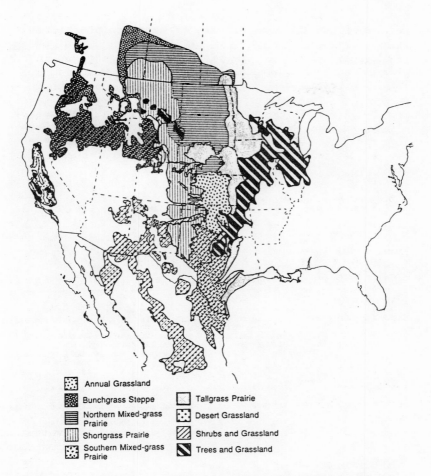

Legend:

- Annual Grassland
- Bunchgrass Steppe
- Northern Mixed-grass Prairie
- Shortgrass Prairie
- Southern Mixed-grass Prairie
- Tallgrass Prairie
- Desert Grassland
- Shrubs and Grassland
- Trees and Grassland

Fig 1.   Major grassland types of North America. Modified from Risser et al. 1981.

Bouteloua and Buchloe in the west, through Agropyron and Stipa to Andropogon, Sorghastrum, and Sporobolus in the east.   Some climatic, floristic and ecological trends are summarized in Table 1.

Secondary uplift of the Rocky Mountains 30 million years ago created an elevational barrier responsible for a massive rain shadow in their eastward lee (Singh et al. 1983).   The development of grasses and grasslands then

51

Table 1. Salient features of American prairies.

Attribute	Shortgrass	Mixed-grass	Tallgrass
Küchler (1964) Veg. Types	64,65	66,67,68,69,70	74,75,76,77,78,81,82
Presettlement Area,* km2	507,970	510,316	745,680
Remaining Area,* km2	332,910	264,070	198,710
Remaining Area,* %	63.6	51.7	26.6
Annual Precipitation,** cm	25-50	40-75	50-100
Potential Evapotranspiration** (P.E.T.), cm/year	89-195	71-160	62-139
Precipitation to P.E.T. Ratio** (during growing season)	0.3-0.5	0.4-0.7	0.6-1.0
Species Richness,*** spp./approx. 50 m2	13-28	37-44	31-57
Canopy Height, cm	15-60	40-120	80-180
Fire Periodicity,+ years	5-10	2-7	1-3
Dominant Grasses:++	Aristida purpurea Bouteloua gracilis Buchloe dactyloides Hilaria spp.	Agropyron spp. Aristida longiseta Bouteloua curtipendula Koeleria cristata Schizachyrium scoparium Stipa spp.	Andropogon gerardi Elymus canadensis Panicum virgatum S. scoparium Sorghastrum nutans Spartina pectinata Sporobolus heterol Stipa spartea
Dominant Forbs:++	Artemisia frigida Opuntia spp. Phlox hoodii Yucca spp.	Chrysopsis villosa Gutierrezia sarothrae Haplopappus spinulosus Psoralea spp. Ratibida columnifera Solidago missouriensis	Amorpha canescens Echinacea pallida Eryngyium yuccifol Liatris punctata Phlox pilosus Ratibida pinnata Silphium spp. Solidago rigida

Principal Sources:
*   Klopatek et al. 1979
** United States Geological Survey 1970
*** Vestal 1949
+   Sauer 1950, Wright and Bailey 1982
++ Weaver 1954, Weaver and Albertson 1956, Gould and Shaw 1983

progressed until their distribution approximated current patterns one to five million years ago (Dix 1964, Stebbins 1981). Pleistocene glaciation subsequently caused massive shifts in the climatic and vegetational zones of the continent (Davis 1976). Repeated advances and retreats of glacial ice and colder climate resulted in countless extirpations and expansions of local populations. Not until the relatively recent hypsithermal (warm and dry) interval of 8300 to 1000 years ago did the grasslands fully reestablish their range in the tallgrass prairie region (Wright 1968).

Although we have scanty evidence of the composition of pre-glaciation grasslands, post-glacial grasslands are clearly composed of a flora with diverse and comparatively recent biogeographic affinities (Stebbins 1981). Many of the common shortgrass genera (Bouteloua, Buchloe, Aristida) are of Mexican and Central American origin and have C_4 photosynthetic pathways (Teeri and Stowe 1976, Risser 1985); on the other hand, common mixed-grass dominants such as Koeleria, Agropyron, Elymus, Poa, and Carex are of northern origin (Clements 1936, Stebbins 1981). Curtis (1959) likewise interprets the species of dry sites within the tallgrass region as derived from the southwestern deserts, while the lowland species have affinities with Alleghenian meadow and southeastern woodland or marshland species. Wells (1970) notes that some eastern coastal lands from Long Island to Florida are floristically similar to tallgrass prairies in the Midwest, being dominated by the same or related species of Andropogon, Schizachyrium, Sorghastrum, Panicum, and Spartina, all of southeastern woodland origin. All three components (southwestern, northern, southeastern) of the Great Plains flora appear to have had their origins in woodland habitats and achieve their greatest diversity there. Yet only in the Great Plains do they achieve physiognomic dominance, along with a marked lack of speciation (Wells 1970). Floristic diversity within a given prairie locality can, however, be rather high (e.g., over 100 native species in prairie remnants of less than two ha), an important consideration in prairie restoration and management.

Theories of Grassland Maintenance--There are two primary theories that attempt to explain why prairies persist, differing in the importance they ascribe to climate and to disturbance, namely fire. Holdridge (1947) defines a "steppe climate" to exist where the mean annual temperatures fall between 6° and $12^\circ C$, where average total precipitation ranges from 250 to 500 mm/yr, and where the ratio of evaporation to precipitation ranges from 1.0 to 2.0. Clements and Shelford (1939) also emphasize the close relationship of grassland distribution to climatic moisture conditions. Borchert (1950) noted the remarkable fit of the central North

53

American grasslands to the "wedge" of westerly air in the rain-shadow of the Rocky Mountains. This region narrows from west to east as moist Arctic air masses influence the Northeast and moist tropical air from the Gulf of Mexico affects the Southeast. The same general boundaries also match critical isopleths of winter precipitation, July rainfall and temperature patterns in drought years (Borchert 1950). The relationship between climate and prairie boundaries was demonstrated by the drought of the 1930s. Thousands of hardwood trees bordering the prairie region died while shortgrass and mixed-grass prairies extended their eastern boundaries by hundreds of kilometers (Weaver and Albertson 1956). Prairie restorations, therefore, are best restricted to drought-prone sites which had once been native grassland.

Climate alone, however, cannot explain the persistence of grasslands because dozens of planted tree species grow well in the "grassland climate." Treelessness in presettlement times was clearly maintained by wildfires (Wright and Bailey 1982). Early European travelers remarked on the extent and frequency of prairie fires, often set by Indians in the fall to drive game, or by lightning strikes (see quotations in Sauer 1950, Curtis 1959). Most juvenile trees and shrubs are killed or repressed by fire, but grasses and many forbs (non-graminoid herbs) recover because their perennating organs are protected beneath the soil. In many ways, this hemicryptophytic growth form (Raunkiaer 1934) represents a general adaptation of grasses to aerial disturbance, effective in coping with fire, drought, and grazing, all of which exerted sharp selective pressure throughout evolutionary history (Stebbins 1981, Anderson 1982). The boundary between grasslands and forests (principally trembling aspen [Populus tremuloides], oak [Quercus spp.] or pine [Pinus spp.]) fluctuates as fires alternately destroy trees and wet periods allow tree seedlings to establish (Gleason 1913). The role of fire seems indisputable, as the suppression of wildfires since European settlement, accompanied by no detectable climatic cooling or moistening in the last 100 years, has resulted in the rapid natural forestation of oak savanna understories in Wisconsin (Curtis 1959), the coalescence of trembling aspen groves in Saskatchewan (Looman 1979), and numerous examples of woody encroachment in present-day prairies.

Prairie fires occur in the spring and fall or during droughts, when accumulated grass litter and standing dead material are more abundant than green foliage. Spring or fall fires retard the growth of such cool-season species with C_3 metabolism as Kentucky bluegrass (<u>Poa</u> <u>pratensis</u>; Curtis and Partch 1948, Engle and Bultsma 1984), smooth brome (<u>Bromus</u> <u>inermis</u>), and many annual weeds. Native warm-season (C_4 metabolism) prairie species are usually dormant at this time and therefore are relatively unharmed. Fire is thus the most powerful tool for excluding (predominantly C_3) exotic and woody invading plant species in remnant and restored prairies, while it promotes the growth of C_4 and native fire-adapted C_3 species (Steuter 1987). Because fire removes shade and ground litter, it stimulates the productivity, vigor, and diversity of native prairie species by allowing the soil and hence the plant roots to warm up more rapidly in the spring. Significant growth is thus initiated when moisture is still plentiful (Rice and Parenti 1978). These positive effects of fire are not universal in grasslands and can instead be negative when the vegetation is already stressed, as is frequently the case in the more drought-prone region west of the 100th meridian (Dix 1960). Surprisingly, the effects of nutrient release from the burning of plant material appear to be negligible (Kucera and Ehrenreich 1962, Risser et al. 1981, Wright and Bailey 1982, Hulbert 1984). Grasslands are "fed from the bottom up," with much nutrient cycling achieved through the death and decomposition of fine roots, thereby producing chernozemic soils rich in organic matter and highly desirable for agriculture.

In summary, neither a droughty climate nor fire alone explains the distribution and maintenance of prairies of the Great Plains: fire in a forest climate retards forest development and may result in scrub; fire in a prairie climate usually helps to maintain and even to enlarge the prairie (Transeau 1935). Although climate can be a critical consideration in choosing appropriate locales and species for prairie restoration, fire is the most powerful tool for the maintenance and enhancement of remnant, degraded and reconstructed grasslands.

<u>Distinctive</u> <u>Properties</u> <u>and</u> <u>Processes</u>--Grassland ecosystems exhibit a number of characteristics that are

often direct or indirect consequences of adaptation by grasses and prairie forbs to the overriding influences of period drought and fire. Unlike forest ecosystems, grasslands tend to have more biomass below the soil surface than above it. Rooting depths of 2 to 5 m are not uncommon in prairie plants with heights less than 0.4 to 2.0 m (Weaver 1954), presumably an evolutionary response to frequent moisture deficits in the surface soil horizons. The crowns of most prairie plants are also at or below the soil surface and are thereby protected from drought, fire, grazing, and severe cold. Unlike the stress-adapted plants of deserts and tundra, however, prairie grasses have the potential for high productivity even under rather adverse conditions.

Because of the sharply seasonal climate, this tremendous aboveground standing crop dies back each fall. Decomposition rates are reduced during the subfreezing or cold-wet winters and droughty summers of the tallgrass region, so about 20 months are required for 50% of the annual litter production to disappear (Kucera et al. 1967). Because aboveground productivity is typically more than 20% greater than the rate of decomposition, litter accumulates (Golley and Golley 1972). Future growth, therefore, will be depressed unless the shading and mechanical barriers associated with this "excess" biomass are removed by grazing or by fire. While grazing and fire appear to be equivalent in their removal of standing dead and litter, the selectivity of grazers and the greater soil disturbance accompanying their activity can result in quite different consequences to prairie community composition (Collins 1987).

Grasslands are also unusual among terrestrial ecosystems in the relative magnitude of grazing and detrital energy pathways. Insects and rodents often consume more foliage than do large ruminant grazers, and the amount of foliage that falls to the ground and is subsequently decomposed by bacteria and fungi can be even greater (McNaughton et al. 1982). Like fire, moderate grazing stimulates the diversity and productivity of grasslands through mechanisms that are not yet completely understood. Trampling by hoofed animals accelerates the breakdown of litter and exposes mineral soil for colonization by ruderal species, today often exotic weeds. Redistribution and concentration of nutrients, particularly nitrogen, in the form of urine and feces also has a stimulatory and heterogenizing effect on vegetation (McNaughton et al. 1982, Yonker and Schimel 1986). Despite the importance of microbial components of the ecosystem, we know little about such basic aspects of microbial biology as substrate specificity and responses of metabolic activity and population growth to changes in environmental conditions. These additional trophic levels have traditionally remained unaddressed in prairie restoration efforts.

GRASSLAND COMMUNITY ORGANIZATION

All autotrophic terrestrial plants use the same basic resources: sunlight, carbon dioxide, soil water, and mineral nutrients suspended in soil water. Since they compete for much the same resources, how are hundreds of plant species able to coexist in the prairie ecosystem, how is diversity maintained, and how can we promote diversity and persistence in reconstructed ecosystems?

Competition and Niche Differentiation--Community diversity and organization can be explained as the products of equilibrial or nonequilibrial processes (Connell 1978). Theories of equilibrium assume that plants sort themselves out according to their inherent attributes or niches and that each species survives and prospers at sites where it is adapted to the local abiotic environment and where it is competitively superior to other species in the acquisition of one or more resources. This sorting process may occur through coevolutionary adaptation (the differential survival and reproduction of interspecifically compatible genotypes; Turkington and Aarssen 1984) or simply by differential mortality among species at each microsite. Because plants must rely on the same basic resources, they partition them by having different optima of resource acquisition in space, time, or abundance. Some grass species, for example, avoid competition during the dry summer by extracting water from different depths; other species (cool-season grasses) grow mostly in the spring and fall (Bazzaz and Parrish 1982). Mycorrhizal fungi, symbiotic nitrogen-fixing bacteria, insect pollinators, and insect or vertebrate seed dispersers are essential resources for some plant groups but not for others,

57

thereby representing further potential for interspecific divergence in resource needs.

Bazzaz and Parrish (1982) propose that coexistence in grasslands occurs (1) by niche separation on the beta-scale, i.e., among habitats within a landscape or region; (2) by alpha-niche differentiation involving coevolution or pre-adaptation to reduce competition for resources among plants sharing the same location or "neighborhood"; and (3) by regeneration characteristics that enable species to become established on disturbed sites. The niche of a species can be envisioned as a multidimensional hypervolume composed of axes that represent all factors important to survival and reproduction (Hutchinson 1957). Species tend to differ in their optimal and tolerable responses to these factors and hence have different niches. The degree of niche overlap between two or more species defines the degree to which they are competing for the same resources or are likely to be interacting in the same place and time. Competition for limited resources, however, is not the only negative interaction between plants. The unknown importance of allelopathic influences in community organization should not be overlooked (Rice 1983).

Beta-niche differentiation in grasslands is governed principally by available soil moisture. The increasing rainfall and decreasing evapotranspiration encountered from the Rocky Mountains eastward to the Mississippi River can be thought of as one large but complex resource gradient. Shortgrass, mixed-grass, and tallgrass communities have developed in response to differences in moisture availability, although some elements of the flora can be found across the gradient. The same effect can be found in a topographic gradient (a catena covering hilltop, slope, and draw) on a more localized scale within the tallgrass region; again distinctive "dry," "mesic," or "wet" communities result (Weaver and Albertson 1956). Many practical guides to prairie restoration (e.g., Schramm 1978, Rock 1981, McClain 1986) use three to five basic moisture-level categories (e.g., wet, wet-mesic, mesic, dry-mesic, and dry) as the primary criteria for matching plant species with site conditions.

Other inter-habitat gradients exist as well, notably temperature and soil factors. Despite some remarkable floristic similarities over as much as 1000 km, north-south differences related to temperature tolerances

58

are clearly found (Gould and Shaw 1983). Differences in soil texture, fertility, and salinity also promote distinctive vegetation within grasslands (Looman 1980). Many of these factors, however, may also be important because of their impact on plant moisture relations: temperature affects stomatal behavior and hence water loss; soil texture determines the amount of water retainable in the soil column; and salinity lowers the water potential of soils (Redmann and Reekie 1982, Risser 1985).

Competition within communities is also reduced by means of niche differentiation in time. Northern, predominantly C_3, grasses may grow and reproduce during the cool, wet spring and fall. Southern, predominantly C_4, grasses are more tolerant of high temperatures and low moisture, and hence grow mostly in midsummer (Teeri and Stowe 1976). Species requiring high nutrient levels may accomplish most of their growth at times of the year when flushes of nitrate are released by soil microorganisms (Russell 1973), but the generality of this phenomenon remains to be demonstrated.

Staggered timing of various growth and reproduction processes is a common method of alpha-niche differentiation. In addition to the differences in growth phenology mentioned above, the range of flowering times varies widely. Species such as Anemone patens and Erythronium mesochoreum grow and reproduce before most grasses have even turned green. Competition for generalist pollinators within a community is reduced when the flowering times are staggered through the season or when flowers open and close at different times of the day or in response to weather-mediated cues (Parrish and Bazzaz 1979). Good reproductive success in a particular plant species may depend on including a number of plant species with flowering times that complement each other, in order to attract and maintain a sufficient population of appropriate pollinators (Parrish and Bazzaz 1979). Selecting plants to ensure a range of flowering times (typically 25% spring, 50% summer, 25% fall) and colors is common in prairie restorations planned for residential landscaping (Diekelmann and Schuster 1982). In this case, species selections made for aesthetic reasons also follow ecological principles of avoiding competition for pollinators.

Other forms of alpha-niche differentiation involve the physical stratification of resource-acquisition organs. Although forests may have tens of meters of aboveground structure within which to "carve out" specialized niches based on shade tolerance and stature, grasslands typically have less than one meter of foliage depth. Grasslands experience wide variation in light penetration and fairly high light intensity at 10 or 20 cm above ground level for much of the year (Old 1969). Canopy stratification nevertheless exists and the range of maximum plant heights in the prairie flora is wide. Many species occupy understory positions and can be expected to have intermediate levels of shade tolerance.

Diversity in growth form is also found belowground. Extensive excavations made by Sperry (1935), Weaver (1954), and others demonstrate that species vary greatly in rooting depth, density, and branching and in the overall distribution of primary rootlets in the profile. The dense fibrous sod of most grasses rarely extends to depths much greater than their maximum canopy height, but many prairie forbs have single taproots that may extend four or five m below the surface (Table 6.5 in Risser et al. 1981). Presumably, plants that have active roots at different locations in the soil profile will not compete so intensely with each other for soil resources. Rootlet density, root turnover rates, and root activity measurements suggest that deep roots function principally in securing water during times of drought.

Differences in the timing of root growth can also be important in avoiding competition (Harris 1967, 1977, Parrish and Bazzaz 1976). It remains to be tested whether a community purposely constructed of species with minimal root overlap is more productive, or more stable, than a random assemblage or a naturally occurring mixture of species.

Disturbance and Random Factors--In contrast to the importance ascribed to competition and niche differentiation in equilibrial theories, nonequilibrial theories place more importance on the randomness of interactions among species (Hubbell 1979) and on disturbance at many different scales (Pickett and White 1985). According to this theory, the persistence of a species in a community depends on its ability either to resist displacement by disturbance (Risser unpublished)

60

or to take advantage of space vacated by disturbance. Once established, plants are considered very difficult to displace, and "squatter's rights" of site occupancy often prevail over competitive ability. Site occupancy and competitive ability are both probably operative to some extent, and both attributes can be useful to prairie restoration. Many plant seedlings tend to "sort themselves out" so that different species attain dominance at sites with different substrate conditions. Nevertheless, established perennial species (whether native or exotic) are also very difficult to displace.

Nonequilibrial processes may operate at several levels to maintain community diversity. Some infrequent prairie species persist by high rates of dispersal in space or time (via a seed bank) to disturbances as small as the mounds created by burrowing mammals and ants or even the mineral soil exposed by hoofprints or bird scratchings. An entire guild of ruderal plant species depends on local disturbance in this manner (Platt 1975, Platt and Weiss 1977, Havercamp and Whitney 1983). These species are typically prolific and disperse widely or have dormancy mechanisms that allow them to take advantage of periodic openings in the canopy. Unfortunately, most native prairie ruderals have been replaced by Eurasian taxa that are particularly widespread as agricultural and roadside weeds.

The dominant prairie species have an impressive set of adaptations to moderate levels of disturbance in the form of drought, fire, and grazing. These adaptations (Table 2) generally allow prairie plants to respond favorably to water shortages, to temperature extremes, and to the removal of shoot material, often through the same "hide-below-ground" mechanism. These adaptations can be used to advantage by those seeking to include the most appropriate native species and to exclude non-native components from artificial prairie communities. Even when the dominant plants are very persistent and resilient, weed species showing rapid growth from seeds will prevail if fresh mineral soil is exposed. Site cultivation prior to planting prairie species is risky unless full weed control can be achieved through repeated shallow disking or by chemical means. Natural disturbances caused by moderate levels of animal activity, however, serve to maintain floristic diversity. Controlling the mode and scale of disturbance, therefore,

Table 2. Physiological-morphological adaptive strategies of grassland plants. From Risser 1985.

Drought
Mechanisms, such as closing of stomata, leaf curling, pubescence, and paraheliotropism, reduce water loss.
More belowground labile carbohydrates are stored under adequate moisture, thus reducing vulnerability of energy storage compounds.
Dark respiration decreases under drought stress conditions, thereby preserving substrate.
Gas exchange processes are maintained under water potentials of -2.0 to -4.0 MPa.
Water use efficiency is increased with C4 pathway, generally favored in drier climates.
Earlier seasonal growth, when moisture is adequate, is characterized by major investment in structural carbohydrates.
Dormancy avoids adverse season.
Germination is delayed over more than one year.
Seed has ability to germinate under relatively dry soil conditions.
Primary root grows rapidly and adventitious roots develop rapidly.
Root strength withstands shrink-swell characteristics of clay soils.

Temperature
Photosynthetic optima are related to carbon fixation pathway and coincident with prevailing temperature regime.
Plant acclimatizes to photosynthetic temperature optimum.
Root respiration temperature optima are correlated with optimum temperatures for photosynthesis.

Nutrients
Rapid nutrient uptake occurs during season when nutrients are available and soil moisture is adequate.
Plant internally stores and recycles nutrients.
Nutrient uptake and consequent increase in forage quality occurs during season when plant is most tolerant to grazing.
Legumes harbor nitrogen-fixation mechanism, and while associated vegetation acquires some nitrogen from legumes, these other herbaceous plants are more efficient than legumes at scavenging soil nitrogen.
Ammonia lost from the soil surface is absorbed by the plant canopy.
Mineral loss of nutrients occurs via leaching from grass leaves.

Grazing
Plants offer various antiherbivore devices: toxic compounds, low palatability, course seed stalks, and short growth cycle.
Intercalary meristems permit continuous regrowth, and buds may be near soil surface and thereby protected from grazing.
Increase in total herbage production and rate of photosynthesis occur with light to moderate grazing, and reduction of inefficient photosynthetic tissue coincides with grazing pressure.
Plant increases allocation of assimilates to young leaves and regrowing tillers, a process that increases photosynthetic capacity, but may account for reduced root growth.
Reduced water supply may increase energy translocation to roots and crowns, but grazing increases energy translocation to young leaves.

Burning
Meristematic tissue is protected from burning.
Plants have rapid regrowth potential, especially in response to elevated soil surface temperatures.
Seed production increases following burning.

is important in maintaining the diversity and integrity of the prairie community and in managing prairie remnants and restorations.

Community Dynamics and Succession--The factors of disturbance, microhabitat heterogeneity, climatic fluctuation, and the regenerative attributes of plant species may be so dynamic and pervasive that compositional equilibrium with the physical environment rarely arises (Pickett and White 1985). An apparently uniform landscape of waving grasses randomly punctuated with the color of wildflowers may be either a highly organized and locally adapted association (as implied by the equilibrial theories) or a dynamic, haphazard jumble of establishing, growing, reproducing, and dying plants. The persistence strategies listed in Table 2 may result in a shifting exchange of propagules and species among patches as all (even climax) species capitalize on their ability to occupy ground. These different modes of community organization probably all operate simultaneously as well, with different equilibrial and nonequilibrial processes predominating under different circumstances. Little research has been done on the relative importance of competition and disturbance in grassland communities, though see Platt (1975), Platt and Weiss (1977) and Collins (1987). The general consensus is that undisturbed prairies are "closed communities" because of the usually dense sod and canopy structure. Although some native prairie species are known to be aggressive increasers when introduced to unvegetated sites, this expansion typically stops after the canopy closes, when sod forms, and when plants attain their mature stature. An established perennial can rarely be replaced without disturbance, a fortunate circumstance that allows us to plan a community and expect it to maintain itself after it is established.

Succession nevertheless occurs in grasslands, and even "mature" prairie is not a static entity. Ecologists and restorationists do not fully understand the successional trends, cycles, and preferences of many prairie species. Although prairies do not exhibit the pronounced changes in growth form and stature typical of forest succession, disturbances usually induce colonization by a suite of species that is eventually replaced over many years as the "climax" community recovers. This concept of community development through domination by successive suites of species is a central paradigm in ecology (McIntosh 1980). In recovering from intensive disturbances such as cultivation or surface mining, most ecosystems, including prairies, go through a loosely predictable sequence of domination by fast-growing annuals, followed by smaller, short-lived perennials, and finally by a self-maintaining ("climax") stand of large-stature, long-lived perennials. Weedy annuals and short-lived perennials currently find refuge in the agricultural fields and roadsides that cover the continent, but at one time they were restricted to gopher mounds, ant hills, buffalo wallows, and dry creek beds (Weaver and Fitzpatrick 1934, Roe 1951, Koford 1958, Curtis 1959, Platt 1975). Following severe drought, overgrazing or (to a lesser extent) fire, these species increase in abundance and hence are termed "increasers" by rangeland managers, for whom they are indicative of poor range conditions (Heady 1975). The differential survival and reinvasion of plant species on the Great Plains during and after the great drought of the 1930s clearly involved species replacement and recovery from disturbance (Weaver et al. 1935, Weaver and Albertson 1943). Fire alone rarely initiates the replacement of species in prairies because the dominant vegetation is well adapted to fire. Under severe environmental conditions such as drought in the semiarid shortgrass steppe region, however, fire can induce the invasion of annual weeds (Clarke et al. 1943, Curtis and Partch 1948, Dix 1960). Because the agricultural cultivation of grasslands typically entails complete destruction of the native vegetation, the recovery of abandoned fields is a slow process often limited by inadequate or negligible seed availability (Costello 1944, Rice et al. 1960, Fitch and Kettle 1980). Depending on the degree of soil degradation, the accumulation of organic matter and buildup of nitrogen (often with the aid of soil cyanobacteria) may facilitate successional development (Rice et al. 1960).

Studies in recent years have complicated this simple theory of succession: (1) the successional series often represent differences in dominance, not necessarily in presence, because the climax species may be present from the start but may take longer to establish; (2) although dramatic changes occur in old-field succession, the native prairie flora evolved in response to such disturbances as fire, drought, and grazing, events that do not induce such distinctive replacement sequences; (3) species replacement, when it occurs, may be the result of microsite modification (resource depletion, microclimate amelioration, shade and organic matter buildup) or may simply be the result of differential competitive ability or longevity; and (4) a dynamic mosaic of large and small disturbances in various stages of recovery is found even in climax communities. True succession, in terms of the replacement of species, may be more important in prairies on the scale of hoof prints and animal burrows than at the level of the landscape.

Some aspects of successional theory may be useful in prairie restoration; at the same time, restoration may also help to resolve a number of theoretical questions regarding succession. For example, colonizing annuals can either inhibit or facilitate the establishment of perennial species and a climax plant community (Iverson and Wali 1982). There is some debate over whether weed control during the first year or two of community reconstruction is worth the effort since the native prairie species (with their superior competitive ability and greater persistence) should eventually prevail. We know that annual cover crops such as wheat and oats can reduce the presence of weeds without persisting in a forage community (Smith 1962), and their use in prairie reconstruction is widespread but sparsely documented. Some authors (e.g., Rock 1981, Burton et al. 1988) suggest using native annuals (e.g., _Ambrosia artemisiifolia_, _Cassia fasciculata_, _Helianthus annuus_) to provide this original cover crop, but these annuals must be vigorous enough to compete successfully with agricultural weeds. Practicing restorationists, however, are reluctant to introduce aggressive or otherwise noxious annual species because these plants may reseed and persist or spread. If we think of successional time as a niche axis, the absence of colonizing annuals in a seed mixture represents an empty niche, an open invitation to unwanted invaders. To fill that niche with native species would, therefore, be best. Another approach is to mow colonizing annuals during the first year of restoration, thereby hastening successional replacement by the planted perennials (Iverson and Wali 1987). Simple experiments are needed to test the long-term compositional effects of diligent manual weeding, of no weed control, of weed control by mowing, of the use of a cereal cover crop such as oats, and of the use of a cover crop of native annuals.

In general, the best guideline to maintaining the stability and quality of a restored prairie after initial seedling establishment is to employ the forces responsible for natural grassland maintenance. This means proper siting to encourage droughtiness (use original prairie land, or south-facing slopes, hill crests, or sandy areas elsewhere), no use of irrigation or fertilizer, and repeated use of controlled fire and perhaps grazing (or its substitute, mowing). If the appropriate species are present, they should persist and thrive under these conditions.

RESTORATION CASE STUDIES FROM ILLINOIS

Numerous approaches to prairie restoration have been tried over the last 40 years. Most have been local "learn-as-you-go" programs, with little published information and no widely accepted practices on which to base plans. Many of these independent efforts have developed effective techniques that are now widely accepted. We discuss several successful prairie reconstructions in Illinois to illustrate three major approaches: (1) large-scale, labor-intensive; (2) large-scale, mechanical; and (3) small-scale. These three case studies represent current practices in prairie restoration, demonstrating methods that vary in their effectiveness and in their underlying ecological assumptions. All restoration efforts are experimental by virtue of their trial-and-error nature, though the "experiments" may not be designed to test any general ecological theories. These and other examples could readily lend themselves to the explicit testing of a number of interesting hypotheses.

Large-scale Labor-intensive Approaches: The Morton Arboretum Prairie--The Morton Arboretum Prairie (now about seven ha in size) near Lisle, Illinois, was planted from 1963 to 1973. It was closely modelled after the Curtis and Greene Prairies established earlier at the University of Wisconsin Arboretum, near Madison, Wisconsin (Greene and Curtis 1953). Whereas parts of the Wisconsin prairie were established by direct seeding of prairie species into a bluegrass turf, all of the plantings at the Morton Arboretum were made into bare soil, primarily with seedlings started in a greenhouse (Schulenberg 1970). This effort has been characterized by a horticultural approach and has relied on dedicated volunteers for seed collection, propagation, transplanting, and weeding. About 6000 m^2 were added to the prairie in this manner every year for ten years (Armstrong 1986).

Seeds were collected from prairie remnants within about 50 km of Chicago, and these areas also served as models for species composition and proportions. Seeds of all species (grasses as well as forbs) were stratified and propagated in greenhouse flats in early winter. Site preparation involved shallow disking three or four times to promote the germination of weeds which were then killed by the next disking. The soil was disturbed as little as possible so that deeply buried weed seeds would not be exposed. Plants were typically outplanted in May. Seedlings were planted on a grid, one plant per ft^2, in a ratio of three grasses to two forbs. Efforts at irregular planting, though more naturalistic, made manual weeding difficult. Weeding was necessary three times in the first year and once in the following spring. Subsequent control of exotics has been principally by annual spring fires. Persistent individuals or small patches of weeds continue to be removed manually or by using a broad-spectrum herbicide such as "Roundup," usually in conjunction with the transplanting of prairie plants into the same areas. Mechanical seeding was attempted, but results were patchy and the larger area was difficult to maintain.

A large corps of volunteers has helped with the prairie since 1979, manually removing weeds, cutting brush, and transplanting greenhouse seedlings of rare species. This approach, with its careful placement of individual plants, a high proportion of forbs, and intensive weeding, has produced an exceptionally diverse and aesthetically pleasing prairie with the appearance of a "wildflower meadow" (Armstrong 1986). The Morton Arboretum Prairie illustrates the value of using local genotypes, spacing seedlings widely so that competition among prairie species does not result in a loss of valuable plant material, and controlling competition from annuals. The key to the management and enhancement of this prairie has been the control of exotics through hand weeding and fire. Succession is not assumed to occur, with exotic weeds being manually replaced by native perennials instead. Tests of density-dependent mortality and weed invasion could be easily incorporated into this approach, as could tests of the stability or invasion-resistance of specific species mixtures.

<u>Large</u>-<u>scale</u> <u>Mechanical</u> <u>Approaches</u>: <u>The</u> <u>Knox</u> <u>College</u>
<u>Field</u> <u>Station</u>--The Knox College Biological Field Station
Prairie (located 32 km east of Galesburg, Illinois) was
started in 1955, but most of it has been established
since 1970 using drill seeding (Schramm 1970, 1978).
Some of the grass seed was originally obtained
commercially from suppliers in Nebraska, but most grass
and forb seed has since been collected from local prairie
remnants. Seed was stratified by mixing it with
vermiculite and storing it at $2^{\circ}C$ in plastic garbage
cans. Following plowing, the site was shallowly disked
and harrowed for a year (or at least at two-to-three-week
intervals during the spring) for weed control. Grasses
and forbs were sown in separate passes or from different
seeder boxes, using a Nesbit seed drill. A mixture of
<u>Andropogon</u>, <u>Schizachyrium</u>, <u>Sorghastrum</u>, and <u>Panicum</u> was
seeded at 50.4 kg/ha using three passes; forbs were
seeded at 22.4 kg/. Rates in each instance refer to the
seed/vermiculite mix. This mixture makes comparison
difficult, but other authors (e.g., McClain 1986)
recommend seeding rates for grasses of 16.8-22.4 kg/ha
for total pure live seed.

Schramm (1978) summarizes a number of strategies to
overcome the weed problem that inevitably arises after
the prairie seed is in the ground. The first is to use
late planting (in Illinois, the first two weeks of June)
to allow mechanical control of the first crop of spring
weeds. After seeding, mowing weeds to 30 cm whenever
they reach 60 to 100 cm prevents most of them from going
to seed during the first year or two. The annual use of
fire (starting 10 or 11 months after seeding, if
possible) every March or April also helps to control
weeds. Finally, Schramm stresses that patience is simply
required if native prairie species are to overtake weeds;
their perenniality, deep rooting, and general tolerance
to stress allows them to establish and eventually to
dominate.

Hand-planting at the Knox College Prairie is reserved
for forb enrichment of the grass matrix and for species
highly sensitive to competition. These species are
planted into hand-weeded areas as hardened seedlings.
Prairie reconstruction by planting successive small areas
every year is recommended in order to avoid committing an
entire site in a single year that may experience

disastrous weather. Small areas also allow manageable weed control in the early stages and permit the testing of alternative methods. Tests of native cover crops, manual or chemical weed control, weed mowing, regular burning and no weed management could be readily incorporated into this framework, as could tests of the stability of different species mixtures.

A program similar to that used at Knox College and based on mechanical matrix planting followed by manual enrichment with forbs is also recommended by McClain (1986). With emphasis on restoring an expansive prairie landscape, the approach places greater faith in succession and the competitiveness of native prairie species, but often (in practice) at the expense of high native diversity.

Small-scale Approaches: Home Landscaping--The most rapidly growing type of prairie restoration is residential and commercial landscaping (e.g., Smith and Smith 1980, Smyser 1982, Diekelmann and Schuster 1982, Diekelmann et al. 1986). While gardeners have long propagated native wildflowers in discrete beds, the reconstruction of entire plant communities under the concept of naturalistic landscaping has become popular only in the last few years. A landscaper or homeowner often tries to recreate the appearance of one or more ecosystems--an open meadow, an alpine rock garden, a woodland stream or understory--relying on a combination of exotic cultivars and native plants. This approach, however, has now developed to the point where the purist desires a landscape composed completely of species once native to the site, and that form of landscaping essentially represents ecosystem restoration on a small scale.

This mode of restoration benefits from a history of landscape design that includes an analysis of local geology, topography, hydrology, soils, climate, and presettlement vegetation, a degree of site analysis that may be lacking in other restoration efforts. Both a "functional analysis" of the anticipated long-term uses of the planting and a "visual analysis" of its imagery can be quite involved. The layout of grasses and forbs can be designed to generate patches of different color combinations at different times of the year, and the selection of plants of varying heights allows the creation of backdrops and depth (Diekelmann et al. 1986). Choosing plants with diverse flowering phenologies may also result in a range of growing periods that maximizes resource use during the year. Such variety inevitably facilitates resource partitioning and high local diversity. The generally smaller scale of a residential prairie makes weed control more practical, although regular burning may be difficult. Because complete weed control is feasible, resource supplementation (irrigation, fertilization) is also permissible, thereby promoting rapid establishment and "community development" with no dependence on succession. A reasonably attractive "prairie" can be established in as little as three years.

Armstrong (1985) recently described her experiences in establishing a prairie at her suburban home in Naperville, Illinois. Based on a desire to create a home that is part of the natural environment, her passive solar house integrates insulative architecture and prairie-savanna landscaping. In addition to carefully planted beds of tall grasses and forbs using the Morton Arboretum method, Armstrong has established a buffalo grass (Buchloe dactyloides) lawn, desirable for its short stature, low moisture requirements, and resistance to trampling (Evander 1986, Knoop 1986). Small swards of this native American grass could represent a nice experimental system for testing the balance of resource levels (water, fertilizer) and initial spacing (plant density) that best maintains the population, perhaps with and without weeding or mowing, under the rich local site conditions.

Armstrong (1985, 1986) advises that watering promotes rapid establishment and flowering of prairie plants, that spring planting (following weed control) is preferable to fall planting, and that natural landscaping--like field-scale restoration efforts--is best undertaken in small parcels. The tasks of seed collection and propagation can be enjoyable in themselves, but weeding is a perpetual chore. Diplomatic explanation or even court battles may be required in dealing with neighborhood objections or municipal weed ordinances that do not distinguish between untended weeds and natural landscaping.

<u>Similarities</u> <u>Among</u> <u>the</u> <u>Three</u> <u>Approaches</u>--The three case studies we have reviewed all share in the application of a number of ecological principles. Some restorationists place more importance than others on the use of locally collected genotypes, but all recognize the importance of carefully selecting species to match the prevailing site conditions. Prairie species clearly exhibit a variety of moisture preferences, rooting depths, canopy structures, temperature optima, and flowering times; these traits should fit the constraints of the site. Further, species should complement each other to minimize competitive interactions. Nearby prairie remnants are frequently a good model for prairie restoration, but other combinations of species are also aesthetically pleasing and apparently just as stable. Promoting high species richness or diversity is a universal goal but has usually been dependent on manual introduction of transplants. The establishment and maintenance of a reconstructed prairie community depend on control of competition by weeds and on using an appropriate disturbance regime such as fire. If a lot of time and seed are available, the processes of natural succession can be allowed to govern prairie establishment and enrichment; human intervention (by weeding, transplanting, even irrigating) can accelerate these processes. All restorations could readily include replicated trials to test different species mixtures or management regimes.

USING PRAIRIE RESTORATION TO
TEST HYPOTHESES OF COMMUNITY ORGANIZATION

Restoration techniques like those described above, in combination with the classic surveys and experiments of such researchers as F. E. Clements, J. E. Weaver, F. W. Albertson, and the International Biological Programme Grassland Biome group, have told us as much about the ecological properties of prairies as we know about any other natural system. Yet prairie restoration efforts are time consuming, frustrating, and prone to failure because of the difficulty in controlling weeds and woody plants while promoting a diverse, self-maintaining association of native species. Given these difficulties, prairie reconstruction should never be considered an alternative to the preservation or ecological enhancement (through selective species removal and addition) of even the most degraded prairie remnants.

Why is the reassembly of this biological community so difficult? Historical changes in a number of ecological factors are clearly important. The current climate is slightly cooler and moister than that of the hypsithermal interval (8300 to 1000 years ago) when the present-day prairie established itself following glacial retreat (Dorf 1960). Such agents of disturbance as wildfires and herds of free-roaming bison are no longer a part of the landscape, although they can be reintroduced on a limited scale. Finally, European settlement has created landscapes dominated by crop monocultures, exposed mineral soil, and a biogeographic explosion of exotic colonizers that thrive in disturbed areas.

Given these de facto changes in the environment, what can be done to enhance the success of restoration efforts? We believe that restoration science would benefit by incorporating ideas from the more academic or theoretical aspects of plant ecology. Restoration science should borrow basic information and approaches from such ecological subdisciplines as autecology (the study of species site relationships and requirements), community organization theory (especially the quantification of interspecific competition and compatibility), and stability theory (with its emphasis on disturbance regimes). There is a general need for an enhanced scientific approach to supplement what has often been an empirical, trial-and-error approach that has focused simply on learning how to grow different plant species. Now that successful propagation techniques have been identified for most prairie species, efforts should be shifted to replicated field trials that test the compatibility and persistence of various combinations of species. In general, restoration efforts would benefit most from a more conscientious application of the scientific method in the many experimental trials now being carried out. All innovations should be replicated (ideally across several soil types, landform types, and even climate regimes) and compared with controls through repeated quantitative monitoring. Results should be assessed statistically and reported in the literature. In turn, theoretical ecology would benefit from such empirical tests of its hypotheses and predictions.

72

Prairie restoration, therefore, offers a useful mechanism for investigating many issues of theoretical community ecology, especially since we have more than 40 years of accumulated information on more than 200 candidate species. In addition, demand is growing for the reintroduction of these species and the restoration of naturalistic prairie landscapes for a variety of scientific, educational, aesthetic, and historical reasons.

Niche Quantification and Resource Partitioning--To illustrate how ecological theory can be applied to prairie restoration, we recently described how niche quantification and site-matching techniques might be used to select plant species that would improve the long-term stability of reconstructed prairie communities (Burton et al. 1988). First, variability in soil moisture (generally the factor governing grassland organization) is described by means of a frequency distribution (histogram) of soil moisture measurements made over time or over space during periods of partial drought. Smoothing this distribution to form a curve, we describe the polygon (the area under the curve) so formed as defining the available "environmental space" (the ES curve in Fig. 2). It approximates the range and frequency of conditions to which plants at this location will be exposed, thereby indicating the range and abundance of resource levels (i.e., soil moisture states) available for exploitation. We then use the results of direct gradient analysis surveys (e.g., Nelson and Anderson 1983) or experimental growth studies to describe the performance of all candidate plant species across the full range of resource levels (soil moisture conditions). These gradient response curves describe the fundamental niche (if based on the experimental performance of species grown in monoculture) or the realized niche (if based on observed performance within the natural vegetation) of each species (sensu Hutchinson 1957). Response curves are standardized so that each species has an optimum performance of 100%; this procedure allows us to compare curve location and shape independent of the magnitude of a given response. The standardized gradient response curves are then overlaid on the environmental space curve, as shown for six graminoid species in Fig. 2.

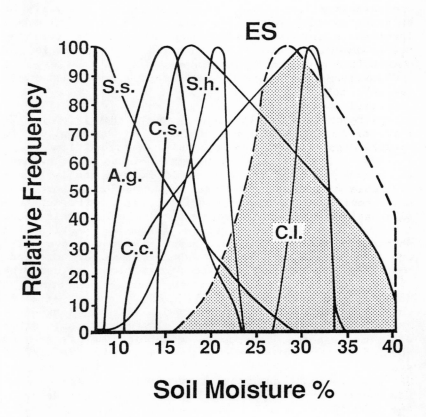

Fig. 2. Overlay of standardized moisture response curves for six graminoid species and a moisture-defined environmental space (ES) for a particular locale. Species abbreviations are as follows: S.s. = Schizachyrium scoparium; A.g. = Andropogon gerardii; C.c. = Calamagrostis canadensis; C.s. = Carex stricta; S.h. = Sporobolus heterolepis; and C.l. = Carex lacustris. Species curves are modified from Nelson and Anderson 1983. The shaded area represents the maximum occupancy (83.15%) of the environmental space possible for this set of species. From Burton et al. 1988.

We now try to fill the environmental space as fully as possible with desired species, on the assumption that the absence of an adapted species at a critical location in space or time (e.g., very wet site conditions) would leave the community open to invasion by exotics that can take advantage of this "vacant niche" with its unexploited resources. The total percentage occupancy of the environmental space (measured by the area under the curves) achieved by selected combinations of six graminoid species is presented in Table 3. The overlap values reported in Table 3 are simple computations of the area of overlap among the standardized curves of specified species, expressed as a percentage of the total

Table 3. Occupancy of environmental space (ES) and interspecific overlap values calculated for selected combinations of species. From Burton et al. 1988.

No. of Spp.	Mixture	Species Composition	Occupancy of ES (%)	Species Overlap (% of ES)	Occupancy Minus Overlap
1	A	Ss, Schizachyrium scoparium	10.64	-	10.64
	B	Ag, Andropogon gerardii	5.44	-	5.44
	C	Cs, Carex stricta	69.92	-	69.92
	D	Sh, Sporobolus heterolepis	9.00	-	9.00
	E	Cc, Calamagrostis canadensis	67.11	-	67.11
	F	Cl, Carex lacustris	28.51	-	28.51
2	G	Ss,Sh	9.36	7.45	1.91
	H	Ag,Cs	69.92	5.44	64.48
	I	Ag,Cl	33.17	0	33.17
	J	Cs,Cc	83.15	53.89	29.26
	K	Sh,Cl	37.51	0	37.51
3	L	Ss,Sh,Cl	14.87	7.81	7.06
	M	Ag,Cs,Cc	83.15	59.33	23.82
	N	Cs,Cc,Cl	83.15	102.97	-19.82
4	O	Ss,Ag,Cs,Sh	69.92	37.25	32.67
	P	Ss,Ag,Sh,Cl	38.79	21.05	17.74
	Q	Ss,Cs,Cc,Cl	83.15	154.70	-71.55
	R	Cs,Sh,Cc,Cl	83.15	153.06	-69.91
5	S	Ss,Ag,Cs,Cc,Cl	83.15	160.14	-76.99
	T	Ss,Ag,Cs,Sh,Cl	76.92	79.94	-3.02
	U	Ss,Cs,Sh,Cc,Cl	83.15	163.70	-80.55
	V	Ag,Cs,Sh,Cc,Cl	83.15	158.50	-75.35
6	W	Ss,Ag,Cs,Sh,Cc,Cl	83.15	169.14	-85.99

area under the environmental space curve. Any of the many mathematical indices designed to measure niche overlap (Giller 1984) could be chosen to measure both environmental space occupancy and interspecific overlap, but we use a simple geometric method here to foster an intuitive interpretation of "overlap area." These calculations allow us to select the best single and multi-species matches to the site. While the average amount of utilized environmental space increases with the number of species, note that maximum occupancy can also be attained with only two species (Carex stricta and Calamagrostis canadensis). Additional species add to the degree of interspecific overlap but not to the overall occupancy of the environmental space. It is worth noting that many wet-mesic prairies in northern Illinois, Iowa and Wisconsin are, in fact, dominated by these same two species (Nelson and Anderson 1983).

A number of theoretical and practical questions regarding the determinants of competitive pressure and community stability can now be raised. Four hypotheses for compositional stability clearly make mutually exclusive predictions that could be tested by establishing and monitoring the compositional stability of the species mixtures listed in Table 3.

(1) If total occupancy of environmental space (first column in Table 3) is a reliable indicator of stability, then mixture G (9.36% occupancy) should rapidly become more weedy than mixture J, also consisting of two species but with 83.15% occupancy.

(2) If diffuse competition or diversity per se is important, then mixture W (six species) should be more stable than mixture J (two species), though each has 83.15% occupancy.

(3) If minimization of overlap among species (second column in Table 3) is important, then mixture M (59.33% overlap within the environmental space) should be more stable than mixture N, another three-species mixture with 102.97% overlap; both mixtures have 83.15% occupancy.

(4) If the difference between occupancy of environmental space and overlap of species (third column in Table 3) is most important, then mixture I (+33.17% net difference) should behave much like mixture O (+32.67% net difference), though they have different occupancy and niche overlap values.

76

This approach can be used with other resource axes as well. Separation of species along a moisture gradient or a moisture-derived environmental space can represent beta-niche or alpha-niche differentiation in terms of the ability of species to withstand various extremes of soil moisture over space or during a season. Other alpha-niche axes worth exploring include the vertical and horizontal deployment of leaves and roots, light intensity (shade tolerance), and the phenology of growth and flowering. Once again, the guiding principle is to occupy the environmental space fully and to minimize deleterious interactions among desired species. The unproven nature of these suggestions means that the efficacy of filling the environmental space and minimizing niche overlap needs to be tested for each niche axis. It is not difficult, however, to imagine highly practical benefits from incorporating this element of design into the prairie restoration process. For example, the persistence of exotic cool-season grasses such as Poa pratensis in restored prairies suggests that there is an "empty" niche in terms of growth form and position on the phenological axis. We suggest testing the use of high densities of fast-growing, native, rhizomatous cool-season graminoid species (e.g., Hierochloe odorata and some Carex spp.) in the original prairie planting in order to more fully occupy the phenological space and thereby retard the invasion of Poa.

The Need for Greater Latitude in Experimentation-- Purists may argue that we cannot experiment with species composition in bona fide restoration efforts because our objective should always be to emulate the pre-existing natural vegetation or some nearby remnant of it. This concern seems unnecessarily restrictive if we consider the great fluidity of species distributions in the Great Plains region. The relatively short history of our modern prairies, their diverse floristic origins, and the low rates of endemism (Wells 1970, Stebbins 1981, Axelrod 1985) all suggest that we could allow greater latitude in the assembly of stable communities than is exhibited by remnant prairies today, themselves often isolated and no longer controlled by natural pressures. Pollen cores retrieved from the sediments of lakes and bogs reveal that forest communities were dismantled and reassembled with little fidelity to the community types we recognize today (Davis 1976, 1981, Delcourt and Delcourt 1987); the same process can be inferred for grasslands.

Some species are naturally restricted to very specific habitats and associations, while other widespread species, such as <u>Schizachyrium scoparium</u>, can be a component of most prairie communities. Benninghoff (1968) has suggested that a history of repeated disturbance has resulted in dominance by broad-niched species capable of coping with great physical stresses through intraspecific variability and plasticity. This theory would explain the remarkable similarity in species composition sometimes found in rather different grassland habitats (Weaver 1954). These observations suggest that common prairie species should be successful in most restoration efforts, but they do not mean that less common species should only be planted with their (present-day) natural associates.

The species assemblages that we understand to typify virgin prairie do not represent an ancient, immutable "super-organism" perfectly synchronized to its environment. Rather, these associations are a few of the countless potential "snapshots" portraying the endless ebb and flow of more or less independently assorting species responding to climate and disturbance (Gleason 1926, 1939). For over 20 million years, species have been mixed and stirred by recurring periods of hot and cold and wet and dry conditions (Risser et al. 1981). Particular species or species groups were alternately favored or repressed by changes in climate, topography, and competitive neighborhood. This interpretation of the dynamic nature of grassland composition and the independent assortment of species is supported by direct observations during and after droughts (Weaver and Albertson 1956, Coupland 1958). Yet floristic dynamism has often been overlooked in the planning of ecosystem restoration efforts because we tend to revere remnants of undisturbed vegetation as perfectly structured ecosystems that define our ideal objectives in restoration. We must guard against the romantic notion that an unplowed patch of vegetation represents an <u>optimal</u> combination of species, genotypes, and interactions for a particular site. Rather, it more probably represents one of any number of stochastic but <u>tolerable</u> combinations.

With some coordination, it would not be difficult to incorporate experiments (such as those proposed above) into the prairie restoration plans of various agencies or institutions. Since restoration is best attempted on small parcels of land, each plot could quite easily and usefully be a replicate for testing one of the many hypotheses posed regarding the role of annual colonizers, the degree to which and rate at which species sort themselves out according to local site differences, the relationships between diversity and stability, the existence of vacant phenological niches, the equivalence of mowing, grazing and fire, and so forth. These experimental plots, on which long-term observations are generally desired, can be part of the desired restored landscape while also providing data which, in turn, could enhance future prairie restoration efforts and our understanding of the principles of community ecology.

In our efforts to conserve genetic diversity, to preserve the prairie landscape, and to learn more about how communities function, we should more often take the initiative to establish and monitor artificial arrays of species and artificial disturbance regimes. While the inquisitive dismantling of ecosystems (reductionism) has proven useful in the past, we may now learn even more by attempting to reassemble these complex systems.

ACKNOWLEDGMENTS

We appreciate the critical comments and discussion offered by E. B. Allen, R. C. Anderson, P. K. Armstrong, F. A. Bazzaz, T. A. Day, A. S. Hodgins, W. E. McLain, R. C. Moran, J. A. D. Parrish, P. Schramm, M. K. Solecki and three anonymous reviewers. Support for the principal author was provided by the Illinois Department of Transportation.

LITERATURE CITED

Aber, J. D., and W. R. Jordan, III. 1986. Restoration ecology (Abstract). Page 73. Program of the Fourth International Congress of Ecology, August 10-16, 1986, Syracuse, New York, USA.

79

Allen, D. L. 1967. The life of prairies and plains. McGraw-Hill, New York, New York, USA.

Anderson, R. C. 1982. An evolutionary model summarizing the roles of fire, climate, and grazing animals in the origin and maintenance of grasslands: an end paper. Pages 297-308 in J. R. Estes, R. J. Tyrl, and J. N. Brunken, editors. Grasses and Grasslands: Systematics and Ecology. University of Oklahoma Press, Norman, Oklahoma, USA.

Armstrong, P. K. 1985. Life at Prairie Sun: weeds, water bans, and worried neighbors. Morton Arboretum Quarterly 21:17-30.

_____. 1986. Lectures presented at the Grand Prairie Friends Prairie Plant Propagation Workshop. April 12, 1986, Penfield, Illinois, USA.

Axelrod, D. I. 1985. Rise of the grassland biome, central North America. Botanical Review 51:163-201.

Bazzaz, F. A., and J. A. D. Parrish. 1982. Organization of grassland communities. Pages 233-254 in J. R. Estes, R. J. Tyrl, and J. N. Brunken, editors. Grasses and Grasslands: Systematics and Ecology. University of Oklahoma Press, Norman, Oklahoma, USA.

Benninghoff, W. S. 1968. Biological consequences of Quaternary glaciations in the Illinois region. Pages 70-77 in R. E. Bergstrom, editor. The Quaternary of Illinois. University of Illinois College of Agriculture Special Publication No. 14, Urbana, Illinois, USA.

Borchert, J. R. 1950. The climate of the central North American grassland. Annals of the Association of American Geographers 40:1-39.

Burton, P. J., K. R. Robertson, L. R. Iverson, and P. G. Risser. 1988. Suggested applications of ecological theory to prairie restoration. Paper 01.16 in A. Davis and G. Stanford, editors. The Prairie: Roots of Our Culture; Foundation of Our Economy. Proceedings of the Tenth North American Prairie Conference, June 22-26, 1986, Denton, Texas. The Native Prairie Association of Texas, Dallas, Texas, USA.

Clarke, S. E., E. W. Tisdale, and N. A. Skoglund. 1943. The effects of climate and grazing practices on short-grass vegetation in southern Alberta and southwestern Saskatchewan. Canadian Department of Agriculture, Publication No. 147, Ottawa, Ontario, Canada.

Clements, F. E. 1936. Origin of the desert climax and climate. Pages 87-140 in T. H. Goodspell, editor. Essays in Geobotany in Honor of William Albert Setchell. University of California Press, Berkeley, California, USA.

Clements, F. E., and V. E. Shelford. 1939. Bioecology. John Wiley & Sons, New York, New York, USA.

Collins, S. L. 1987. Interaction of disturbances in tallgrass prairie: a field experiment. Ecology 68:1243-1250.

Connell, J. H. 1978. Diversity in tropical rain forests and coral reefs. Science 199:1302-1310.

Costello, D. F. 1944. Natural revegetation of abandoned plowed land in the mixed prairie association of northeastern Colorado. Ecology 25:312-326.

Coupland, R. T. 1958. The effects of fluctuations in weather upon the grasslands of the Great Plains. Botanical Review 24:273-317.

Curtis, J. T. 1959. The vegetation of Wisconsin. University of Wisconsin Press, Madison, Wisconsin, USA.

Curtis, J. T., and M. L. Partch. 1948. Effect of fire on the competition between blue grass and certain prairie plants. The American Midland Naturalist 39:437-443.

Davis, M. B. 1976. Pleistocene biogeography of temperate deciduous forests. Geoscience and Man 13:13-26.

_____. 1981. Quaternary history and the stability of forest communities. Pages 132-153 in D. C. West, H. H. Shugart, and D. B. Botkin, editors. Forest Succession: Concepts and Application. Springer-Verlag, New York, New York, USA.

Delcourt, P. A., and H. R. Delcourt. 1987. Long-term Forest Dynamics of the Temperate Zone: a Case Study of Late-Quaternary Forests in Eastern North America. Springer-Verlag, New York, New York, USA.

Diekelmann, J., J. Harrington, and E. A. Howell. 1986. An approach to residential landscaping with prairie. Pages 242-248 in G. K. Clambey and R. H. Pemble, editors. The Prairie-Past, Present and Future: Proceedings of the Ninth North American Prairie Conference, 29 July-1 August 1984. Tri-College University, Moorhead, Minnesota, USA.

Diekelmann, J., and R. Schuster. 1982. Natural landscaping: designing with native plant communities. McGraw-Hill, New York, New York, USA.

Dix, R. L. 1960. The effects of burning on the mulch structure and species composition of grasslands in western North Dakota. Ecology 41:49-55.

_____. 1964. A history of biotic and climatic changes within the North American grassland. Pages 71-89 in D. J. Crisp, editor. Grazing in Terrestrial and Marine Environments. Blackwell Scientific Publications, Oxford, England.

Dorf, E. 1960. Climatic changes of the past and present. American Scientist 48:341-364.

Engle, D. M., and P. M. Bultsma. 1984. Burning northern mixed prairie during a drought. Journal of Range Management 37:398-401.

Evander, J. 1986. Buffalograss as a low-maintenance lawn turf. Tenth North American Prairie Conference Abstracts, June 22-26, 1986, Denton, Texas. The Native Prairie Association of Texas, Dallas, Texas, USA.

Fitch, H. S., and W. D. Kettle. 1980. Ecological succession in vegetation and small mammal population on a natural area of northeastern Kansas. Pages 117-121 in C. L. Kucera, editor. Proceedings of the Seventh North American Prairie Conference, August 4-6, 1980. Southwest Missouri State University, Springfield, Missouri, USA.

Giller, P. S. 1984. Community structure and the niche. Chapman and Hall, London, England.

Gleason, H. A. 1913. The relation of forest distribution and prairie fires in the Middle West. Torreya 13:173-181.

_____. 1922. The vegetational history of the Middle West. Annals of the Association of American Geographers 12:39-85.

_____. 1926. The individualistic concept of the plant association. Bulletin of the Torrey Botanical Club 53:7-26.

_____. 1939. The individualistic concept of the plant association. The American Midland Naturalist 21:92-110.

Golley, P. M., and F. B. Golley, editors. 1972. Papers from a symposium on tropical ecology with an emphasis on organic productivity. Institute of Ecology, University of Georgia, Athens, Georgia, USA.

Gould, F. W., and R. B. Shaw. 1983. Grass systematics. Second edition. Texas A&M University Press, College Station, Texas, USA.

Greene, H. C., and J. T. Curtis. 1953. The re-establishment of an artificial prairie in the University of Wisconsin Arboretum. Wild Flower 29:77-88.

Harris, G. A. 1967. Some competitive relationships between Agropyron spicatum and Bromus tectorum. Ecological Monographs 37:89-111.

_____. 1977. Root phenology as a factor of competition among grass seedlings. Journal of Range Management 30: 172-177.

Havercamp, J., and G. G. Whitney. 1983. The life history characteristics of three ecologically distinct groups of forbs associated with the tallgrass prairie. American Midland Naturalist 109:107-119.

Heady, H. F. 1975. Rangeland management. McGraw-Hill, New York, New York, USA.

Holdridge, L. R. 1947. Determination of world plant formations from simple climatic data. Science 105:367-368.

Hubbell, S. P. 1979. Tree dispersion, abundance, and diversity in a tropical dry forest. Science 203:1299-1309.

Hulbert, L. C. 1984. Causes of fire effects in tallgrass prairie (Abstract). Bulletin of the Ecological Society of America 65:180.

Hutchinson, G. E. 1957. Concluding remarks. Cold Spring Harbor Symposia on Quantitative Biology 22:415-427.

Iverson, L. R., and M. K. Wali. 1982. The reclamation of coal mined lands: the role of Kochia scoparia and other pioneers in early succession. Reclamation and Revegetation Research 1:123-160.

Iverson, L. R., and M. K. Wali. 1987. Mowing of annual colonizers to enhance revegetation after surface mining in North Dakota. Reclamation and Revegetation Research 6:157-161.

Jenkins, R. 1973. Ecosystem restoration. Pages 23-27 in L. C. Hulbert, editor. Third Midwest Prairie Conference Proceedings. Kansas State University, Manhattan, Kansas, USA.

King, J. E. 1981a. Late Quaternary vegetational history of Illinois. Ecological Monographs 51:43-62.

_____. 1981b. The prairies of Illinois. The Living Museum 43:42-45.

Klopatek, J. M., R. J. Olson, C. J. Emerson, and J. L. Joness. 1979. Land-use conflicts with natural vegetation in the United States. Environmental Conservation 6:191-199.

Knoop W. E. 1986. Buffalograss for home lawns. Tenth North American Prairie Conference Abstracts, June 22-26, 1986, Denton, Texas. The Native Prairie Association of Texas, Dallas, Texas, USA.

Koford, C. B. 1958. Prairie dogs, whitefaces, and blue grama. Wildlife Monographs 3:1-78.

Kucera, C. L., R. C. Dahlman, and M. R. Koelling. 1967. Total net productivity and turnover on an energy basis for tallgrass prairie. Ecology 48:536-541.

Kucera, C. L., and J. H. Ehrenreich. 1962. Some effects of annual burning on central Missouri prairie. Ecology 43:334-336.

Küchler, A. W. 1964. Potential natural vegetation of the conterminous United States. American Geographical Society, New York, New York, USA.

Lemon, P. C. 1970. Prairie ecosystem boundaries in North America. Pages 13-18 in P. Schramm, editor. Proceedings of a Symposium on Prairie and Prairie Restoration. Knox College, Galesburg, Illinois, USA.

Looman, J. 1979. The vegetation of the Canadian Prairie Provinces. 1. An overview. Phytocoenologia 5:347-366.

_____. 1980. The vegetation of the Canadian Prairie Provinces. II. The grasslands, Part 1. Phytocoenologia 8:153-190.

McClain, W. E. 1986. Illinois prairie: past and future: restoration guide. Illinois Department of Conservation, Springfield, Illinois, USA.

McIntosh, R. P. 1980. The relationship between succession and the recovery process in ecosystems. Pages 11-62 in J. Cairns, Jr., editor. The Recovery Process in Damaged Systems. Ann Arbor Science Publishers, Ann Arbor, Michigan, USA.

McNaughton, S. J., M. B. Coughenour, and L. L. Wallace. 1982. Interactive processes in grassland ecosystems. Pages 167-193 in J. R. Estes, R. J. Tyrl, and J. N. Brunken, editor. Grasses and Grasslands: Systematics and Ecology. University of Oklahoma Press, Norman, Oklahoma, USA.

Nelson, D. C., and R. C. Anderson. 1983. Factors related to the distribution of prairie plants along a moisture gradient. The American Midland Naturalist 109:367-375.

Old, S. M. 1969. Microclimate, fire, and plant production in an Illinois prairie. Ecological Monographs 39:355-384.

Oosting, H. J. 1956. The study of plant communities. Second edition. W. H. Freeman and Co., San Francisco, California, USA.

Parrish, J. A. D., and F. A. Bazzaz. 1976. Underground niche separation in successional plants. Ecology 57:1281-1288.

Parish, J. A. D., and F. A. Bazzaz. 1979. Difference in pollination niche relationships in early and late successional plant communities. Ecology 60:597-610.

Pickett, S. T. A., and P. S. White, editors. 1985. The ecology of natural disturbance and patch dynamics. Academic Press, New York, New York, USA.

Platt, W. J. 1975. The colonization and formation of equilibrium plant species associations on badger disturbances in a tallgrass prairie. Ecological Monographs 45:285-305.

Platt, W. J., and I. M. Weis. 1977. Resource partitioning and competition within a guild of fugitive prairie plants. American Naturalist 111:479-513.

Raunkiaer, C. 1934. The life forms of plants and statistical plant geography. Clarendon, Oxford, England.

Redmann, R. E., and E. G. Reekie. 1982. Carbon balance in grasses. Pages 195-231 in J. R. Estes, R. J. Tyrl, and J. N. Brunken, editors. Grasses and Grasslands: Systematics and Ecology. University of Oklahoma Press, Norman, Oklahoma, USA.

Rice, E. L. 1984. Allelopathy. Second edition. Academic Press, New York, New York, USA.

Rice, E. L., and R. L. Parenti. 1978. Causes of decreases in productivity in undisturbed tall grass prairie. American Journal of Botany 65:1091-1097.

Rice, E. L., W. T. Penfound, and L. M. Rohrbaugh. 1960. Seed dispersal and mineral nutrition in succession in abandoned fields in central Oklahoma. Ecology 41:224-228.

Risser, P. G. 1985. Grasslands. Pages 232-256 in B. F. Chabot and H. A. Mooney, editors. Physiological Ecology of North American Plant Communities. Chapman and Hall, Ltd., London, England.

Risser, P. G., E. C. Birney, H. D. Blocker, S. W. May, W. J. Parton, and J. A. Wiens. 1981. The True Prairie Ecosystem. Hutchinson Ross Publishing Co., Stroudsburg, Pennsylvania, USA.

Risser, P. G., J. R. Karr, and R. T. T. Forman. 1984. Landscape ecology: directions and approaches. Illinois Natural History Survey Special Publication No. 2, Champaign, Illinois, USA.

Rock, H. 1981. Prairie propagation handbook. Sixth edition. Milwaukee County Department of Parks, Recreation and Culture, Wehr Nature Center, Whitnall Park, Hales Corners, Wisconsin, USA.

Roe, F. G. 1951. The North American buffalo: a critical study of the species in its wild state. University of Toronto Press, Toronto, Ontario, Canada.

Russell, E. W. 1973. Soil conditions and plant growth. Tenth edition. Longham, London, England.

Sauer, C. O. 1950. Grassland climax, fire, and man. Journal of Range Management 3:16-21.

Schramm, P. 1970. A practical restoration method for tall grass prairie. Pages 63-65 in P. Schramm, editor. Proceedings of a Symposium on Prairie and Prairie Restoration. Knox College, Galesburg, Illinois, USA.

_____. 1978. The "do's" and "don'ts" of prairie restoration. Pages 139-150 in D. C. Glenn-Lewin and R. Q. Landers, Jr., editors. Proceedings of the Fifth Midwest Prairie Conference, August 22-24, 1976. Iowa State University, Ames, Iowa, USA.

Schulenberg, R. 1970. Summary of Morton Arboretum prairie restoration work, 1963-1968. Pages 45-46 in P. Schramm, editor. Proceedings of a Symposium on Prairie and Prairie Restoration. Knox College, Galesburg, Illinois, USA.

Singh, J. S., W. K. Lauenroth, and D. G. Milchunas. 1983. Geography of grassland ecosystems. Progress in Physical Geography 7:46-80.

Smith, D. 1975. Forage management in the north. Third edition. Kendall/Hunt Publishing Company, Dubuque, Iowa, USA.

Smith, J. R., and B. S. Smith. 1980. The prairie garden: seventy native plants you can grow in town or country. University of Wisconsin Press, Madison, Wisconsin, USA.

Smyser, C. A. 1982. Nature's design: a practical guide to natural landscaping. Rodale Press, Emmaus, Pennsylvania, USA.

Sperry, T. M. 1935. Root systems in Illinois prairie. Ecology 16:178-202.

Sprague, H. B., editor. 1974. Grasslands of the United States: their economic and ecologic importance. Iowa State University Press, Ames, Iowa, USA.

Stebbins, G. L. 1981. Coevolution of grasses and herbivores. Annals of the Missouri Botanical Garden 68:75-86.

Steiger, T. L. 1930. Structure of prairie vegetation. Ecology 11:170-217.

Steuter, A. A. 1987. C_3/C_4 production shift on seasonal burns--northern mixed prairie. Journal of Range Management 40:27-31.

Stevenson, A. J., directing editor. 1972. Webster's new geographical dictionary. G. & C. Merriam Co., Springfield, Massachusetts, USA.

Teeri, J. A., and L. G. Stowe. 1976. Climatic patterns and the distribution of C_4 grasses in North America. Oecologia 23:1-12.

Transeau, E. N. 1935. The prairie peninsula. Ecology 16: 423-437.

Turkington, R., and L. W. Aarsen. 1984. Local-scale differentation as a result of competitive interactions. Pages 107-127 in R. Dirzo and J. Sarukhan, editors. Perspectives on Plant Population Ecology. Sinauer Associates, Sunderland, Massachusetts, USA.

United States Geological Survey. 1970. The national atlas of the United States of America. U.S. Department of the Interior, Washington, D.C., USA.

Vestal, A. G. 1949. Minimum areas for different vegetations, their determinations from species-area curves. Illinois Biological Monographs 20(3):1-129.

Weaver, J. E. 1954. North American prairie. Johnsen Publishing Co., Lincoln, Nebraska, USA.

Weaver, J. E., and F. W. Albertson. 1943. Resurvey of grasses, forbs, and underground plant parts at the end of the great drought. Ecological Monographs 13:63-117.

Weaver, J. E., and F. W. Albertson. 1956. **Grasslands of the Great Plains.** Johnsen Publishing Co., Lincoln, Nebraska, USA.

Weaver, J. E., and T. J. Fitzpatrick. 1934. The prairie. Ecological Monographs 4:109-295.

Weaver, J. E., L. A. Stoddart, and W. Noll. 1935. Response of the prairie to the great drought of 1934. Ecology 16:612-629.

Wells, P. V. 1970. Historical factors controlling vegetation patterns and floristic distributions in the Central Plains region of North America. Pages 211-221 in W. Dort, Jr. and J. K. Jones, Jr., editors. Pleistocene and Recent Environments of the Central Great Plains. Department of Geology, University of Kansas, Special Publication 3, Lawrence, Kansas, USA.

Wright, H. A., and A. W. Bailey. 1982. Fire ecology: United States and southern Canada. John Wiley and Sons, New York, New York, USA.

Wright, H. E., Jr. 1968. History of the prairie peninsula. Pages 78-88 in R. E. Bergstrom, editor. The Quaternary of Illinois. University of Illinois, College of Agriculture Special Publication No. 14, Urbana, Illinois, U.S.A.

Yonker, C., and D. S. Schimel. 1986. Geomorphology and grassland biogeochemistry (Abstract). Page 361. Program of the Fourth International Congress of Ecology, August 10-16, 1986, Syracuse, New York, USA.

5. Some Trajectories of Succession in Wyoming Sagebrush Grassland: Implications for Restoration

ABSTRACT

An understanding of successional processes is essential to land reconstruction, which can also be viewed as an attempt to hasten the rate of succession to a late seral stage. Where restoration, or a return to the predisturbance ecosystem is the goal, promoting succession may be especially important.

The assumption is usually made that natural succession will result in a predisturbance state. Three pictoral models are presented to illustrate that succession may result in different rates, patterns, and trajectories, depending on the initial as well as later seral conditions. These are illustrated with examples from the literature and from my research in sagebrush grassland. According to the models, different rates and patterns will eventually result in a predisturbance vegetation, while a different trajectory will result in a system with different species composition. The discussion will focus on different trajectories that are caused by loss of topsoil, introduction of nonindigenous plant species, and absence of mycorrhizal fungi. Where initial conditions alter the trajectory of succession restoration of the predisturbance system may not be possible, although reclamation or rehabilitation may be viable goals.

Because successional studies are always time-limited, it is often not possible to determine whether a site conforms to the model of rate, pattern or succession. For the purposes of restoration, a site that shows deviation from the desired course of succession, whether because of

rate, pattern, or especially trajectory, will require
special effort to establish and maintain a desirable
community.

INTRODUCTION

The study of succession is central to an
understanding of ecosystem reconstruction. Where the
goal is to restore the predisturbance ecosystem, one
management strategy is to hasten the rate of succession.
This is generally attempted by planting late seral
species, in the hope that the vegetation and associated
biotic and abiotic components will continue in the same
trajectory of succession as would the undisturbed system.
However, it is not clear from either natural or
manipulated ecosystems that succession will necessarily
lead to a system that resembles the land before
disturbance. In this chapter I review some of the
concepts pertaining to succession in arid and semi-arid
lands that deal with the trajectories of succession
toward similar or dissimilar vegetation, and give two
examples from my own research on experimental
manipulations to observe trajectories of succession. One
deals with the long-term effects of introduced Eurasian
weeds on disturbed sagebrush grassland in Wyoming, and
the other deals with changes in plant species composition
caused by mycorrhizal fungi on reclaimed sagebrush
grassland.
Many prominent early theories of succession allowed
little flexibility in what the final outcome of
disturbance would be; it was assumed that the original
vegetation would reestablish. This was true whether a
"monoclimax" (e.g., Clements 1916) or edaphic
"polyclimaxes" (e.g., Tansley 1939, Daubenmire 1968)
were espoused. The main difference between these two
theories was whether one regional climax or many climaxes
based on soil-vegetation relationships existed, but
disturbances in a region or within a soil type eventually
succeeded to the predisturbance vegetation. Theories
based on plant population patterns along gradients
(Gleason 1939, Whittaker 1953) were also not concerned
with whether the same or different populations would
eventually assemble along a disturbed gradient. Instead,

90

they were an attempt to explain more realistically the patterns of largely undisturbed vegetation.

Another approach to succession involves changes in the initial conditions of a site after a disturbance that alters the trajectory of succession (e.g., MacMahon 1983). Implicit in this view is that the original vegetation may return, but several alternative vegetation types may establish also. Dyksterhuis (1958) was one of the earliest to note that disturbance may be so severe in some cases as to cause edaphic conditions that no longer sustain the original vegetation. His observations included highly eroded soils and induced high water tables that required a new classification for the resultant vegetation. It is difficult to determine why earlier theories of succession did not usually incorporate alternative trajectories. In some cases the researchers did not include a range of disturbed sites in their observations, but in others they assumed the sites would eventually return to their original state during the succession process, no matter what the disturbance. The belief that the same climax vegetation could be achieved after disturbance may be in part the basis for the "restoration ethic" that land should not be disturbed for resource extraction unless complete restoration is possible (Bradshaw and Chadwick 1980).

A more theoretically based view of alternative trajectories of succession comes from modeling theory, where the concepts of multiple stable equilibria and resilience were developed (Holling 1973, Westman 1978). For several decades now the concepts of convergence of seral sites versus changing trajectories have existed in the literature sometimes as opposing schools of thought. In arid lands Westoby (1979) noted that vegetation often did not return to its original state after severe defoliation by domestic animals, based on a number of reasons, including invasion by alien plant species, severe changes in the soil, and selective grazing followed by stable coexistence of remaining species. Other writers on arid lands still espouse convergence (Daubenmire 1968, Meeker and Merkle 1984, Carpenter et al. 1986). Similar differences of opinion exist in the literature from mesic lands, as exemplified by contributors to the volume by West et al. (1981). For instance, Horn (1981) espoused convergence while Shugart et al. (1981) and Franklin and Hemstrom (1981) suggested that the initial conditions of succession will determine the trajectory. A related debate is whether succession consists of repeated or predictable species sequences after disturbance (e.g., Connell and Slatyer 1977) or simply a change with no inherent pattern (MacMahon 1980).

To summarize the courses of succession that may be found in the literature, I have constructed pictoral models to represent rates, patterns, and trajectories of succession (Fig. 1). The following discussion includes examples that illustrate each of the three models, with special reference to arid and semiarid lands. Different rates of succession (Fig. 1a) are illustrated by observations in grasslands during the drought of the 1930's (Costello 1944, Weaver 1954), where the annual weed stage was lengthened in duration because of drought. Grazing of recently disturbed sites similarly lengthened the annual weed stage (Costello 1944). Low soil nitrogen caused by erosion was thought to increase the duration of the early successional stages in Oklahoma grassland and in the Transvaal of South Africa (Roux and Warren 1963), and the degree of disturbance was related to rate of recovery in the Mojave Desert (Webb et al. 1987).

Different patterns of succession followed by convergence (Fig. 1b) are perhaps best illustrated by the models of Horn (1975, 1981) where different early successional tree species colonized initially, but each site was finally dominated by beech. In North American grasslands a number of observations indicated that different species of early seral annuals colonized different sites, but they were typically succeeded by the same late seral grasses (e.g., Clements 1916, Weaver and Albertson 1944, Weaver 1954). The large deviations in pattern of the intermediate seral stages that are seen in eastern deciduous forest are not to be expected in arid lands where there are few, and sometimes only one, seral stages.

Different trajectories of succession (Fig. 1c) are caused by different initial conditions, or by some permanent stress or change in conditions that do not allow the ecosystem to return to its original state. Huston and Smith (1987) modeled changes in environmental conditions that lead to different successional trajectories, even if the same initial species are present. Initial establishment of the shrub <u>Viburum</u>

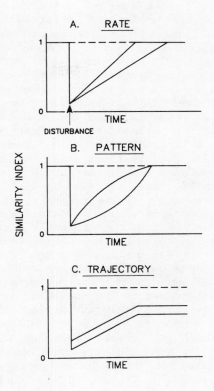

Fig. 1.   Three models showing the course of succession
when different rates, patterns, or trajectories are
involved.   In the first two models a disturbed site
resembles the original vegetation with time (similarity
index = 1), but in the third the predisturbance
vegetation is never achieved.

lentago caused succession to be "arrested" for 55 years
in eastern deciduous forest (Niering et al 1986).   In the
Great Basin an annual grass from Europe, _Bromus tectorum_,
is becoming the successional dominant.   Early
observations from abandoned plowed land by Piemeisel
(1938, 1951) that were continued into the fourth decade

of succession by Hironaka and Tisdale (1963) showed that recolonization by native grasses and shrubs was sparse where B. tectorum has colonized. Partially to combat this undesirable grass, the perennial Asian grass, Agropyron desertorum, has been planted for the past half century and appears to be stable: some native shrubs, especially Artemisia tridentata, but very few other plant life forms, have colonized even the oldest stands of A. desertorum (Johnson 1986). Another example of the influence of introduced species on the trajectory of succession comes from planted African Eragrostis species in southwestern Arizona that have resisted invasion by native species for 50 years (Bock et al. 1986).

Other examples of different trajectories of succession in arid lands come from a variety of disturbances. Fire in Coleogyne ramossisimum shrublands more frequently resulted in replacement by other native shrub species rather than the original C. ramossisimum, even after thirty years (Callison et al. 1985). Grazing by domestic animals has in some regions of the western United States increased the abundance of Artemisia tridentata, but discontinuing grazing even for 13 years did not cause an increase in the associated grass species (West et al. 1984). Soil compaction by motorized vehicles caused early seral species to persist after forty years in the Mojave desert (Prose et al. 1987), and initial deficits in plant density were not overcome in spring, as compared to fall, burned Quercus coccifera garrigue (Malanson and Trabaud 1987). Westman and O'Leary (1986) suggested that frequent fire is needed to extirpate weak sprouters in California coastal sage scrub, thereby altering the trajectory of succession. Surface mining is one of the most severe disturbances and has resulted in some of the most unusual plant communities. The vegetation as well as the mycorrhizal fungal populations of abandoned mine spoils in SW Wyoming did not resemble the native communities nearby after thirty years (Waaland and Allen 1987). Analyses of vegetation on abandoned spoils near Calgary, Alberta, indicated that it had no resemblance at all to any known vegetation types (Russell and La Roi 1986).

The three models (Fig. 1) are presented in their simplest form. It is of course possible to have combinations of rates, patterns and trajectories. For instance, two sites may simultaneously have different species turnover rates and different trajectories, or they may have different rates and patterns at the same time.

The remainder of this chapter is concerned with two research projects that I initiated to study the effects of introduced annual weeds and vesicular-arbuscular mycorrhizal fungi on succession. These were controlled field experiments with manipulations to create the initial conditions of succession, and long-term observations to observe the trajectory of succession. These two manipulations were chosen in part because both colonizing weeds and VA mycorrhizae are important factors to consider in the restoration of degraded arid lands, as discussed below.

INTRODUCED WEEDY ANNUALS AND
THE TRAJECTORY OF SUCCESSION

Eurasian weeds have been a component of western U.S. vegetation for approximately a century now (Young et al. 1972, Baker 1974). Their effects on native vegetation is difficult to assess because they have colonized many areas so completely that few or no strictly native communities still exist. One region that has until recently been subject to little invasion by alien plants is the Powder River Basin of northeastern Wyoming. Much of the area is _Artemisia_ _tridentata_-grassland which is suitable for grazing but too arid for cultivation. Because the area is underlain by strippable coal, surface mining has expanded in the last dozen years coupled with an increase in Eurasian annuals.

An experiment was initiated in northeastern Wyoming in 1975 to determine what the effects of the introduced annuals, primarily _Salsola_ _kali_, would be on the development of native vegetation. An area was disturbed by discing, and _S._ _kali_ seeds were planted in one-half of 144 0.5 m^2 sampling quadrats. Only a few other introduced species colonized naturally, each with <1% cover. Site descriptions and details of the methods are given in Allen and Knight (1984), including control sites near croplands where introduced weeds colonized abundantly.

The experiment was monitored for ten years (Fig. 2), after which it was destroyed by mining. The introduced weeds, primarily S. kali, as well as the less abundant native annuals, peaked in percent cover after 2-4 years and then declined. However, there were residual effects of these annuals on the perennial vegetation that continued into the tenth year (Fig. 2). Specifically, Opuntia polyacantha and Artemisia tridentata (grouped in the "forbs and shrubs" category in fig. 2, where forbs formed less than 1% of the ground cover in any year, and A. tridentata was the only shrub species) had increased coverage after ten years where S. kali was absent in the early years. Conversely, the grass species (primarily Stipa comata, Agropyron smithii, and Bouteloua gracilis, in that order of abundance) had increased coverage where S. kali had been present. The herbaceous Artemisia frigida showed no significant difference due to weeds in any year (Fig. 2).

The causes of these different trajectories for different native species or groups of species is perhaps easiest to explain for Opuntia. Discing the soil to initate succession caused Opuntia pads and pieces of pads to be left scattered on the surface of the ground. Dense stands of S. kali and the other introduced weeds reduced the ability of these propagules to establish (Allen and Knight 1984). Where S. kali was not planted Opuntia propagules took root. Changes in A. tridentata and the grasses are not as straightforward to explain, especially as significant differences did not occur until the fourth and fifth years, respectively. The explanation may lie in the ability of the grasses to spread vegetatively, while A. tridentata requires establishment of seedlings. After S. kali became inabundant during the normal course of succession in the fourth year, the already established grasses were perhaps able to take advantage of this "biological vacuum" and expand vegetatively. A vacuum was created because S. kali had previously suppressed native annuals (Fig. 2). Artemisis tridentata, by contrast, did not begin (visible) seedling establishment until the third year. After this time, the rapidly spreading grasses may have inhibited further seedlings, as the density of A. tridentata was lower where grass density was higher (Allen unpublished).

The changes in trajectories of the various groups of species in this experiment can be seen as a sequence of events, where the successional decline of S. kali was

96

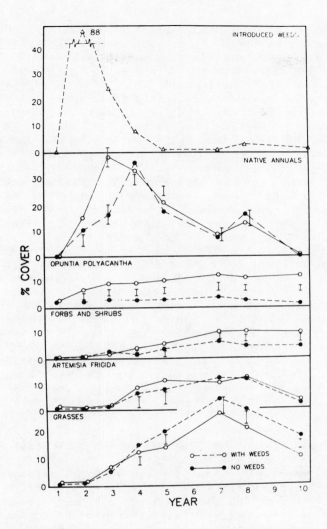

Fig. 2.   Changes in different species and groups of species ten years after discing sagebrush grassland in northwestern Wyoming. The introduced annuals consisted primarily of the planted <u>Salsola</u> <u>kali</u> and 1% cover of other   colonizers.   The forbs and shrubs category consisted mainly of <u>Artemisia</u>   <u>tridentata</u> and assorted forbs (1%) in the later years. The grasses were   all native perennials.

followed by an increased vegetative spread of grasses, which in turn reduced the establishment of A. tridentata. The net effect in this vegetation type was to form a grass-dominated community where S. kali and other introduced weeds colonized, and an A. tridentata community where weeds were initially absent.

The introduction of S. kali into this region has important implications both for succession and restoration. Plowed land abandoned during the drought of the 1930's is still dominated by grasses rather than A. tridentata. The contrast can be seen along old "plow lines," where shrubs have scarcely colonized swards of native grasses which established after abandonment (DeAnda 1977 and personal observations). In the most liberal interpretation of these data, the long term effects of S. kali may be to change a shrub-grassland to a grassland. The implications for reclamationists are that shrubs may be more difficult to establish where introduced weeds invade. Indeed, the low success of A. tridentata establishment is well documented for reclamation, especially in a dense matrix of grasses (Blaisdell 1949, Richardson et al. 1986). In deciding the goal for a reconstructed community, it is important to consider what is ecologically feasible. If shrub densities comparable to undisturbed communities are desired, it would be necessary to reduce either the coverage of the weed stage or the grass stage, or both, to allow shrub establishment.

VA MYCORRHIZAE AND THE TRAJECTORY OF SUCCESSION

An experiment was performed on mine spoil to determine the effects of vesicular-arbuscular (VA) mycorrhizal fungi on the trajectory of succession. These fungi form a mutualistic association with the roots of 90% or more of species from arid and semiarid lands (Trappe 1981), whereby the plant obtains nutrients from the fungus and the fungus in return receives carbohydrates (e.g., Harley and Smith 1983). Mycorrhizae may be especially important in arid lands to increase water uptake and drought stress tolerance (Allen and Boosalis 1983).

The hypothesis that VA mycorrhizae may hasten the rate of succession or restoration has been proposed a number of times (Janos 1980, Reeves et al. 1979, Williams and Allen 1984). The rationale for constructing such a hypothesis lies in the physiological response to mycorrhizae infection of plant species from different seral stages. Many of the colonizing annuals in arid lands do not form a mycorrhizal association (are nonmycotrophic, e.g., Chenopodiaceae, Brassicaceae, Amaranthaceae, Zygophyllaceae), and thus may be well adapted to disturbed soils where mycorrhizal inoculum is low or absent. Later seral species are facultatively mycorrhizal with varying degrees of response to infection, and in some areas, especially the tropics, the late successional species are obligately mycorrhizal (Janos 1980).

The physiological responses to VA mycorrhizae were tested for a number of dominant species of Wyoming sagebrush-grassland (Table 1). The species are listed in order of their appearance in succession, and show a continuum of greater physiological change with infection from early to late succession. The two nonmycotrophic annuals, <u>Salsola</u> <u>kali</u> and <u>Atriplex</u> <u>rosea</u>, actually had reduced growth and water vapor conductance when mycorrhizal fungi were present in their rhizospheres, even though they do not form mycorrhizal infection. <u>Bromus</u> <u>tectorum</u> is an annual grass that may dominate in the next stage of succession, and although it forms VA mycorrhizae, it has shown no physiological response when grown in soils from field sites. The next four species on the list are perennial grasses that have sequentially greater response to mycorrhizae with later seral stage. The two shrub species from the final stage of succession, show the greatest response to mycorrhizae.

A reconstruction model was formed based on the physiological response to mycorrhizae of species from different seral stages (Fig. 3). This model simulates succession as well as reconstruction, since it it based on the dominant stages that are frequently found in sagebrush-grassland. The inoculum of VA mycorrhizal fungi is reduced when the soil is disturbed, whether by mining (Rives et al., 1980, Allen and Allen 1980), agriculture (Allen and Boosalis 1983), soil erosion (Powell 1980), or pesticides (Menge 1982). Thus the "bare soil" stage of succession (Fig. 3) represents reduced or eliminated mycorrhizal inoculum. Annual

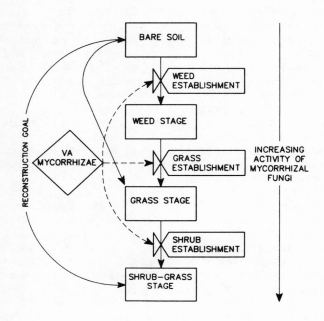

Fig. 3. A model of succession indicating that an increasing activity of VA mycorrhizal fungi may hasten succession from the nonmycotrophic weed stage to facultatively mycorrhizal grasses and then to shrubs.

weeds, many of them nonmycotrophic, will establish fungi readily on bare soil whether mycorrhizal inoculum is present or not. The VA mycorrhizae are the driving variable in the model, so the persistence of the weed stage is regulated by the fungi. Direct evidence for this comes from a decreased abundance of _Salsola kali_ when inoculated in the field (Allen and Allen 1988). In addition, a long persistent stage of nonmycotrophic annuals such as _S. kali_ can form a positive feedback whereby the inoculum has no host plant on which to establish, and succession to later stages may be slowed because inoculum does not build up naturally (Allen and Allen 1980, 1988)..

The goal of reconstruction is to reduce the dominance of the annual weed stage and to hasten establishment of a shrub-grass or possibly a grass stage (Fig. 3). Mycorrhizae may in part control successful establishment of both of these stages. There is evidence that they have a greater effect on shrubs than grasses (Lindsey 1984). In addition, shrubs had a greater percentage of their root length infected with the fungi than co-occuring grasses at a southwestern Wyoming reclamation site (Waaland and Allen 1987).

Several field sites were set up to test the combined effects of mycorrhizal inoculum and removal of nonmycotrophic annuals on succession in a reclamation study. Results from two of the sites will be discussed here, one on stored topsoil and the other on overburden (sedimentary parent material). Mycorrhizal inoculum was extremely low in the stored topsoil and absent from the overburden soil. Inoculum was added as a thin (1-2 cm) layer of fresh topsoil to sampling quadrats at both sites, and colonizing weeds were removed by hand in a 2 X 2 factorial experimental design. Grasses and shrubs were seeded.

On the topsoil site, the planted grasses (several _Agropyron_ species) had no increase in their percent cover when they were infected with mycorrhizal fungi (Allen and Allen 1986). Mycorrhizal _Agropyron_ _smithii_ did, however, have decreased stomatal resistance to water vapor during periods of drought. In addition, the negative effect of _S. kali_ on the stomatal resistance of _A. smithii_ was alleviated by mycorrhizae in this field experiment. A previous greenhouse study showed that mycorrhizae could also alleviate the negative effects of _S. kali_ competition on biomass of _A. smithii_ (Allen and Allen 1984). The data suggest that mycorrhizae may be most important for these facultatively mycorrhizal grasses under conditions of stress such as moisture or competition, but neither of these stresses were severe during the field study. Normally this site receives less precipitation than the years under observation (Allen et al. 1987). Mycorrhizae may be important as a driving variable that affects the abundance of the grass stage of succession during normal or low precipitation years.

On the overburden site the very abundant _S. kali_ experienced both reduced percent cover and density when inoculated with mycorrhizae (Allen and Allen 1988), as previous greenhouse experiments implied would happen to this nonmycotrophic annual (Table 1). However, the reduction in weeds did not improve grass establishment. The overburden site differed from the topsoil site in another important aspect in that it was located on the top of a ridge and was subject to intense winds, often stronger than 10 m/sec. The S. kali "tumbleweed" litter actually formed a microsite of reduced wind and increased snow capture that enabled increased grass seedling establishment (Allen and Allen 1988). Inoculation, which caused a reduction in the weed "cover crop," also resulted in reduced establishment of facultatively mycorrhizal grasses. This implies that on this harsh site mycorrhizae may slow the early stages of succession. The outlook for the shrub stage of succession may be different. If reduced grass establishment increases shrub establishment as was suggested from the northeastern Wyoming weed succession study discussed in the previous section, then the net effect of inoculation may be to reduce the grass stage but encourage the shrub stage. Neither of these reclaimed sites is yet in the later seral shrub stage, but it is clear that mycorrhizae may influence rates, patterns, and possibly trajectories of succession by changing initial species composition.

INTERACTIONS OF WEEDS AND MYCORRHIZAE

The combined effects of introduced weeds and VA mycorrhizae on the trajectory of succession are summarized in a model (Fig. 4). The possible trajectories represent seral vegetation, since the sites described above were observed from 6-10 years. For instance, where the density of weed colonization was high and mycorrhizal activity (defined as inoculum density plus percentage of root infection) was low, annual nonmycotrophic weeds persisted up to ten years, as given in examples above (Allen and Allen 1980, 1988). In the opposite extreme, low weeds and high mycorrhizal activity, shrubs dominated as in the northeastern Wyoming successional study where weeds had not been seeded (Fig.

Table 1.--Relative responses of plant species from different seral stages in Wyoming sagebrush grassland to VA mycorrhizal infection. 0 = no change, - = decrease, + = increase, CO_2 = rate of photosynthesis. g_s = stomatal conductance, P = phosphorus.

	DRY MASS	CO_2	g_s	P	SOURCE
SALSOLA KALI	-,0		-,0	0	ALLEN AND ALLEN (1984, 1988)
ATRIPLEX ROSEA	-,0		-		ALLEN (1984)
BROMUS TECTORUM	0		0	0	ALLEN (1984, UNPUBL.)
HORDEUM JUBATUM	+		+	0	ALLEN (UNPUBL.)
AGROPYRON DASYSTACHYUM	+,-,0		+,0	0	ALLEN AND ALLEN (1986 AND UNPUBL.)
AGROPYRON SMITHII	+,0	+	+	+,0	ALLEN ET AL. (1984) ALLEN AND ALLEN (1984)
BOUTELOUA GRACILIS	+,0	++	++	+	ALLEN ET AL. (1981) ALLEN ET AL. (1984)
ARTEMISIA TRIDENTATA	+++			+	CALL AND MCKELL (1985) LINDSEY (1984)
ATRIPLEX CANESCENS	+++			+	CALL AND MCKELL (1985) LINDSEY (1984), ALDON (1975)

2, Allen unpubl.). Where both weed density and mycorrhizal activity were high, grasses dominated (Fig. 2, Allen unpubl.). The fourth combination, low weeds and low activity, is best represented by the reclamation study on topsoil where a high density of grasses was planted and shrubs established poorly. Mycorrhizal activity was not very high here even with inoculation, possibly a consequence of very high precipitation (Allen and Allen 1986). The question marks between grass and shrub stages indicate that without more time to observe these different seral communities, the final composition is speculative. The sites may remain in the grass stage but also may become dominated by shrubs with time.

RELEVANCE OF AN UNDERSTANDING OF TRAJECTORIES OF SUCCESSION TO RESTORATION

The question marks in Fig. 4 suggest the central problem in determining whether time-limited observations of courses of succession will finally be characterized by different rates, patterns, or trajectories. It is tempting after observing sites such as those that have been dominated for 40-50 years by Bromus tectorum, (Hironaka and Tisdale 1963), Agropyron desertorum (Johnson 1986), or Eragrostis species (Bock et al. 1986), to conclude that these truly represent different trajectories of succession caused by accidental or purposeful species introductions. Although these altered vegetations have not been colonized appreciably by native species either in the past or more recently, a conservative approach to the problem would be to assume that they are still capable of reverting to native vegetation. It could be argued, for instance, that the necessary sequence of environmental conditions has not occured to allow native colonization. What may be needed is a series of dry years which opens gaps in the existing vegetation followed by wet years that allow colonization by native species. This hypothesis is testable by making the appropriate experimental manipulations and observing population dynamics of native species, whereas it is not possible to observe a site forever. Intervention by man in the form of restoration may also alter the trajectory of succession of some artificial communities, but it is doubtful that a

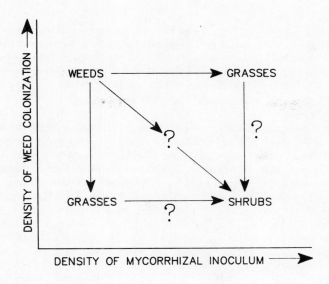

Fig. 4. Possible trajectories of succession in sagebrush-grassland as affected by introduced weeds and mycorrhizal inoculum after 6-10 years. The question marks indicate that sites must be observed longer, or appropriate experiments must be carried out, to determine whether the next stage of succession will be achieved or whether a permanent change in the vegetation has taken place due to initial conditions.

ubiquitous, persistent colonizing annual such as <u>Bromus tectorum</u> could be completely eliminated.

The changes induced in seral vegetation by manipulations of <u>Salsola kali</u> and mycorrhizal fungi are more subtle than, for instance, invasions of nearly pure stands of <u>Bromus tectorum</u> or removal of topsoil. Both of these manipulations merely caused changes in densities of weeds, grasses, and shrubs rather than an entire turnover in species composition. It could be argued that the different initial treatments would eventually become similar by future shifts in species' abundances. To support this argument in the case, for instance, of the <u>S. kali</u> planting and succession study (Fig. 2), one would have to assume differential population dynamics of

<u>Artemisia</u> <u>tridentata</u> seedlings in the two treatments. Seedlings would need to establish at a higher rate over time in the weed quadrats to achieve the higher densities in the non-weed quadrats. An experiment to test this could be done by studying <u>A.</u> <u>tridentata</u> establishment rates in a grass matrix of varying densities.

The unusual plant communities that establish naturally on severely disrupted soils such as mine spoils or eroded soil may arguably be called early seral stages that represent different patterns but not different trajectories of succession. Perhaps after thousands of years of topsoil formation the original vegetation may reestablish and will resemble the undisturbed sites. However, this conclusion is based on several unrealistic assumptions, including no change in climate, no changes in the undisturbed vegetation and soils, and no evolutionary changes during the soil formation period. For practical and theoretical considerations, a site that has been denuded of topsoil will undergo a different trajectory of succession.

Even though the theoretical problem of successional convergence versus different trajectories will remain until more long term and experimental data are available, knowledge of the course of the first several decades of succession will assist in ecosystem reconstruction. The same factors that may theoretically alter the trajectory of succession, such as changes in edaphic factors or species introductions, will also affect succession on a reconstructed site. Even if their long term effects cannot be predicted with accuracy, such factors will certainly operate over the short time scale after replanting a disturbed site and will dictate what practical measures (e.g., irrigation, seeding density, weeding) must be taken to establish vegetation. In setting a goal of restoration, it is necessary to know what is realistic in terms of the possible trajectory of succession, especially where this trajectory may not conform to the vegetation of the undisturbed ecosystem. Reclamation or rehabilitation need to be considered where restoration is not possible.

ACKNOWLEDGMENTS

This research was supported by U.S.D.A. grants 83-CRCR-1-1229, 83-CRSR-2-2274, and 85-CRSR-2-2719, and D.O.E. grant DE-AC02-78EV04963.

LITERATURE CITED

Aldon, E.F. 1975. Endomycorrhizae enhance survival and growth of four-wing saltbush on coal mine spoils. U.S.D.A. Forest Research Note RM-294.

Allen, E.B. 1984. VA mycorrhizae and colonizing annuals: implications for growth, competition, and succession. Pages 41-59 in S.E. Williams and M.F. Allen, editors. VA mycorrhizae and reclamation of arid and semiarid lands. University of Wyoming Agricultural Experiment Station Scientific Report No. SA1261.

Allen, E.B. and M.F. Allen. 1980. Natural reestablishment of vesiculararbuscular mycorrhizae following stripmine reclamation in Wyoming. Journal of Applied Ecology 17:139-148.

Allen, E.B. and M.F. Allen. 1984. Competition between plants of different successional stages:mycorrhizae as regulators. Canadian Journal of Botany 62:2625-2629.

Allen, E.B. and M.F. Allen. 1986. Water relations of xeric grasses in the field: interactions of mycorrhizas and competition. New Phytologist 104:559-571.

Allen, E.B. and M.F. Allen. 1988. Facilitation of succession by the nonmycotrophic colonizer Salsola kali (Chenopodiaceae) on a harsh site: effects of mycorrhizal fungi. American Journal of Botany 75:257-266.

Allen, E.B. and D.H. Knight. 1984. The effects of introduced annuals on secondary succession in sagebrush grassland, Wyoming. The Southwestern Naturalist 29:407-421.

Allen, M.F., E.B. Allen and P.D. Stahl. 1984. Differential niche reponse of Bouteloua gracilis and Pascopyrum smithii to VA mycorrhizae. Bulletin of the Torrey Botanical Club 111:361-365.

Allen, M.F., E.B. Allen and N.E. West. 1987. Influence of parasitic and mutualistic fungi on Artemisia tridentata during high precipitation years. Bulletin of the Torrey Botanical Club 114:272-279.

Allen, M.F. and M.G. Boosalis. 1983. Effects of two species of VA mycorrhizal fungi on drought tolerance of winter wheat. New Phytologist 93:67-76.

Allen, M.F., W.K. Smith, T.S. Moore, and M. Christensen. 1981. Comparative water relations and photosynthesis of mycorrhizal and non-mycorrhizal *Bouteloua gracilis* (H.B.K.) Lag ex Steud. New Phytologist 88:683-693.

Baker, H.G. 1974. The evolution of weeds. Annual Review of Ecology and Systematics 5:1-24.

Blaisdell, J.P. 1949. Competition between sagebrush seedlings and reseededgrasses. Ecology 30:512-519.

Bock, C.E., J.H. Bock, K.L. Jepson, and J.C. Ortega. 1986. Ecological effects of planting African lovegrasses in Arizona. National Geographic Research 2:456-463.

Bradshaw, A.D. and M.J. Chadwick. 1980. The Restoration of Land. University of California Press, Berkeley.

Call, C.A. and C.M. McKell. 1985. Endomycorrhizae enhance growth of shrub species in processed oil shale and disturbed native soil. Journal of Range Management 38:258-261.

Callison, J., J.D. Brotherson, and J.E. Bowns. 1985. the effects of fire on the blackbrush (*Coleogyne ramosissima*) community of southwestern Utah. Journal of Range Management 38:535-538.

Carpenter, D.E., M.G. Barbour and C.J. Bahre. 1986. Old field succession in Mojave Desert scrub. Madrono 33:111-122.

Clements, F.E. 1916. Plant Succession. Carnegie Institute of Washington Publication Number 242.

Connell, H.G. and R.O. Slatyer. 1977. Mechanisms of succession in natural communities and their role in community stability and organization. American Naturalist 111:1119-1144.

Costello, D.F. 1944. Natural revegetation of abandoned plowed land. Ecology 25:312-326.

Daubenmire, R. 1968. Plant Communities. Harper and Row, New York.

DeAnda, V.R.A. 1977. Plant succession on abandoned and other disturbed areas in the Powder River Basin, Wyoming. M.S. Thesis University of Wyoming, Laramie.

Franklin, J.F. and M.A. Hemstrom. 1981. Aspects of succession in the coniferous forests of the Pacific Northwest. Pages 219-229 in D.C. West, H.H. Shugart, and D.B. Botkin, editors. Forest Succession. Concepts and Applications. Springer-Verlag, New York.

Gleason, H.A. 1939. The individualistic concept of the plant association. American Midland Naturalist 21:92-110.

Dykersterhuis, E.J. 1958. Ecological principles in range evaluation. Botanical Review 24: 253-272.

Harley, J.L. and S.E. Smith. 1983. Mycorrhizal Symbiosis. Academic Press, New York.

Hironaka, M. and E.W. Tisdale. 1963. Secondary succession in annual vegetation in southern Idaho. Ecology 44:810-812.

Holling, C.S. 1973. Resilience and stability of ecological systems. Annual Review of Ecology and Systematics 4:1-23.

Horn, H.S. 1975. Markovian properties of forest succession. pp. 196-211. in M.L. Cody and J.M. Diamond, editors. Ecology and Evolution of Communities. Harvard University Press, Cambridge, Massachusetts.

Horn, H.S. 1981. Some causes of variety in patterns of secondary succession. Pages 24-35 in D.C. West, H.H. Skugart and D.B. Botkin, editors. Forest Succession. Concepts and Applications. Springer-Verlag, New York.

Huston, M. and T. Smith. 1987. Plant succession: life history and competition. American Naturalist 130:168-198.

Janos, D.P. 1980. Mycorrhizae influence tropical succession. Biotropica 12:56-64.

Johnson, K.L., editor. 1986. Crested Wheatgrass: Its Values, Problems and Myths; Symposium Proceedings. (1983). Range Science Department, Utah State University, Logan, Utah.

Lindsey, D.L. 1984. The role of vesicular-arbuscular mycorrhizae in shrub establishment. Pages 52-67 in S.E. Willams and M.F. Allen, ditors. VA Mycorrhizae and Reclamation of Arid and Semiard Lands. University of Wyoming. Agricultural Experiment Station. Laramie, Wyoming U.S.A.

MacMahon, J.A. 1980. Ecosystems over time: succession and other types of changes. Pages 27-58 in R.H. Waring, editor. Forests: Fresh Perspectives from Ecosystem Analysis. Proceedings of the 40th Annual Biology Colloquium (1979). Oregon State University Press, Corvallis, Oregon.

MacMahon, J.A. 1983. Nothing Succeeds Like Succession: Ecology and the Human Lot. 67th Faculty Honor Lecture, Utah State University Press, Logan, Utah.

Malanson, G.P. and L. Trabaud. 1987. Ordination analysis of components of resilience of Quercus coccifera garrigue. Ecology 68:463-472.

Meeker, D.O. Jr. and D.L. Merkel. 1984. Climax theories and a recommendation for vegetation classification -- a viewpoint. Journal of Range Management 37:427-429.

Menge, J.A. 1982. Effect of soil fumigants and fungicides on vesicular-arbuscular fungi. Phytopathology 72:1125-1132.

Niering, W.A., G.D. Dreyer, F.E. Egler, and J.P. Anderson, Jr. 1986. Stability of a Viburnum lentago shrub community after 30 years. Bulletin of the Torrey Botanical Club 113:23-27.

Piemeisel, R.L. 1938. Changes in weedy plant cover on cleared sagebrush land and their probable causes. USDA Technical Bulletin Number 654.

Piemeisel, R.L. 1951. Causes affecting change and rate of change in a vegetation of annuals in Idaho. Ecology 32:53-72.

Powell, D.L. 1980. Mycorrhizal infectivity of eroded soils. Soil Biologyand Biochemistry. 12:247-250.

Prose, D.V., S.K. Metzger, and H.G. Wilshire. 1987. Effects of substrate disturbance on secondary plant succession: Mojave Desert, California. Journal of Applied Ecology 24:305-313.

Reeves, F.B., D. Wagner, T. Moorman, and J. Kiel. 1979. The role of endomycorrhizae in revegetation practices in the semi-arid west. I. A comparison of incidence of mycorrhizae in severely disturbed versus natural environments. American Journal of Botany 66:6-13.

Richardson, B.Z., S.B. Monsen, and D.M. Bowers. 1986. Interseeding selected shrubs and herbs on mine disturbances in southeastern Idaho. Pages 134-139 in Proceedings-Symposium on the Biology of Artemisia and Chrysothamnus (1984) Provo, Utah USDA General Technical Report NT-200. Ogden, Utah.

Rives, C.S., M.I. Bajwa, A.E. Liberta and R.M. Miller. 1980. Effects of topsoil storage during surface mining on the viability of VA mycorrhiza. Soil Science 129:253-257.

Roux, E.R. and M. Warren. 1963. Plant succession on abandoned fields in central Oklahoma and in the Transvaal Highveld. Ecology 44:576-579.

Russell, W.B. and G.H. La Roi. 1986. Natural vegetation and ecology of abandoned coal-mined land, Rocky Mountain Foothills, Alberta, Canada. Canadian Journal Botany 64:1286-1298.

Shugart, H.H., D.C. West and W.R. Emmanuel. 1981. Patterns and dynamics of forests: an application of simulation models. Pages 74-94 in D.C. West, H.H. Shugart and D.B. Botkin, editors. Forest Succession. Concepts and Applications. Springer-Verlag, New York.

Tansley, A.G. 1939. The British Islands and their Vegetation (Second Edition). Cambridge University Press, Cambridge, England.

Trappe, J.M. 1981. Mycorrhizae and productivity of arid and semi-arid rangelands. Pages 581-599 in J.T. Manassah and E.J. Briskey, editors. Advances in Food Producing Systems for Arid and Semi-arid Lands. New York, Academic Press.

Waaland, M.E. and E.B. Allen. 1987. Relationships between VA mycorrhizal fungi and plant cover following surface mining in Wyoming. Journal of Range Management 40:271-276.

Weaver, J.E. and F.W. Albertson. 1944. Nature and degree of recovery of grassland from the great drought of 1933 to 1940. Ecological Monographs 14:393-479.

Weaver, J.E. 1954. A seventeen year study of plant succession in prairie. American Journal Botany 41:31-38.

Webb, R.H., J.W. Steiger, and R.M. Turner. 1987. Dynamics of Mojave Desert shrub assemblages in the Panamint Mountains, California. Ecology 68:478-490.

West, D.C., H.H. Shugart and D.B. Botkin, editors. 1981. Forest Succession. Concepts and Applications. Springer Verlag, New York.

West, N.E., F.D. Provenza, P.S. Johnson, and M.K. Owens. 1984. Vegetation change after 13 years of livestock grazing exclusion on sagebrush semidesert in West Central Utah. Journal of Range Management 37:262-264.

Westman, W.E. 1978. Measuring the inertia and resilience of ecosystems. Bioscience 28:705-710.

Westman, W.E. and J.F. O'Leary. 1986. Measures of resilience: the response of coastal sage scrub to fire. Vegetatio 65:179-189.

Westoby, M. 1979. Elements of a theory of vegetation dynamics in arid rangelands. Israel Journal Botany 28:169-194.

Whittaker, R.H. 1953. A consideration of climax theory: the climax as a population and pattern. Ecological Monographs 23:41-78.

Williams, S.E. and M.F. Allen, editors. 1984. VA Mycorrhizae and Reclamation of Arid and Semi-arid Lands. University of Wyoming Agricultural Experiment Station Science Report Number SA 1261. Laramie, Wyoming.

Young, J.A., R.A. Evans and J. Major 1972. Alien plants in the Great Basin. Journal of Range Management 25:194-201.

6. Belowground Structure: A Key to Reconstructing a Productive Arid Ecosystem

ABSTRACT

Plant establishment and productivity in arid lands are primarily limited by water availability, nutrients and soil instability, which are in turn regulated by belowground interactions of roots, microorganisms and soils. In arid ecosystems, succession appears to initiate in patches as "islands of fertility", rather than in large, homogeneous units. Understanding the factors that regulate development of these islands may be critical to revegetating disturbed arid lands. Major changes occur in soil and microbial spatial patterning following disturbances. Nutrients become low and diffuse, soil vertical structure is destroyed, and soil aggregation is diminished. Root systems change architectures due both to genetic capacity and the altered soil structure. Following plant establishment, microorganisms and the processes they regulate reestablish around the roots and where litter accumulates. The reformation of a desirable ecosystem depends not only upon the establishment of plants, but on the concentrating of initially diffuse nutrients to plant foci both horizontally (by surface roots, mycorrhizae and wind deposition) and vertically (by deep rooted species and their microbial associations). Thus, I hypothesize that efficient land reconstruction may depend not only on planting highly productive species, or genetically-engineering "better" organisms, but also on replacing the structural characteristics of mature ecosystems.

113

INTRODUCTION

Dynamics that control the stability and productivity of arid ecosystems are complex and interactive. However, one point is clear: light is rarely a limiting resource in a desert landscape, so the limits to productivity tend to be the resources available from below the surface of the soil. Despite this obvious situation, more research has concentrated on describing the leaf or herbivore reactions to limiting resources than on understanding how plants gain soil resources. Even when those efforts are made, they tend to focus on one aspect alone (e.g., root structure or production) and rarely on the integrative characteristics of soils, plant roots and microorganisms. It is these components and their dispersion in soil which I will attempt to discuss in the context of restoring a self-sustaining community.

LIMITS TO RECONSTRUCTION

Water deficiency is the major factor that characterizes an arid ecosystem. Broadly, a desert is defined as an area in which precipitation is less than 25 cm per annum coupled with a high evaporational demand compared to the precipitation input. Despite this definition, predicting the key processes that limit production is not simple. Agriculturalists have often relied on simple evapotranspiration models to predict irrigation needs and production limits. However, plants depend upon the entire continuum (soil-plant-atmosphere) to maintain an appropriate water balance to fix carbon. That continuum is heavily dependent upon the water storage capacity and release characteristics of the soil throughout the entire rooting profile. Those characteristics are affected not only by the soil physical characteristics and by the root distribution alone, but also by the expansion of the water uptake zones via mycorrhizal fungi and by the altered water release curves generated by the organic matter in the rooting zones.

Although water shortage is the most obvious limiting resource in deserts, others have suggested that the importance of water at the ecosystem level lies primarily in its regulations of nutrient dynamics. The critical roles of water in arid land N processes (fixation, nitrification, denitrification, ammonification ...) has been well documented (e.g., Skujins 1981). Also, recent work (see Whitford et al. 1981, Allen 1983) has demonstrated that the importance of seasonal activities of the biota and how they interact with specific precipitation events might be as or more important than overall water balance. Regardless of the specific process affecting plant production, the use and liberation of soil resources, regulated by belowground biota, are the dominant processes that determine ecosystem functioning.

Despite the emphasis on production, stability may be the more important variable in attempting to maintain viable ecosystem activities of arid habitats. In arid systems, stability might be related to environmental variability and the ability of the biota to withstand that variability by retaining resources in accessible locations and forms. Walker et al. (1981) suggested that if a system reaches a point where nutrients are no longer accessible, retrogressive succession can occur and only a severe disturbance or climate change can improve this site. MacMahon (e.g., 1981) suggested that in arid systems, the variability in temperature and precipitation is an overriding feature regulating ecosystem processes. Water inputs into soils are unpredictable both in time and space resulting in a high potential for plant death and nutrient loss by leaching, erosion and volatilization (in the case of N). Not only is the climate highly variable, but spatial variability due to topographic changes and microbial organization patterns around individual plants create radical microscale variability in soils and microclimates. For example, slope bottoms have different soil depths and particle sizes, nutrient concentrations, daily irradiance, wind directions and intensity, and water input, storage and demand than do upland sites (e.g., Shmida et al. 1986). Other data indicate that these changes may be as great over a few cm around an individual shrub as they are across a site. These patterns create a microbial and plant resource organizational pattern that interact within a few cm (Allen and MacMahon 1985). All of these differing conditions exist within the reaches of an individual plant and can differentially affect establishment of its diaspores.

Plants adapt to arid regions in a variety of ways but all depend upon transfer of water to leaves via belowground biotic components, and on retention and transfer of nutrients. A wide variety of organisms are involved in these processes from all trophic levels. Plants fix carbon and transfer much of that reduced carbon belowground, most directly to roots (albeit reluctantly, see Caldwell 1976). Vesicular-arbuscular (VA) mycorrhizal fungi, mutualistic associates with most arid-land plant species (Trappe 1981), and N-fixing prokaryotes immobilize nutrients and transfer them to the plant in exchange for a large fraction of that carbon. Decomposers (both fungal and bacterial) mineralize much of the carbon and immobilize nutrients for renewed uptake by plants. (More detail on the interactions of the soil trophic structure can be found in the chapter by Whitford in this volume).

Despite the clear roles of the biota in these processes that operate over small scales, many researchers continue to use a "watershed" approach to describe production and nutrient cycling processes in deserts. This approach provides valuable data on past changes, but it has questionable predictive capability for reconstructing lands because it often fails to describe the behavior of the key organisms that regulate the functioning of those land units (see Shachak et al. 1987 for a contrary example). I suggest that a first and basic need for predicting successful management practices in a disturbed arid ecosystem is to know the key organisms and their spatial dispersion patterns in desirable ecosystems. Describing how they might be manipulated to reestablish those patterns in disturbed lands would follow.

BELOWGROUND STRUCTURE

The structure of the belowground components of a productive, stable ecosystem needs to be described at several scales. Plants and their associated microorganisms respond to variations in microhabitat that select against the individual. Arid lands can have complex land forms as do other ecosystems and the selective pressures on the organisms are different across a landscape. Microorganisms respond to individual root segments that are their carbon sources. Therefore, to restructure a disturbed habitat, the entire range of scales must be considered: landscape, plant patches, individual plants, and individual root segments.

Landscape scale structure and soil resources have been studied and utilized by agriculturalists for millenia. Water harvesting systems such as those at Avdat, Israel (Evenari et al. 1971) and elsewhere (e.g., Boers and Ben-Asher 1982) demonstrate the utilization of slope dynamics to gain water and nutrient resources. Erosion zones (arroyas and wadis) have quite different resources from uplands, resulting in different communities (Phillips and MacMahon 1978, Shmida et al. 1986). More importantly, even small changes in slope aspect or distance down the slope can radically alter resource availability. Even small slopes can create turbulence patterns that drive moisture deposition and soil erosion, thereby creating quite differing environments on a single disturbance site (Figs. 1,2). These slopes, in turn, determine not only plant-available moisture but plant growth and seedling recruitment (e.g., Steinberger and Whitford 1984, Allen et al. 1987). Thus, with the exception of extreme arid lands, e.g., the allochthonous ecosystems dependent upon detrital carbon inputs (Alaily et al. 1987, Bornkamm 1988), the mosaic of ridges, wadis (arroyas), and slopes differentially regulate the availability of soil resources which leads to high physical/chemical/biological diversity of any potential disturbance site.

Plants also have the ability to alter their local environment, to "liberate" unavailable resources or to move them from considerable distances. Some plants can send out roots several meters (horizontally) to gain water (e.g., Kummerow 1981). They then deposit organic matter under the canopy and change the local water and nutrient availability for microorganisms involved in nutrient turnover and uptake. Other species have roots that extend deeply into the soil to reach the buried water table. At that depth (sometimes 4 m), a whole array of microbial associates can be found, including symbiotic N-fixing organisms and mycorrhizal fungi (Virginia et al. 1986), which ultimately regulate the nutrient characteristics under the canopy of that plant (Virginia and Jarrell 1983). Plants not only move resources via root growth, they also alter the air turbulence structure, thereby regulating patterns of deposition and retention of snow, microbes, and organic matter (West and Caldwell 1983, Fig. 3). These biotic-driven systems result in horizontal (Fig. 4) and vertical (Fig. 5) resource structuring at the scale of individual plants or clumps of plants at any location within the landscape.

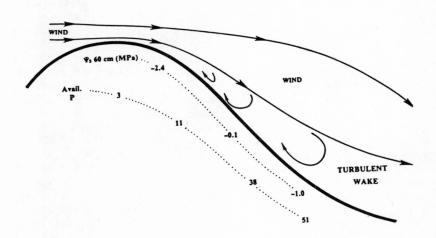

Fig. 1. Effect of landscape structure on atmosphere and soil characteristics at the Kemmerer Reconstruction Site (see descriptions in Allen 1983, Allen and MacMahon 1985, Allen et al. 1987). The wind at this site is predominately from the west, resulting in the wind and turbulence structure shown (from Neuber 1984). This terrain and wind determines the moisture structure (shown as the deep soil moisture) both as a function of snow deposition (Fig. 2) and increasing plant production down the slope (Allen et al. 1987). Also soil nutrients tend to increase down the slope (expressed as available phosphorus, Allen unpublished data), presumably due to wind erosion, particle deposition, and altered nutrient cycling characteristics of the sites with greater moisture.

The scale at which microorganisms must be studied is the most problematical. As with any organisms, microbes establish and grow in response not to average climate, but rather to the immediate microconditions. The spatial variation in soil resources "perceived" by microbes appears to be extremely high in arid lands. For example, in the early morning, soils can range from saturated

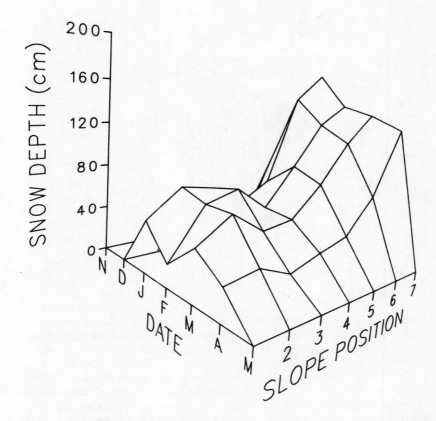

Fig. 2. Snow deposition patterns down the slope at the Kemmerer Site during the winter of 1983-1984, a high snow year. This snow pattern results from the wind turbulence shown in Fig. 1 and results in the soil moisture pattern also shown in Fig. 1.

under a rock to extremely dry at the edge of the rock
creating a whole range of conditions for microorganisms.
Indeed, studies on soil fungal communities show a much
higher richness per number of isolates with increased
aridity in grassland habitats (Christensen 1981) and
higher richness in sagebrush steppe communities than in
more mesic habitats (Allen 1985). Microbes also respond

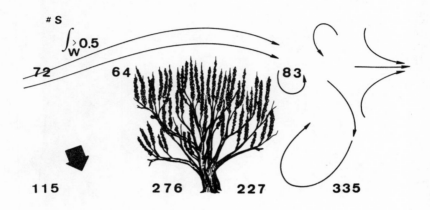

Fig. 3.   An example of the turbulence structure
created by an individual shrub and its influence on
deposition of particles in the 30-100 um diameter range
(from Hipps and Allen, in preparation).   Shown above the
shrub are the number of seconds out of 2 minutes in which
the standard deviation of the wind vertical velocity ($\int_w$)
was greater than 0.5, a high degree of turbulence.   Shown
below are the number of particles in the 30-100 um
diameter range that were deposited in the spatial
arrangement shown.   These data show that there is a dead
air zone associated with the shrub, that results in a
greater particle deposition under as opposed to in front
of the shrub and high turbulence (especially downward air
movement) behind the shrub.   These air flow patterns
control the horizontal structural characteristics shown
in Fig. 4.

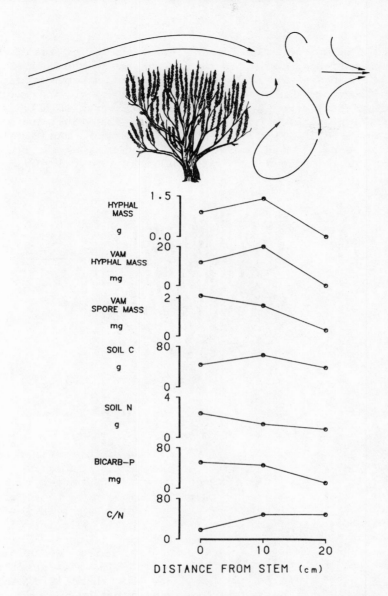

Fig. 4.   The horizontal structure of soil microbial and nutrient characteristics down wind from a shrub (data from Allen and MacMahon 1985).   Litter is concentrated under and near the edge of the canopy and the microbes are most active in association with this zone.

directly to roots by forming gradients of species and trophic groups, both from the rhizoplane to the bulk soil and from the old suberized roots to the root tips (Coleman et al. 1983). Different plant roots differentially regulate mycorrhizal activity and nutrient depletion dynamics (e.g., Caldwell et al. 1985, Allen and Allen 1986). Mycorrhizal fungi, in turn, change the surrounding physical and chemical structure of the soils from the rhizoplane out into the bulk soils by binding

depth (cm)	VAM infection	spore density (# /g)	LPi	Phosphorus (mg/kg) LP$_o$	Total
10	++	16	16	53	668
12	++	13	17	26	764
25	++	32	14	31	821
45	+	14	13	46	731
75	+	20	14	9	646

Fig. 5. The vertical structure of VA mycorrhizae and soil phosphorus below a shrub. These data indicate that both microbial and active nutrient dynamics occur deep in the profile at the Kemmerer site. LPi = labile inorganic phosphorus, LPo = labile organic phosphorus.

122

soil particles and increasing available soil nutrients (Jurinak et al. 1986, Thomas et al. 1986).

In summary, belowground organisms respond to their microenvironment at the scale of the organism not the scale that humans observe. Those conditions vary over both microscales (individual roots) to landscape scales (hilltop to wadi). All are important in describing how ecosystem processes operate and in reconstructing desirable lands.

EFFECTS OF DISTURBANCE

In almost any disturbance, some microorganisms survive. Less severe disturbance results in greater survival with the potential for more rapid recovery of the soil processes important to the establishment of a desirable ecosystem. The retention of topsoil in many current mine reclamation practices is an example of utilizing surviving residuals to improve land reconstruction (e.g. Allen and Allen 1980, Fresquez et al. 1986, Tate and Klein 1985). Some soil organisms will be lost even with minimal disturbance. After they are lost, few of these organisms can be purposefully reintroduced. VA mycorrhizal fungi cannot be cultured without a host, and current nursery practices (pot cultures) are far too bulky and costly to allow reintroduction at the scale of most land disturbances (Wood 1984). Saprophytes are too diverse to reinoculate, and the soils are different enough following disturbance such that new organisms are probably better adapted to the new conditions. For example, Allen and MacMahon (1985) noted that the dominant saprophytic microfungi changed from taiga-affiliated species in the undisturbed soils to desert species following surface mining in a cold desert as the exposed soils became drier and hotter. Soil animal populations and trophic structure can change significantly, depending upon the relative rates of survival of both plants and microbial associates (e.g., Stanton and Krementz 1982). If residuals survive, it is possible that reestablishment of the belowground system can recover rapidly resulting in minimal significant loss of desirable ecosystem properties.

A greater concern than decreases in species richness after disturbance, is the loss of spatial structure

(Allen and MacMahon 1985). Dispersion of free-living and symbiotic soil organisms is tightly regulated by the dispersion and growth patterns of associated plants. The chances of long term survival of the organisms as well as the impacts they have on the environment is dependent on whether they are in an appropriate spatial pattern.

Establishment by both residuals and migrating diaspores of microorganisms will occur. Organisms establish in habitats where they can survive despite rigors in the physical or biotic environment (Gleason 1939). Although several long distance dispersal or saltation mechanisms have evolved in desert systems, movement by desirable organisms to an appropriate location for establishment is chancy at best. In addition, many soil organisms not only must reach the appropriate locations but they also must get below the surface of the ground to initiate growth and development. This is especially important following disturbance but it continues even in so-called climax communities where there is small scale disturbance by animals (Koide and Mooney 1987) and die-back with unfavorable environmental conditions (Allen et al. 1987) that alter soil biota such as mycorrhizal fungi. If the establishment of organisms capable of retaining existing nutrients does not occur relatively rapidly, the potential for resource depletion to occur and permanent desertification is high (e.g., Allen 1987).

RESPONSES WITH POOR RECONSTRUCTION

Despite the reclamation laws, environmental concerns, and research efforts (especially of the last decade), numerous examples of unsuccessful reclamation efforts are available, even in the so-called developed countries. Most result from a lack of consideration of basic ecosystem processes, such as the need to balance productivity and mineralization and to retain organisms important to the immobilization process (e.g., Fig. 6). Interestingly, many less desirable long-term reclamation efforts may result from practices deemed favorable, including even-aged stand plantings of highly productive species, fertilization, and irrigation (Allen 1985). These practices tend to reduce or eliminate mycorrhizal fungi and to result in high quantities of standing dead

litter that immobilize nutrients important to new growth.
Grasses are most often chosen for reclamation because
they are easiest to establish. However, grasses have
shallow roots that are capable of utilizing irrigation
water but do not initiate deeper roots and provide the
vertical structure for associated deep microbes important
to long-term stability. Alternatively, lack of
consideration to establishing plants can result in weed
cover or no plants at all. These sites lose mineral
nutrients and are subject to severe, continuous erosion
and the potential for permanent degraded land. Examples
of both types of sites can be found in the Western United
States and elsewhere (Allen 1985).

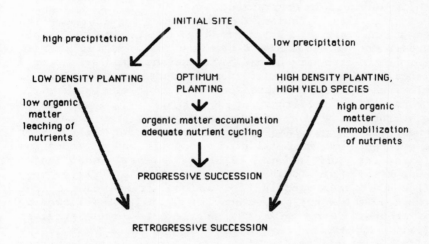

Fig. 6. Three possible outcomes of reconstruction
efforts depending on the nutrient cycling and
productivity dynamics of the system (from Allen 1985).
Two of the scenarios result in retrogressive succession,
decreasing productivity with unavailable nutrients. Only
when moisture, nutrient cycling rates and productivity
are matched will successful restoration occur.

125

TECHNOLOGICAL FIXES

Several technological fixes have been proposed to aid in reconstruction efforts for disturbed arid lands. These range from the use of new equipment for seeding or furrowing to genetically-engineered plants and microorganisms with improved drought tolerance and greater plant production. Some of these have potential in developed countries. For instance, salt-tolerant microorganisms still capable of fixing nitrogen or transporting phosphorus to the host plant will be important to plant establishment in saline habitats. However, there are significant limits to these technologies within the context of reconstructing large disturbed arid areas. These include our current lack of understanding of survival mechanisms of organisms and the non-linear interactive parameters that organisms alter in their surrounding environment.

The first problem, environmental requirements for the survival of specific organisms, is not well understood for existing microorganisms, and far less so for engineered organisms. Transplant studies in arid lands have indicated that even the short-term survival of microbes is highly unpredictable. For example, when we transplanted seedlings of _Hedysarum_ _borealis_ onto a disturbed site in 1983 (a wet year), the local VAM endophyte, _Glomus_ _fasciculatum_, survived for the two year experiment and improved plant survival and reproduction (Carpenter and Allen, 1988). However, when three endophytes (the local _G_. _fasciculatum_, _G_. _macrocarpum_ from the Laramie basin, and an undescribed fungus from the Mojave desert) were transplanted in 1986, followed by a drought year, only the hot-desert fungus survived (Allen and Friese, unpublished data). No statistically significant effects on the host _Agropyron_ _smithii_ plants were detected. These and similar studies suggest that we cannot yet describe the relative survival potential of local versus introduced endophytes, the first step in utilization of specific microbes for land reconstruction.

The second problem is predicting how microorganisms affect their environment, particularly in the myriad of non-linear interactions. For example, ice-nucleating bacteria not only cause plant losses to frost, but they also have a beneficial role as nucleating centers for

forming of raindrops (Odum 1985). Escape of desirable
organisms into undesirable situations occurred before
with unpredictable consequences (Halvorson et al. 1985)
This suggests that a better understanding of basic
microbial ecology is necessary before using specific
microorganisms for ecological manipulations.

SUCCESSIONAL APPROACHES TO STRUCTURAL RESTORATION

In successional arid sites, shrub establishment
appears to occur in clumps as opposed to being regularly
distributed across the landscape (Phillips and MacMahon
1981). In 1983, I proposed that this approach could be
used for restoring disturbed arid ecosystems as the
aerodynamic qualities of shrub clumps would allow for
entrapment of snow, blowing VAM and saprophytic fungal
spores, and organic matter (see Allen 1985, Skujins and
Allen 1986, Allen 1987). Subsequently, we have
demonstrated that individual shrubs superimpose small-
scale turbulence on the air flow, which increases the
deposition and reduces entrainment of 20-150 um particles
in the canopy wake (Hipps and Allen, in prep.). Also,
patterns of litter retention and snow depth around
individual shrubs show associations with the described
wind dynamics (Fig. 7). Additionally, our recent data
suggest that shrubs, when planted closely enough,
interact and affect wake size and particle deposition
(Allen, Hipps and Mullen, unpublished data). Thus, the
potential importance of utilizing planting patterns,
based on natural successional processes, appears to be
one effective way to enhance the establishment potential
of arid land plants. These processes, however, are
affected by the landscape on which restoration is
attempted. We have shown that spores of VAM fungi can
move from as far as 2 km onto a disturbed site (Warner et
al. 1987). However, the deposition of those spores is
dependent upon the daily wind intensity coupled with
terrain complexity (Fig. 8). If those wind dynamics and
terrain interactions are known, it should be possible to
predict and utilize those predictions to promote input of
naturally-dispersed particulates (spores, soil, organic
matter) important to ecosystem restoration.

Unfortunately, propagule input does not equal organism establishment. Root growth appears to be faster than mycorrhizal hyphal growth. This fact coupled with an altered soil structure (even with topsoil respreading) means that the fungal hyphae cannot keep up, vertically with root growth. Thus, the vertical characteristics found with plants on a disturbed site do not resemble those from the undisturbed area (Fig. 9). Our data suggest that animals play a small or insignificant role in the horizontal structuring of the belowground portion of this ecosystem (e.g., animals have only a small role in moving VA mycorrhizal fungi onto the site, Allen, 1988). However, ants, beetles, and cicadas can transport inoculum vertically (Friese and Allen unpublished data). Other reports indicate that animals influence the

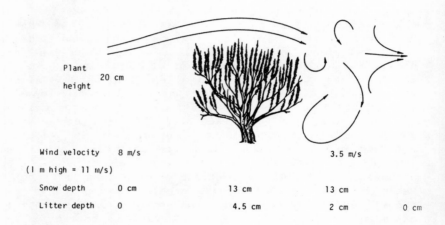

Fig. 7. Patterns of snow and litter accumulation around a planted shrub on the Kemmerer site. No litter accumulation occurred during the first four years of shrub growth as the shrub was not large enough to produce adequate litter or alter wind turbulence. After the shrub was ~20 cm diameter and 20 cm tall litter and snow began to accumulate. I predict that this patterning will ultimately result in the horizontal characteristics resembling those shown in Fig. 4.

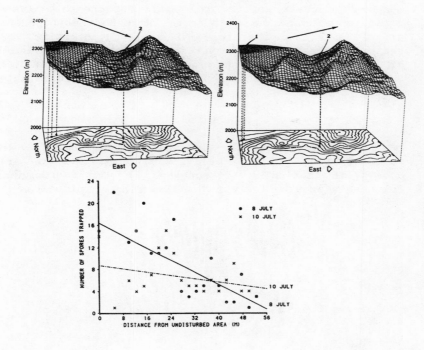

Fig. 8. Landscape scale wind and particle deposition
characteristics at the Kemmerer site. Although the wind
direction is virtually always from the west, it can come
in two manners, slowly in which the upper and valley
flows are coupled (left) or fast when from the west,
while the valley flows are to the north (right). These
flows result in different patterns of VA mycorrhizal
spore movement (and presumably other particles of similar
sizes). When the winds are coupled (e.g., 8 July 1983),
there are decreasing spores numbers moving up the slope
of the disturbed site (location A) and none reach the lee
side (location B). When winds are uncoupled (e.g., 10
July 1983), spores move all across the site and up over
onto the lee side of the slope. These patterns dictate
the types of particles moving across the restoration area
and the potential for utilizing natural-moving microbial
inoculum.

129

ecosystem more than just their energy flows would suggest because of their ability to regulate processes such as establishment and turnover (e.g., MacMahon 1981, Shachak et al. 1987). Therefore, I would hypothesize that restoring the belowground vertical structure might be one of the more important animal attributes in the successional process and important to any restoration effort.

CONCLUSIONS

In summary, several points can be made regarding the reconstruction of the belowground component of arid ecosystems following disturbance. The belowground components provide the water and nutrients that drive the

depth	phosphorus (mg/kg)		VAM spore density	infection	root mass (g)
0-12 cm	LPi	TP			
	18	850	11	+	49
>12	39	800	0	0	14

Fig. 9. Shown is the vertical structure under a shrub on the reclaimed Kemmerer site. Despite the fact that many aspects of the horizontal structure dictated by the wind are recovering (Fig. 7) there appears to be little redevelopment of the vertical structure resembling that of the undisturbed area (Fig. 5) even after the 5 years of plant growth. I hypothesize that animals may be important to this restructuring but the specific dynamics involved are not known. LPi = labile inorganic P, TP = total P.

system. They have distinctive structures at both the individual plant and landscape scales that are destroyed with disturbance. Finally, the reestablishment of that structure is dependent upon the interactions of plants, animals, and the physical features of each habitat. As belowground organisms become recognized as biological entities rather than just parts of nutrient cycles or soils, their genetic and ecological potential can become known, predictable and tapped to the extent that reconstruction efforts can become a scientifically-based process rather than an art form with unpredictable consequences.

ACKNOWLEDGMENTS

I thank Carl Friese, Lawrence Hipps, Karen Leunk, Nancy Warner, and Wendy Jones for technical help and data interpretation of various aspects of the research presented here. Support was provided by grants from the National Science Foundation no. BSR 83-17358 and the United States Department of Agriculture nos. 83-CRCR-1-1229 and 85-CRSR-2-2179.

LITERATURE CITED

Alaily, F. R. Bornkamm, and M. Renger. 1987. Evaluation of land in SW-Egypt. Berliner Geowissenschaftliche Abhandlungen 75:517-544.

Allen, E.B. and M.F. Allen. 1980. Natural reestablishment of vesicular-arbuscular mycorrhizae following stripmine reclamation in Wyoming. Journal of Applied Ecology 17:139-147.

Allen, E.B. and M.F. Allen. 1986. Water relations of xeric grasses in the field: interactions of mycorrhizas and competition. New Phytologist 104:559-571.

Allen, M.F. 1983. Formation of vesicular-arbuscular mycorrhizae in Atriplex gardneri (Chenopodiaceae): seasonal response in a cold desert. Mycologia 75:773-776.

Allen, M.F. 1985. Spatial patterning and soil saprophytic microbiota: impact of strip mining, importance and management strategies. Pages 322-326 in Second Annual Meeting of the American Society for Surface Mining and Reclamation, Proceedings.

Allen, M.F. 1987. Mycorrhizae and rehabilitation of disturbed arid lands. in J.J. Skujins and O.M. El-Tayeb, editors. Microbiology and organic matter in desert rehabilitation. U.N.E.P., Nairobi, in press.

Allen, M.F. 1988. Re-establishment of VA Mycorrhizae following severe disturbance: comparative patch dynamics of a shrub desert and a subalpine volcano. Proceedings of the Royal Society of Edinburgh (section B): in press.

Allen, M.F., E.B. Allen, and N.E. West. 1987. Influence of parasitic and mutualistic fungi on _Artemisia tridentata_ during high precipitation years. Bulletin of the Torrey Botanical Club 114:272-279.

Allen, M.F. and J.A. MacMahon. 1985. Impact of disturbance on cold desert fungi: comparative microscale dispersion patterns. Pedobiologia 28:215-224.

Boers, T.M. and J. Ben-Asher. 1982. A review of rainwater harvesting. Agriculture Water Management 5:145-158.

Bornkamm, R. 1987. Allochthonous ecosystems. Landscape Ecology 1:119-122.

Caldwell, M.M. 1976. Root extension and water absorption. Pages 63-85, in O.L. Lange, L. Kappen, and E.-D. Schulze, editors, Ecological Studies, Analysis and Synthesis, Vol. 19, Water and Plant Life, Springer-Verlag, Berlin.

Caldwell, M.M., D.M. Eissenstat, J.H. Richards, and M.F. Allen. 1985. Competition for phosphorus: differential uptake from dual-isotope-labeled soil interspaces between shrub and grass. Science 229:384- 386.

Carpenter, A.T. and M.F. Allen. 1988. Responses of _Hedysarum_ _boreale_ to mycorrhizas and _Rhizobium_: plant and soil nutrient changes. New Phytologist, in press.

Christensen, M. 1981. Species diversity and dominance in fungal communities. Pages 201-232, in D.T. Wichlow and G.C. Carroll, editors. The fungal community. Marcel Dekker, Inc. New York.

Coleman, D.C. C.P.P. Reid, and C.V. Cole. 1983. Biological strategies of nutrient cycling in soil systems. Advances in Ecological Research 13:1-55.

Evenari, M., L. Shanan, and N.H. Tadmor. 1971. The Negev: the Challenge of a Desert. Harvard University Press, Cambridge, MA.

Fresquez, P.R., E.F. Aldon, and W.C. Lindemann. 1986. Microbial re-establishment and the diversity of fungal genera in reclaimed coal mine spoils and soils. Reclamation and Revegetation Research 4:245-258.

Gleason, H.A. 1939. The individualistic concept of the plant association. American Midland Naturalist 21:92-110.

Halvorson, H.O., D. Pramer, and M. Rogul. 1985. Engineered organisms in the environment: scientific issues. American Society for Microbiology, Washington D.C. .pa

Jurinak. J.J., L.M. Dudley, M.F. Allen, and W.K. Knight. 1986. The role of calcium oxalate in the availability of phosphorus in soils of semiarid regions: a thermodynamic study. Soil Science 142:255-261.

Koide, R.T. and H.A. Mooney. 1987. Spatial variation in inoculum potential of vesicular-arbuscular mycorrhizal fungi caused by formation of gopher mounds. New Phytologist 107:173-182.

Kummerow, J. 1981. Structure of roots and root systems. Pages 259-288, in F. diCastri, D.W. Goodall and R.L. Specht, editors, Mediterranean-type shrublands. Elsevier Scientific Publishing Co., Amsterdam.

MacMahon, J.A. 1981. Successional processes: comparisons among biomes with special reference to probable roles of and influences on animals. Pages 277-304, in D.C. West, H.H. Shugart and D.B. Botkin, editors. Forest Succession, Concepts and Application. Springer-Verlag, New York.

Neuber, H. 1984. Comparisons of snow depth, soil temperature, matric potential and quasi-friction velocity between a windward and a lee shelter in a cold desert. M.S. Thesis, Utah State University, Logan, Utah.

Odum, E.P. 1985. Biotechnology and the biosphere. Science 229:1338.

Phillips, D.L. and J.A. MacMahon. 1978. Gradient analysis of a Sonaran Desert Bajada. Southwestern Naturalist 23:669-680.

Phillips, D.L. and J.A. MacMahon. 1981. Competition and spacing patterns in desert shrubs. Journal of Ecology 69:97-115.

Shachak, M., C.G. Jones, and Y. Granot, 1987. Herbivory in rocks and the weathering of a desert. Science 236:1098-1099.

Shmida, A. M. Evenari, and I. Noy-Meir. 1986. Hot desert ecosystems: an integrated view. Pages 379-387, in M. Evenari et al., Hot deserts and arid shrublands, B. Elsevier Science Publishers, Amsterdam.

Skujins, J.J. 1981. Nitrogen cycling in arid ecosystems. Ecological Bulletins (Stockholm) 33:477-491.

Skujins, J.J. and M.F. Allen. 1986. Use of mycorrhizae for land rehabilitation. MIRCEN Journal 21:161-176.

Stanton, N.L. and D. Krementz. 1982. Nematode densities on reclaimed sites on a cold desert shrub-steppe. Reclamation and Revegetation Research 1:233-241.

Steinberger, Y. and W.G. Whitford. 1984. Spatial and temporal relationships of soil microarthropods on a desert watershed. Pedobiologia 26:275-284.

Tate, R.L. III, and D.A. Klein. 1985. Soil reclamation processes, microbiological analyses and applications. Marcel Dekker, Inc., New York.

Thomas, R.S., S. Dakessian, R.N. Ames, M.S. Brown, and G.J. Bethlenfalvay. 1986. Aggregation of a silty clay loam soil by mycorrhizal onion roots. Soil Science Society of America Journal 50:1494-1499.

Trappe, J.M. 1981. Mycorrhizae and productivity of arid and semiarid rangelands. Pages 581-599, in J.T. Manassah and E.J. Briskey, editors, Advances in food producing systems for arid and semiarid lands. Academic Press, New York.

Virginia, R.A. and W.M. Jarrell. 1983. Soil properties in a mesquite-dominated Sonoran Desert ecosystem. Soil Science Society of America Journal 47:138-144.

Virginia, R.A., M.B. Jenkins, and W.M. Jarrell. 1986. Depth of root symbiont occurrence in soil. Biology and Fertility of Soils 2:127-130.

Walker, J., C.H. Thompson, I.F. Fergus, and B.R. Tunstall. 1981. Plant succession and soil development in coastal sand dunes of subtropical Eastern Australia. Pages 107-131, in D.C. West, H.H. Suguart, and D.B. Botkin, editors. Forest Succession, concepts and application. Springer- Verlag, New York.

Warner, N.J., M.F. Allen, and J.A. MacMahon. 1987.
Dispersal agents of vesicular-arbuscular mycorrhizal
fungi in a disturbed air ecosystem. Mycologia 79:722-
730.

West, N.E. and M.M. Caldwell. 1983. Snow as a factor in
salt desert shrub vegetation patterns in Curlew Valley,
Utah. American Midland Naturalist 109:376- 379.

Whitford, W.G., V. Meentmeyer, T.R. Seastedt, K. Cromack,
Jr., D.A. Crossley, Jr., P. Santos, R.L. Todd, and J.B.
Waide. 1981. Exceptions to the AET model: deserts and
clear-cut forest. Ecology 62:275-277.

Wood, T. 1984. Commercialization of VAM inocula: the
reclamation market. Pages 21-27, in S.E. Williams and
M.F. Allen, editors. VA mycorrhizae and reclamation of
arid and semiarid lands. University of Wyoming
Agriculture Experiment Station, Laramie.

Walter G. Whitford

7. Decomposition and Nutrient Cycling in Disturbed Arid Ecosystems

ABSTRACT

Several studies focused on the effects of organic mulches on soil biota and soil processes in surface mined areas are reviewed. The effects of overgrazing and subsequent rangeland degradation on soil processes are described. Amending mine spoil materials with recalcitrant mulch materials, bark and wood chips, resulted in increased abundances and diversity of soil microflora and microfauna which resulted in decomposition rates similar to unmined soils. Other organic mulches, straw and sewage sludge, had short term or no effect on biota and decomposition. On surface mined areas reconstructed by contouring with a surface layer of topsoil amended with straw, the soil biota and processes were most similar to unmined soil the first year post restoration and diverged greatly by the fourth year. This restoration procedure failed to maintain a viable soil biota. Addition of organic amendments to intact but degraded rangeland had no long-term effect on soil processes, soil biota or vegetative production. In arid rangelands the shift in vegetation from grassland to shrubland has resulted in lowered nitrogen availability as evidenced by low total soil nitrogen and reduced nitrogen mineralization potential.

INTRODUCTION

Most of the arid and semi-arid land areas in the
United States have been subjected to a variety of
man-induced disturbances over the past 120 years. The
historical disturbance of natural ecosystems in the
southwestern U.S. began with the introduction of domestic
livestock by the Spanish settlers in the Rio Grande
valley in the 16th century.   From the 1870's to the
present time, the establishment of an extensive livestock
industry throughout the western U.S. has resulted in
rapid changes in vegetation with increases in woody
species and species that are undesirable as livestock
forage.   There are numerous studies of the deterioration
of arid and semiarid rangeland that document these
changes and demonstrate that the deterioration is
continuing, albeit at a lower rate, at the present time
(Buffington and Herbel 1965, York and Dick-Peddie 1969,
Rogers 1982, Gross and Dick Peddie 1979).   All other
disturbances of arid and semiarid ecosystems   in North
America are imposed on systems already disturbed by
overgrazing. One of the more recent kinds of disturbances
and one that is affecting increasingly larger areas of
land is surface mining.   Surface mining completely
destroys native ecosystems.   Re-establishment of stable
ecosystems on surface mined lands depends upon
development of a soil and those soil processes that
affect water and nutrient availability.   An active
microflora is necessary for the development of mine
spoils into soils (Visser et al. 1979) and numerous
studies have shown that mineralization of nutrients from
decomposing organic matter is dependent upon soil
microfauna (Parker et al. 1984, Ingham et al. 1985).
There are few studies of reclamation of mine spoils that
have focused on decomposition processes (Carell et al.
1979, Visser et al. 1979, Lawery 1977).   However, there
have been a number of studies of soil microflora (Cundell
1977, Fresquez and Lindemam 1982, Hersman and Klein 1979,
Parkinson 1979, Miller et al. 1979, Olson et al. 1981).
Few studies have examined the activities of the soil
fauna in reclaimed spoils (Cross and Wilman 1982).
Based on the basic research findings on the
interrelationships of soil microfauna and microflora in
decomposition and nutrient cycling processes (Santos and
Whitford 1981, Elkins et al. 1982, Parker et al. 1984),

137

we designed a series of studies to evaluate the efficacy of current restoration procedures in developing a viable soil. We hypothesized that a mature soil microflora and microfauna would produce higher rates of decomposition and nitrogen mineralization than successional or incompletely developed soil biota. In a study of the efficacy of organic amendments in increasing the rate of soil development from raw spoil material, we hypothesized that the addition of recalcitrant organic matter would be more effective than addition of readily decomposable organic matter in the development of soil biota and that decomposition and subsequent mineralization would be highest in areas amended with recalcitrant organics (Elkins et al 1984). In a second study we assessed the direction of the soil development process on restored areas that had been subjected to the same restoration procedures 1-4 years prior to our studies. These studies form the basis of my assessment of decomposition and nutrient cycling in reclaimed strip mines (Parker et al. 1987).

Our studies of decomposition and nutrient cycling processes in arid ecosystems of southern New Mexico (Parker et. al. 1984), and studies by Coleman and his associates with semiarid short grass prairie soil ecosystems (Ingham et al. 1985) led us to hypothesize that efforts to reconstruct a soil that will support productive vegetation must include all of the components of the below ground subsystem and of the processes of decomposition and nitrogen cycling that are essential processes in all ecosystems. We hypothesized that addition of organic materials to rangelands or more severely disturbed soils would provide an energy and nutrient source for the soil biota that are responsible for the essential soil processes. In this chapter I review several separate studies on a variety of disturbed semiarid ecosystems that focused on the belowground subsystem. Since the general approach was similar in these studies it should be possible to examine the efficacy of added organic mulches as energy and nutrient sources for soil biota.

Historically, rangeland management procedures were developed from the concept that vegetation is in equilibrium with climate and soil: the climax community concept (Clements 1916, Tansley 1935, Weaver and Clements 1938). Rangeland management has therefore focused on the idea that manipulating stocking rates and or controlling the undesirable "increasers" can force vegetation from a "disclimax" species assemblage or degraded state towards the more productive and desirable "climax" situation. There has been little effort focused on the maintenance relationships between soil processes and re-establishment of rangeland vegetation.

Many of the rangelands of the southwestern U.S. are in what could be classified as a degraded state. Cover of dominant C_4 grasses has been reduced, cover of unpalatable shrubs has increased and erosion from such areas ladens rivers with silt during periods of intense summer rains. If vegetation of degraded rangelands is to be forced back toward an equilibrium with climate and soil, the soil properties and processes characteristic of a climax grassland must be achieved. One result of overgrazing and loss of perennial cover is the reduction in soil organic matter and concomitant changes in soil microflora and microfauna. Regeneration of the perennial grasses probably requires rebuilding the soils. We hypothesized that addition of organic materials to degraded rangeland soils would stimulate activity of the soil biota, increase soil organic matter and soil nutrients especially nitrogen fixers and by modifying the physical environment, i.e., infiltration and soil temperatures.

Here I review studies of decomposition processes, soil biota and some aspects of nitrogen cycling as indicators of the relative success of reclamation procedures in restoring soil ecosystem processes and degree of divergence of soils in ecosystems impacted by grazing from soils of undisturbed ecosystems.

Our studies on reclaimed surface mined lands were conducted at the McKinley Coal Mine 30 km northwest of Gallup, New Mexico. The pre-mining vegetation was sagebrush (<u>Artemisia</u> <u>tridentata</u>) in the valleys and open pinon-juniper woodland on the hill slopes. Mean annual precipitation is 300 mm. Studies of rangelands subject to varying degrees of degradation by grazing of domestic livestock were conducted on the New Mexico State University Ranch and Jornada Experimental Range (U.S.D.A.), which are located approximately 40 km northeast of Las Cruces, New Mexico. Vegetation includes a variety of grasslands and shrublands. Mean annual precipitation is approximately 230 mm per year. The

139

studies of organic amendments on degraded rangeland were conducted 20 km south of Cuba, New Mexico on an area with blue grama grass and scattered shrubs.

REVIEW OF SOIL BIOTA ASSOCIATED WITH
DECOMPOSITION AND MINERALIZATION PROCESSES
IN ARID AND SEMIARID ECOSYSTEMS

Before discussing specific studies that were designed to evaluate restoration procedures and procedures for enhancing rangeland productivity, it will be useful to briefly review our knowledge of soil processes in arid ecosystems. This review will address only those processes occurring in the soil, not those occurring in plant debris on the soil surface.

Santos and Whitford (1981a) and Santos et al. (1981b) used selected biocides to study decomposition of litter buried in a desert soil. They found that the initial stages of decomposition were mediated by a yeast and bacteria that were grazed by bacteriophagous nematodes and protozoans. In the absence of predatory tydeid mites, the nematodes overgrazed the microflora and reduced decomposition. Thus nematode populations were regulated by tydeid mites. In the absence of soil microarthropods and nematodes, the rates of mass loss (decomposition) were significantly reduced. In a subsequent study, Parker et al. (1984) found that the later stages of decomposition were mediated primarily by fungi. The fungi growing on the dead plant materials immobilized nitrogen. Fungal grazers, that is fungivorous nematodes and small tarsonemid and pygmephorid mites were found to be important in nitrogen mineralization. When the fungivorous mites were eliminated, nitrogen mineralization rates were markedly reduced. The populations of fungivorous mites were regulated by predatory mesostigmatid and prostigmatid mites. Under favorable conditions, soil dwelling collembolans also grazed on the fungi thereby affecting mineralization rates. Thus two key soil processes in arid ecosystems, decomposition and mineralization, are dependent upon activities of soil microfauna which act as regulators of the soil microflora as shown in Fig. 1.

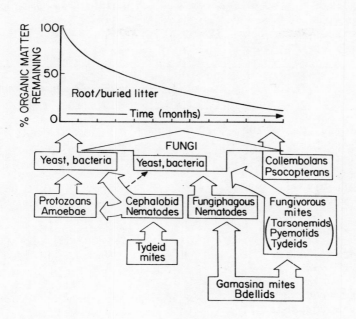

Fig. 1. Relationship between the time course and mass loss of roots and/or buried litter and the trophic structure of the decomposer community in the soil.

EFFECTS OF ORGANIC MULCHES ON SOIL BIOTA AND PROCESSES IN RESTORED SURFACE MINE SPOILS

In the studies on the mine spoils, populations of bacteria increased more rapidly in the sites with organic amendments, but there were no significant differences in protozoan populations or fungal biomass two years after amendments were applied (Table 1). Populations of nematodes and fungal feeding microarthropods were significantly higher in the unmined soils and in the bark-wood chip amended spoils than on the other sites (Table 1). Total numbers of microarthropods increased rapidly in the decomposing straw buried in the unmined

Table 1. Average numbers of soil biota per litter bag from straw buried in minespoils amended with indicated materials. (Data from Parker et al. 1987 and Elkins et al. 1984).

	Topsoil	Bark	Straw	Unmined
Bacteria, No. x 10^4	10.3	13.0	9.4	5.5
Protozoans, No. x 10^4	800	810	830	100
Fungi, hyphal length m x 10^4	12.7	20.0	13.0	10.3
Nematodes	1282	1729	1119	497
Predatory micro-arthropods (1)	9	50	36	41
Fungivorous microarthropods (2)	160	417	538	3930
Omnivorous micro-arthropods (3)	63	243	101	71

(1) Mesostigmata plus Bdellidae, Cheyletidae, Stigmaeidae
(2) Tarsonemidae and Pygmephoridae
(3) Nonorchestidae, Tydeidae, Cryptostigmata: Scheloribates spp. Aphelacarus spp. Collembola, Psocoptera

soil and had a lower rate of increase in straw buried in the bark-wood mulched spoil (Fig. 2). The total population size of the microarthropods in the spoils amended with mulches were not significantly different at the end of the study (Fig. 2). However, the composition differed with the wood-bark amended spoil having higher populations of the omnivorous microarthropods that feed not only on fungi but also consume the plant material (Table 1).

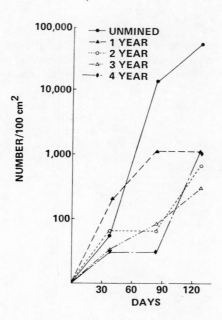

Fig. 2. Changes in total numbers of microarthropods in decomposing straw buried in mine spoils amended with organic mulches, or left without amendment (data from Elkins et al. 1984).

Rates of barley straw decomposition were significantly higher in spoil mixed with bark and wood chips than in any of the other treatments and not significantly different from decomposition rates in unmined soils (Table 2). When these rates were compared with the microflora and microfauna, we found that there were no significant differences in numbers and biomass of bacteria, fungi, or protozoans but there were significant differences in free living nematodes and microarthropods (Tables 1 and 2). The nematode and microarthropod populations were higher in the wood-bark amended spoils and unmined soils than in the other treatments. Considering these data with respect to our knowledge of trophic relationships of arid region soil biota during decomposition and their role in mineralization (Santos and Whitford 1981a, Santos et al. 1981, Elkins et al. 1982, Parker et al. 1984), I suggest that microfloral activity is highest in the unmined soils and wood chip

Table 2. Average mass losses from barley straw buried for 90 days (June - October) and decomposition rates in mine spoils treated with organic mulches (data from Elkins et al. 1984)

Amendment or area	Average Percent Mass Loss	Decomposition Rate (K)
Unmined	17.0	$0.624 \cdot yr^{-1}$
Bark	17.3	$0.661 \cdot yr^{-1}$
Topsoil	9.7	$0.340 \cdot yr^{-1}$
Straw	10.2	$0.341 \cdot yr^{-1}$
None	8.4	$0.324 \cdot yr^{-1}$

bark amended spoil because grazing by the microfauna maintains the populations of microflora in an active growth phase, and microfloral grazer populations are regulated by the microarthropod predators. In addition the diversity of the soil microarthropod fauna in the wood-chip bark amended spoils was closer to that of the unmined soils than were any of the other treatments. This suggests that the taxonomic diversity of the microflora was also higher in this treatment since the diversity of the microfauna is almost certainly related to the diversity of the microflora.

CHANGES IN SOIL BIOTA THROUGH TIME ON RESTORED MINE SPOILS

Population estimates of microflora involved in nitrogen cycling processes can provide an index of the degree of similarity or difference in N cycle processes. When we compared nitrogen cycle bacteria in 1-4 year old restored sites we found that populations of denitrifying bacteria and N fixing Azotobacter decreased with time

Table 3. Soil microorganisms in developing soils on reclaimed coal mine spoils and unmined soil, June 1980. Values in a column followed by the same letter are not significantly different (P = 0.05). (Data from Parker et al. 1987).

Time Since Restoration	Total Bacteria (no.x10^8/g)	Fungi (m/g)	Azotobacter (no.x10^6/g)	Nitrosomonas (no.x10^3/g)	Nitrobacter (no.x10^3/g)	Denitrifiers (no.x10^3/g)
Unmined	5.40b	63.9b	2.39b	2.02a	0.29a	256bc
4 years	3.39ab	10.2a	0.70a	8.38b	13.93b	46a
3 years	2.89a	42.1ab	1.45ab	10.57b	13.45b	94ab
2 years	3.47ab	14.5a	1.82ab	13.39b	6.03b	954cd
1 year	4.84b	17.2a	1.74b	14.88b	9.81b	2013d

145

after restoration but populations of nitrifying bacteria (<u>Nitrosomonas</u> spp. and <u>Nitrobacter</u> spp.) were higher on restored sites than on the unmined area (Table 3). Rates of decomposition of barley straw were highest in the unmined soils and inversely related to time since restoration (Table 4). There was net immobilization of nitrogen in the decomposing straw after two months in the field (Table 4) and net mineralization in straw in the unmined and two and three year old restored areas after four months in the field. The populations and biomass of microflora and microfauna were generally higher on straw buried in the most recently restored areas and unmined sites (Fig. 3). However, the soil microarthropod populations were one to two orders of magnitude higher in straw buried in the unmined sites than in any of the restored sites (Fig. 4) These differences were primarily due to population densities of small fungiphagous mites (Table 5).

The results of both studies on restored strip mined lands reinforce the view that a complete soil biota are needed for normally functioning soil processes. The addition of recalcitrant organic matter in the form of bark and wood chips to raw spoils allowed for the establishment of tarsonemid mites in that area and subsequent colonization of decomposing material by those mites. Tarsonemid mites feed on fungi and have been found to be important in nitrogen mineralization (Parker et al. 1984). The recalcitrant organic mulch mixed into raw spoil provided a better habitat for the soil microfauna than the topsoil alone. The correlation between decomposition rates and diversity and density of soil microfauna is not accidental as demonstrated experimentally by Santos et al (1981), Elkins et al. (1982) and Parker et al. (1984). Not all organic amendments produce soil environments conducive to establishment of soil fauna, e.g. the straw mulch as shown by Elkins et al. (1984). The importance of the trophic relationships among the soil biota (Fig. 1) and key taxa of this biota in decomposition and mineralization cannot be emphasized too much. Restoration research that fails to consider the biota of the entire soil sub-system will fail in any attempt to evaluate success of restoration procedures. Qualitative (species composition) as well as quantitative data on soil fauna can provide a useful index of the relative

Table 4. Percent mass loss after 120 days (June - October) of barley straw buried in an unmined area and in areas restored by stored topsoil with straw mulch 1-4 years prior to the study and average changes in straw nitrogen (N) during that period (data from Parker et al. 1987).

	% Loss ± SD	Mean Change Straw N 0-90 days	Change in Straw N 90-120 days
Unmined	16.3 ± 1.0	+3 mg $\cdot$ g^{-1}	-16 mg $\cdot$ g^{-1}
1 year	10.6 ± 0.9	+11 mg $\cdot$ g^{-1}	-2 mg $\cdot$ g^{-1}
2 years	14.7 ± 1.1	+3 mg $\cdot$ g^{-1}	-15 mg $\cdot$ g^{-1}
3 years	8.0 ± 0.7	+3 mg $\cdot$ g^{-1}	-7 mg $\cdot$ g^{-1}
4 years	6.5 ± 1.1	+18 mg $\cdot$ g^{-1}	+3 mg $\cdot$ g^{-1}

success of reclamation procedures in restoring soil microflora and soil processes.

In the study comparing soil processes and biota on spoils restored by standard procedures over five years, there were large discrepancies between the rates of soil processes and populations of soil biota. For example, while the densities of bacteria, fungi and protozoans were lower in decomposing straw in the unmined site than in the restored sites, rates of decomposition were highest in the unmined site. Numbers and/or biomass do not necessarily reflect metabolic activity especially with reference to soil microflora. The activity and/or turnover of soil microflora is dependent upon grazers, the microflora, and it is the activity of the microflora, not the biomass that is important in both decomposition and nutrient cycling.

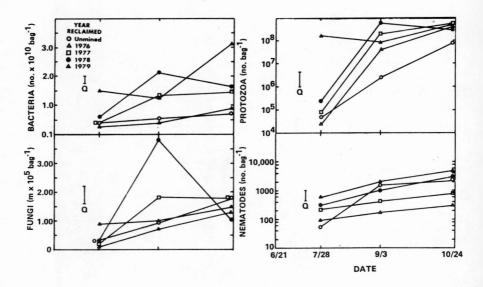

Fig. 3. Changes in soil biota in decomposing straw in litter bags buried in sites restored by standard methods 1 year (1979) to four years (1976) prior to the study in comparison to bags buried in unmined soils (data from Parker et al. 1987).

SOIL BIOTA, ORGANIC AMENDMENTS, DECOMPOSITION AND NITROGEN CYCLING IN DEGRADED RANGELANDS

Overgrazing by livestock affects the soil sub-system by reducing organic matter inputs and increasing erosion. The effects of reduced organic matter and topsoil loss on the soil biota are profound. For example the diversity and abundance of soil microfauna that are essential for effective mineralization vary directly with soil depth and soil organic matter (Cepeda, 1986). A similar relationship is seen in soil nitrogen on a desert watershed. Based on these limited data, we hypothesized that vegetation degradation (in terms of grass herbage yield) has resulted in the loss of biological diversity in the soil biota and consequently reduced rates of critical soil processes. We hypothesized that the addition of organic materials to degraded rangeland would stimulate the activity of soil biota and increase the rates of processes such as decomposition and nitrogen mineralization.

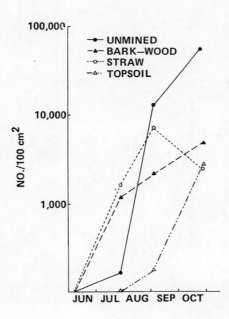

Fig. 4. Changes in number of soil microarthropods in decomposing straw in litter bags buried in sites restored by standard methods 1-4 years prior to the study in comparison to bags buried in unmined soils (data from Parker et al.).

Adding organic amendments to intact but degraded rangeland had only a short term effect or no effect on soil processes and soil biota. Decomposition rates were higher on plots amended with bark and wood chips during the first year of study but were not significantly different from the control or other amendments during the second year (Table 6). Straw mulch and sewage sludge had no effect on decomposition rates. Bark and straw amendments produced an initial increase in soil respiration followed by a decrease. Sewage sludge generally suppressed soil respiration during the first year after amendments were added and initially caused an increase in soil nitrogen in readily usable forms such as ammonia, nitrate and urea. That nitrogen was rapidly lost from the soil by plant uptake, volatilization or

149

Table 5. The effect of time after restoration on microarthropods extracted from decomposing barley straw on unmined and reclaimed soils on the McKinley Mine. The columns labeled 1yr - 4yr refer to elapsed time since the site was reclaimed. Letters next to numbers in a line indicate significantly higher population densities of a taxon for that sample date (p < .05). *Due to the low number of species of the Prostigmata: Bdellidae, Cheyletidae, Cunaxidae and Stigmaeidae were summed as predator species; Cryptostigmata included Scheloribates spp. and Aphelacarus spp.; Mesostigmata included Laelapidae and Rhodacaridae. (Data from Elkins et al. 1984).

$\bar{X}$ No. x bag^{-1}

Taxa	Unmined	1yr	2yr	3yr	4yr	Unmined	1yr	2yr	3yr	4yr	Unmined	1yr	2yr	3yr	4yr
ACARI:															
Prostigmata															
Predator species*	7			4	5	20	5	4	1	1	15	10	15	2	25
Nanorchestidae	18					30					81				
Tudeidae	2	207a	8	9	3	21	57a	8	13	10	16	88a	55a	15	13
Tarsonemidae	10	34	11	1	2	2328a	147b	9	2	1	9350a	89	98	104	48
Pygmaphoridae		5	1	5	4	27	58	3	14	3	72	30	26	439a	507a
Cryptostigmata						21					5				
Mesostigmata*	1	18	2	1	10	51a	42a	11	1	1	19	31	31	8	4
INSECTA:															
Collembola															
Onychiuridae	8					13		102	38				46	16	5
Isotomidae						7		351	111				3	1	17
Entomobryidae	1					2		53	12	6	12		1	3	4
PSOCOPTERA:															
Liposcellidae	4		3		4	5			1				3	4	23
TOTAL	51	264	25	20	28	2525	336	541	193	22	9570	248	278	592	646

150

Table 6. Average percent mass of wheat straw remaining in the litter bags placed on plots mulched with organic amendments. * indicates significant difference at P < .05. (Data from Whitford et al. 1988).

	Straw	Bark	Sludge	Control
November 1	100	100	100	100
March 5	82.7	85.6	87.0	86.0
July 8	72.5	58.2*	65.8	4.8
September 11	58.3	47.5*	55.5	56.7
December 12	63.2	47.8*	57.0	55.6

denitrification, and soil nitrogen remained constant from September until the end of the study. There were no transitory or longer term effects of organic mulches on the biomass of soil microflora or protozoans (Table 7). There were significant increases in numbers of soil nematodes in mulched soils during the first year but these effects were not present during the second year of the study. The only effect of the amendments on micro-arthropods was a reduction in numbers of prostigmatid mites in sludge amended soils when compared to the other mulches and unmulched soil. As with the nematodes even this difference disappeared in year two (Figure 5). The bark mulched plots had significantly higher production of blue grama grass (Bouteloua gracilis) biomass during the first year but there were no differences in total net aboveground biomass production when forbs were included (Table 8).

The results of this two year study of the effects of adding organic mulches to natural vegetated rangeland demonstrated that organic amendments have no long-lasting effect on soil processes or on soil biota. This is in sharp contrast to the results from studies of mulches on stripmined spoils. However, such studies are not strictly comparable. In the study at the mine the organic

Table 7. The effects of organic mulches on soil microflora and microfauna data are averages for the growing season. There were no significant differences during the growing season. (Data from Whitford et al. 1988).

	Straw	Bark	Control	Sludge
Protozoans No.· g^{-1} dry soil	47,334 ± 15,183	46,354 ± 16,267	43,125 ± 16,064	47,723 ± 23,189
Bacteria mg C`g^{-1} dry soil	39.1 ± 9.0	41.8 ± 15.2	46.0 ± 16.3	48.0 ± 31.6
Fungi mg C`g^{-1} dry soil	201.2 ± 153.3	154.9 ± 100.3	214.6 ± 149.6	234.8 ± 167.0
Yeast mg C`g^{-1} dry soil	107.7 ± 76.5	108.2 ± 36.8	111.5 ± 38.0	103.3 ± 48.8

amendments were disced into the regraded spoil as well as applied to the surface as a mulch. In the rangeland study the organics were applied only as surface mulches on the soil. In the strip mine study, there was no vegetation present initially, whereas in the rangeland, the vegetation consisted of elements of the climax community. Spoil restoration involves successional processes from the first stages of succession i.e. immigration, establishment and site modification whereas amendments added to degraded rangelands are aimed primarily at site modification. In mine restoration it is evident that adding recalcitrant organics, such as wood and bark, to the spoil material increased the rate of establishment of microflora and microfauna and enhanced the establishment of soil processes such as decomposition. Such procedures are therefore useful as methods that decrease the time required for re-establishment of a relatively stable vegetation. However, costs of adding organic matter to rangeland soils in order to increase nitrogen availability and

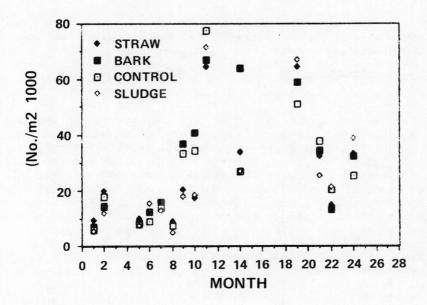

Fig. 5. Variation in soil microarthropod populations on a semiarid blue grama (<u>Boutiloua</u> <u>gracilis</u>)
grassland mulched with a variety of organic mulches (data
from Whitford et al. 1988).

Table 8. The effects of organic mulches on primary
production (peak standing crop biomass in g m^{-2}) of blue
grama (<u>Bouteloua</u> <u>gracilis</u>). (Data from Whitford et al.
1988). *Significantly different at p < .01.

	1981	1982
Straw	60.0	14.4
Bark	109.0*	15.7
Sludge	46.7	12.3
Control	68.5	14.8

enhance recovery by grasses are too expensive and too transitory to be feasible.

RANGELAND NITROGEN AVAILABILITY

The data on nitrogen in rangeland ecosystems suggests that loss or reduction in grass cover and increase in cover of woody perennials results not only in loss of forage for livestock but also results in reduction in soil nitrogen and nitrogen availability. Whitford (1986) has presented evidence that productivity in Chihuahuan desert ecosystems is nitrogen limited. Non-symbiotic nitrogen fixers appear to be dependent upon grass roots for their energy source. Grass root turnover and exudation apparently provide sufficient energy for maintenance of these microbial populations while root systems of woody shrubs do not. This may be a function of the diffuse nature of woody shrub roots in comparison to the high density of fine fibrous roots of perennial grasses. This hypothesis is consistent with the data on N fixation, and data on application of organic mulches to rangeland soils is also consistent with the hypothesis that the nitrogen cycling microflora are limited by sources of organic matter.

We have studied soil processes and soil biota in a number of sites on a desert watershed in Southern New Mexico. Portions of the watershed have been overgrazed, resulting in increasing cover by woody perennials and marked reduction in cover of perennial grasses. Other portions of the watershed have been lightly grazed or ungrazed for nearly 20 years and have good cover of perennial grasses Bouteloua eriopoda, black grama, and Eragrostis lehmanniana, Lehman's love grass. Recently we have been studying N fixation by non-symbiotic rhizosphere microorganisms. We have isolated strains of Azotobacter, Azospirillum and Clostridium from the rhizospheres of grasses. Surveys of roots of two abundant shrubs (Larrea tridentata (creosotebush) and Xanthocephalum spp. (snakeweed) failed to document populations of N fixing bacteria (Azotobacter, Azospirellum spp.) in the rhizosphere of the shrubs. We therefore conclude that nitrogen fixing bacteria were virtually absent from the roots of two common shrubs. The lack of N fixers in the rhizospheres of shrubs suggests that associative N fixation contributes virtually nothing to the N economy of shrubs. We have also measured acetylene reduction by rhizosphere organisms associated with grass roots. There is significant associative N fixation as measured by acetylene reduction in the rhizospheres of the perennial grasses (Table 9).

Studies currently being conducted in the greenhouse have shown that N fixation by the rhizosphere Azospirillum contributes significantly to the productivity of the perennial grass, Sporobolus flexulosus (El Shahaby unpublished data).

In an earlier section of this chapter, I described the rangeland degradation process as one in which perennial grasses were replaced by woody shrubs concomitant with soil losses. The changes in root densities and physiological characteristics of the dominant species undoubtedly interact with the soil affecting the soil nutrient cycling processes. A shift from grasses to shrubs affects N fixation by rhizosphere

Table 9. Nitrogen fixation by free living N-fixing bacteria in the rhizospheres of several desert grasses, root free soil and an herbaceous annual estimated by acetylene reduction. Data are n mols ethylene $\cdot$ g $^{-1}$ dry roots or soil $\cdot$ hr^{-1} for the 24 hour or 48 hour incubation. (Data courtesy of Ahmed El Shahaby)

Species	24 hrs.	48 hrs.
Erioneuron pulchellum (fluff grass)	455.2	528.1
Sporobolus flexulosus (dropseed)	65.1	50.2
Bouteloua eriopoda (black grama)	31.0	45.3
Erogrostis Lehmanni (Lehman's love grass)	102.3	59.1
Baileya multiradiata (desert marigold)	225.4	ND
Root-free Soil	15.0	13.0

bacteria, reducing nitrogen inputs and affecting soil nitrogen status.

In areas dominated by shrubs total soil nitrogen is low and nitrogen mineralization is low (Fig. 6; Table 10). Loss of grass cover also undoubtedly affects sheet flow during intense storms, redistributing litter and feces, hence affecting soil organic matter patterns. Shrub dominated sloping terrain has low soil organic matter when compared to grasslands regardless of slope, and on gravelly or sandy soils. When these factors are combined, it is evident that reduction in grass cover by grazing initiated trends toward low fertility soil by reduction in N fixation and, loss of organic matter that reduced quantities of nitrogen cycled from the mineralization of decomposing plant material. The subsequent loss of soil fertility by disruption of N cycling and changes in soil properties have probably affected attempts to re-establish grasslands on such areas.

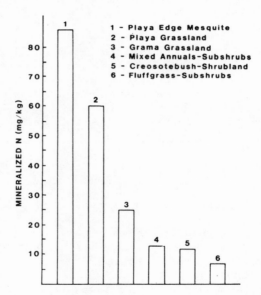

Fig. 6. Variation in nitrogen mineralization potential of soils in a variety of plant communities on a desert watershed (Data from Jornada LTER project courtesy F. Fisher).

Table 10. Comparison of total soil nitrogen in a series of vegetation zones ranging from sandy soils of a black grama, _Bouteloua eriopod_ grassland to clay-silt of an ephemeral lake bed (playa). (Unpublished data from the Jornada LTER project, courtesy of Frederick Fisher.)

	Total Soil N mg kg^{-1} soil
Playa center (clay-silt; perennial grass)	1385 ± 186
Playa edge (clay-silt; perennial grass)	2401 ± 260
Mid-basin slope (sandy loam; sub-shrub annuals) *overgrazed former grassland	374 ± 43
Bajada (sandy soil, _Larrea tridentata_ shrubland)	363 ± 79
Grassland (sandy soil, _Bouteloua eriopoda_ grassland)	482 ± 25

We have also examined patterns of N mineralization on a desert watershed. Highest rates of N mineralization are in the playa lake soils and associated mesquite fringe which are areas of organic matter accumulation. When the slope areas are compared, the ungrazed grassland soils have higher rates of N mineralization than the soils of the shrubland or overgrazed basin slope (Fig. 6). These data are consistent with the idea that overgrazing has had a deleterious effect on nitrogen cycling in arid ecosystems.

CONCLUSIONS

What generalizations can be drawn from the available data? First it is clear that critical processes such as decomposition and mineralization require an intact soil biota. The absence of key groups of soil animals results in low rates of decomposition and mineralization and will probably affect the stability of the ecosystem. Current restoration procedures that utilize stored topsoils and mulches over surface mine spoils followed by seeding and often irrigation and fertilization are not inducing the development of a complete soil biota. Indeed in the one case that we studied in Northwestern New Mexico the restored soil system appeared to be gradually deteriorating (Tables 4 and 5, Figs. 3 and 4)! Mulching or incorporating organic matter can induce development of a relatively complete soil biota even on raw spoils amended with such material and also results in higher rates of decomposition and mineralization. However, the organic material must be recalcitrant, that is it must decompose slowly. An example of such material is wood chips and bark that add a low but continuous source of organic matter and appear to stimulate both establishment of soil biota and the processes they mediate.

In order for a complete and complex soil biota to develop there must be not only a non-toxic physical environment but a supply of energy and nutrients. The limiting nutrient is frequently nitrogen, and nitrogen fixing and transforming microorganisms require a source of energy. The addition of recalcitrant organic matter can provide a long term source of energy to the microbes perhaps for sufficient time for development of root systems that provide energy by root decomposition and exudation.

ACKNOWLEDGMENTS

The writing of this chapter was supported by Grant No. BSR 821539 from the National Science Foundation. Discussion with Earl Aldon, Diana Freckman, Ned Elkins, Fred Fisher and Larry Parker contributed to the ideas expressed in this chapter. Fred Fisher and Ahmed El Shahaby kindly made available unpublished data from their studies.

LITERATURE CITED

Buffington, L.C. and C.H. Herbel. 1965. Vegetation changes on a semi-desert grassland range. Ecological Monographs 35: 139-164.

Carrel, J. E., K. Wieder, V. Leftwich, S. Weems, C.L. Kucera, L. Bouchard, and M. Game. 1979. Strip mine reclamation: Production and decomposition of plant litter. Pages 670-676 in M. K. Wali, editor. Ecology and Coal Resource Development. Pergamon Press, New York.

Cepeda, J. 1986. Spatial and temporal patterns of decomposition and microarthropod assemblages in decomposing surface leaf litter on a Chihuahuan Desert watershed. Ph.D. Thesis, New Mexico State University, Las Cruces, New Mexico.

Clements, F.E. 1916. Plant succession: an analysis of the development of vegetation. Carnegie Institution of Washington, Publication 242: 1-512.

Cross, E.A. and J.M. Wilman. 1982. A preliminary study of the refoundation of alkaline shale coal surface mine spoil by soil arthropods. Pages 353-358 in 1982 Symposium on Surface Mining Hydrology, Sedimentology, and Reclamation. University of Kentucky, Lexington, Kentucky.

Cundell, A.M. 1977. The role of microorganisms in the revegetation of strip-mined lands in the western United States. Journal of Range Management 30:299-305.

Elkins, N.Z., Y. Steinberger and W.G. Whitford. 1982. The role of microarthropods and nematodes in decomposition in a semi-arid ecosystem. Oecologia 55: 303-310.

Elkins, N.Z., L.W. Parker, E.F. Aldon and W.G. Whitford. 1984. Responses of soil biota to organic amendments in stripmine spoils in northwestern New Mexico. Journal of Environmental Quality 13:215-219.

Fresques, P.R. and W.C. Lindemann. 1982. Soil and rhizosphere microorganisms in amended coal mine spoils. Soil Science Society of America Journal 46: 751-755.

Gross, F. A. and W. A. Dick-Peddie. 1979. A map of primeval vegetation in New Mexico. Southwestern Naturalist 24: 115-122.

Hersman, L.E. and D.A. Klein. 1979. Retorted oil shale effects on soil microbiological characteristics. Journal of Environmental Quality 8: 520-524.

Ingham, R.E., J.A. Trofymow, E.R. Ingham and D.C. Coleman. 1985. Interactions of bacteria, fungi and their nematode grazers: effects on nutrient cycling and plant growth. Ecological Monographs 55: 119-140.

Lawery, J.D. 1977. The relative decomposition potential of habitats variously affected by surface coal mining. Canadian Journal of Botany 55: 1544-1552.

Miller, R.V., E.E. Staffeldt and B.C. Williams. 1979. Microbial populations in undisturbed soils and coal mine spoils in semi-arid conditions. U.S.D.A. Forest Service Research Note RM-372. Rocky Mountain Forest and Range Experiment Station, Fort Collins, Colorado.

Olson, G.T., G.A. McFeters and K.L. Temple. 1981. Occurrence and activity of iron- and sulfer-oxidizing microorganisms in alkaline coal strip mine spoils. Microbiological Ecology 7: 39-50.

Parker, L.W., P.F. Santos, J. Phillips and W.G. Whitford. 1984. Carbon and nitrogen dynamics during the decomposition of litter and roots of a Chihuahuan desert annual, Lepidium lasiocarpum. Ecological Monographs 54: 339-360.

Parker, L.W., N.Z. Elkins, E.F. Aldon and W.G. Whitford. 1987. Decomposition and soil biota after reclamation of coal mine spoils in an arid region. Biology and Fertility of Soils 4:109-114.

Parkinson, D. 1979. Microbes, mycorrhizae and mine spoil. Pages 634-642 in M.K. Wali, editor. Ecology and Coal Resource Development. Pergamon Press, New York.

Rogers, G. F. 1981. Then and now: A photographic history of vegetation change in the central Great Basin Desert. University of Utah Press, Salt Lake City, Utah.

Santos, P.F., J. Phillips and W.G. Whitford. 1981a. The role of mites and nematodes in early stages of buried litter decomposition in a desert. Ecology 62: 664-669.

Santos, P.F. and W.G. Whitford. 1981b. Litter decomposition in the desert. Bioscience: 145-146.

Tansley, A. G. 1935. The use and abuse of vegetational concepts and terms. Ecology 16: 284-307.

Visser, S., J. Zak and D. Parkinson. 1979. Effects of surface mining on soil microbial communities and processes. Pages 643-651 in M.K. Wali, editor. Ecology and Coal Resource Development. Pergamon Press, New York.

160

Weaver, J.E. and F.E. Clements. 1938. Plant Ecology. McGraw Hill, New York.

Whitford, W.G. 1986. Pattern in desert ecosystems: water availability and nutrient interactions. Pages 109-117 in Z. Dubinsky and Y. Steinberger, editors. Environmental Quality and Ecosystem Stability, Vol. III, Bar Ilan University Press, Ramat Gan, Israel.

York, J.C. and W.A. Dick-Peddie. 1969. Vegetation changes in southern New Mexico during the past 100 years. Pages 157-166 in W. O. McGinnies and B. J. Goldman, editors, Arid Lands in Perspective, University of Arizona Press, Tucson, Arizona.

Edward J. DePuit, Edward F. Redente

8. Manipulation of Ecosystem Dynamics on Reconstructed Semiarid Lands

ABSTRACT

Reconstruction of disturbed shrub and grassland ecosystems in semiarid regions is a dynamic process involving ecological succession. Reconstruction is influenced by factors related to physical (climate, soil, physiography and disturbance) and biological (plants, animals and microorganisms) conditions of the site. Certain of these factors may be anthropogenically manipulated to influence the rate and direction of the reconstruction process.

Site factors may be altered for various reasons, such as improving the substrate for biological organisms. Topsoiling and fertilization are two approaches to this type of site modification. The introduction of biotic propagules comprises a broad approach to manipulation of biological conditions. Studies on disturbed shrub and grasslands have shown that different site and biotic manipulations can be used to induce corresponding differences in plant community productivity, composition and diversity over the short-term, as well as microbiological function. Longer-term ecosystem dynamics, however, are less well understood because of the limited duration of most research. Nonetheless, various site management practices may prove effective for longer-term manipulation of site and biotic factors. Research suggests grazing management to be one promising approach for maintained influence over plant community and soil development.

Successful manipulation of the factors that influence ecosystem reconstruction depends upon ecological propriety of practices implemented. Such propriety requires a theoretical understanding of the reconstruction process and its long-term dynamics. This understanding, however, is limited for disturbed semiarid shrub and grasslands, and must be addressed by long-term ecological research with proper emphasis on functional rather than purely empirical relationships.

INTRODUCTION

The development of ecosystems can be strongly influenced by the pattern and magnitude of ecological disturbances imposed upon such systems (Picket and White 1985). Modern man has added variety, frequency and intensity to ecological disturbance of shrub and grasslands in the semiarid West. Many such disturbances (e.g., mining) may be termed "drastic" in the sense of completely destroying pre-existing ecosystems (Box 1978). The recovery of drastically disturbed lands is of interest both ecologically and environmentally. Ecosystem reconstruction is essential to mitigate adverse environmental impacts of drastic disturbances.

Ecosystem recovery following drastic disturbance is complex, and must be conceptualized and approached from a total ecosystem perspective (Brisbin 1982, Wali 1975, Whitford and Elkins 1986). It is a dynamic rather than static phenomenon, involving the interrelated processes of plant succession and soil genesis (Moore et al. 1977, Schafer and Nielsen 1978).

Natural (i.e., non-augmented by man) ecosystem recovery has often been slow and unpredictable in the semiarid West (Mackey and DePuit 1985). Consequently, most disturbed lands are treated with a variety of reclamation practices to "induce" ecosystem recovery. The basic functions of applied practices are to both accelerate and direct ecosystem reconstruction.

Dynamics of recovering ecosystems are influenced by a wide array of factors and processes interacting over time. In ecosystem reconstruction, practices are applied to manipulate successional factors and processes to influence the rate and direction of recovery. Such practices must be properly based upon ecological principles to be effective. Therefore, the reconstruction of drastically disturbed ecosystems is an integration of basic and applied ecology.

This paper will first briefly review the nature of ecosystem recovery on drastically disturbed shrub and grasslands in the semiarid West, with particular emphasis on lands impacted by mining disturbances. The array of factors influencing the recovery process will be discussed, as will principles and practices for anthropogenic manipulation of such factors. Examples will be drawn from selected studies of ecosystem reconstruction, primarily on mined lands, to illustrate ecological effects of certain manipulations.

NATURE OF ECOSYSTEM RECONSTRUCTION ON DISTURBED SHRUB AND GRASSLANDS

Ecological succession is the dynamic process in which ecosystems evolve toward a state of equilibrium between living organisms and their physical environment. The reconstruction process on drastically disturbed lands may have elements of both primary and secondary succession depending on substrate characteristics. Succession on unweathered mine spoil or waste material that did not previously support vegetation would be classififed as primary, and consequently may be relatively slow. Conversely, succession on weathered, previously vegetated topsoil replaced over unweathered material is more similar to secondary succession, and consequently is more rapid. The thickness and physical, chemical and biological characteristics of topsoil will determine whether succession is primary, secondary or intermediate in nature.

Succession that is driven by the organisms inhabiting the site is termed autogenic succession, while allogenic succession is influenced by environmental changes beyond the control of indigenous organisms (Barbour et al. 1980). Succession on disturbed lands in the West may be governed both autogenically and allogenically, as is succession in other disturbed environments (White 1979). Anthropogenic influences, such as site modification, biotic propagule introduction and site management, may be conceptualized as allogenic in nature initially, but nonetheless may affect autogenic processes.

The successional process provides an important mechanism by which disturbed lands progress toward a state of dynamic equilibrium (Whitford and Elkins 1986). During this process, plant species composition changes, ecosystem diversity may increase for a time, and nutrient cycling becomes more closed. Ultimately, a new "climax" community will be established as a result of succession, with attributes reflecting abiotic and biotic factors interacting on the site.

Fig. 1 illustrates the types of changes associated with early years of plant succession on seeded mined lands in semiarid southeastern Montana (DePuit et al. 1978). Highly productive annual species tend to dominate initially, stabilizing the soil and adding organic matter to the system. Annuals decline to insignificant levels in subsequent years, with a corresponding increase in composition of perennials. Composition among perennials shifts from early dominance by seeded grasses to later co-dominance by seeded grasses and slower-developing forbs and shrubs. Floristic richness increases concomitant with this change in dominance, primarily due to progressive establishment of non-seeded species. Concurrent pedogenic studies (Schafer et al. 1979) have shown soil development also to be dynamic during early years of succession. However, while interrelated with plant succession, certain facets of soil genesis were shown to proceed far more slowly in the above studies.

Ecosystem development on drastically disturbed lands is unique because of the nature and severity of the disturbance and the intense efforts of man to influence the successional process. Drastic disturbances, such as mining activity, may yield substrates dramatically different from those prior to disturbance. Such differences may affect the rate of succession, and also may chronically alter its direction (Schafer 1984). Succession may also be influenced by man's efforts to modify abiotic and biotic conditions of the site. However, ecological research on manipulation of disturbed ecosystems is but a recent development in the semiarid West (DePuit 1985). In consequence, while considerable progress has been made, such progress has related primarily to short-term, initial aspects of the recovery process. The longer term ramifications of initial

165

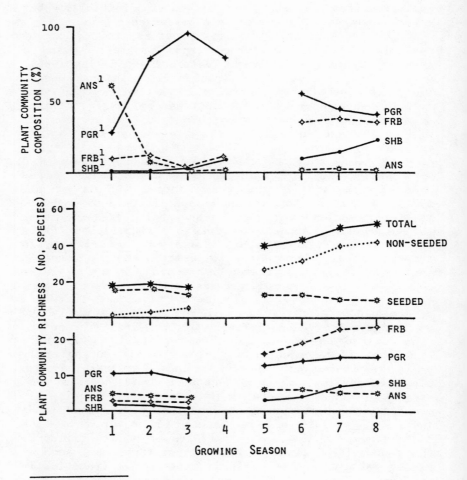

Fig. 1. Trends in plant community composition and richness during early years of succession on seeded coal mined lands in southeastern Montana. Derived from published and unpublished data of DePuit et al. (1978).

manipulations of ecosystem reconstruction must therefore remain conjectural until revealed by future research.

FACTORS INFLUENCING ECOSYSTEM RECONSTRUCTION

Site factors influencing ecosystem reconstruction are defined here to include effects of abiotic site characteristics that are expressed both initially and over time, and exogenous perturbations (both biotic and abiotic) throughout the reconstruction period. Biotic factors are related to effects of organisms themselves, which may be both autogenically expressed and mediated by site factors. It is necessary to briefly review the influence these varied factors can have on ecosystem reconstruction before progressing to an analysis of their manipulation.

Site Factors--Site factors such as climate, edaphic conditions, and size and intensity of a disturbance strongly influence the reconstruction process. In aggregate, such factors comprise the physical base upon which succession acts to eventually produce a stable ecosystem. The nature of these factors influences the type of ecosystem ultimately achievable (i.e., successional direction), and may affect the rate of succession as well. Reclamation practices that are selected and implemented are based, in part, upon site conditions, and these conditions in many cases will determine the intensity of the reconstruction process and its success.

Understanding how climate influences the interaction of abiotic and biotic processes is essential to the successful reconstruction of disturbed ecosystems. Climate and weather have both long- and short-term implications and influences that cannot be divorced from one another. Over the short-term, weather factors (precipitation, temperature, insolation, wind, and their variability and interaction) will exert strong influence over the initiation and subsequent nature of biotic processes. Over the long-term, climate may also influence other site factors (e.g. soils and topography), which in turn will affect biotic processes. The cumulative effects of such direct and indirect climatic influences may be expressed in both the rate and

167

direction of ecosystem recovery. Shrub and grasslands in the semiarid western United States are characterized by several prevalent climatic constraints to ecosystem recovery--most notably limited and unpredictable water availability and, secondarily, extreme temperature fluctuation. These and other site-specific climatic constraints must be recognized and addressed by reclamation practices.

The reconstruction potential of a site is related not only to climate, but also to the specific soil and topographic conditions present. Soil genesis and plant succession are interdependent processes on disturbed lands (Schafer and Nielsen 1978). Initial edaphic conditions (physical, chemical and biological) will determine whether succession is primary or secondary in nature, thereby influencing the rate of succession. Physical and chemical properties of soils will also partially determine the direction of soil genesis and plant succession (Schafer 1984), although certain properties may prove modifiable over time. Common initial edaphic constraints to ecosystem recovery in the semiarid West include elemental deficiencies or excesses, inimical hydraulic or textural characteristics, and limited biological function. Topographic characteristics of a site also affect the process of ecosystem reconstruction (Stiller et al. 1980, Toy 1984). Topography interacts with macroclimate to produce the microclimate that influences both soil genesis and plant succession at any specific site (Wollenhaupt and Richardson 1982). The combined influence of edaphic and topographic conditions on ecosystem reconstruction is therefore great; such conditions must be considered in conjunction with climate when practices are designed to manipulate the reconstruction process.

The degree and extent to which pre-existing soils and topography are altered (i.e., disturbance intensity and size) varies considerably among disturbances. Under certain drastic disturbances, conditions may be changed so markedly as not only to retard the rate of recovery, but also to direct recovery toward a different type of ecosystem than that originally present (Denslow 1985). For instance, Biondini et al. (1985a) noted that varied intensities of soil disturbance in Colorado produced dramatically different types of plant communities after six years of succession. Nielsen and Peterson (1972) found the direction of soil genesis on severely altered Utah minesoils (e.g., tailings) to be different from that on natural soils.

Size and intensity of disturbance therefore play an important role in the dynamics of ecosystem reconstruction (Denslow 1985). For example, the larger the size of the disturbance, the less influence the surrounding ecosystem may have in providing a source of plant propagules and soil microorganisms. This alteration in propagule supply could substantially retard the successional process. In similar fashion, as the intensity of the disturbance increases, the level of destruction to the biological components of the ecosystem increases and their initial role in succession declines. Drastic disturbances can result in nearly sterile conditions with virtually no indigenous organisms present for purposes of recovery.

Biotic Factors--Ecosystem reconstruction is strongly influenced by a number of plant, animal and microorganism related factors. All biotic factors can be directly or indirectly mediated by the site factors discussed above.

Migration of biotic propagules to disturbed sites is an initial precursor to succeeding processes of ecosystem reconstruction (Denslow 1985). At the outset of ecosystem recovery, establishment of organisms following propagule migration is governed by site factors (e.g., climatic, edaphic and physiographic conditions) in concert with autecological attributes of organisms. With time, the influence of organisms becomes progressively greater. Hence, initial biotic establishment and composition are functions of site conditions, migration and autecological attributes of migrant organisms, while subsequent succession is also influenced by autogenic processes.

Several biological processes must be considered in any analysis of ecosystem reconstruction and its manipulation. The first relates to modifications of site factors by organisms. The colonization of denuded sites by plants and microorganisms is essential for initiation of site modification processes, such as soil stabilization, organic matter enrichment, initiation of nutrient cycling and soil structural development (Whitford and Elkins 1986). Further site modification continues as plants, microorganisms and animals interact to change their environment.

Concurrent with, and possibly influenced by, site modification occur organism-induced changes in ecosystem structure and function. For example, interrelations between plants and microorganisms may govern the occurrence, composition and functions of each within developing ecosystems (Allen and Allen 1984, Cundell 1977, Tate and Klein 1985, Williams and Allen 1984). Synecological relationships among plant species (e.g., competition, mutualism, allelopathy, etc.) have often been cited as partial determinants of plant compositional changes over time (Allen and Knight 1984, Grime 1979, Iverson and Wali 1982a). Interactions between plants and animals have also been shown to influence biotic composition and function as disturbed ecosystems develop (DePuit and Coenenberg 1980, Majer 1984, Majer et al. 1984, Hintgen and Clark 1984).

ANTHROPOGENIC MANIPULATION OF SITE AND BIOTIC FACTORS

Nearly all manipulations of ecosystem reconstruction by man may be classed within one of the following categories: 1) initial modification of site factors, 2) initial supply of biotic propagules, and 3) ongoing site management. The following sections will review principles, objectives and practices within each class of manipulation, and provide research-derived examples of ecological effects of selected practices.

Site Modification--Numerous approaches are possible to modify climatic, edaphic and topographic conditions of disturbed sites, and thereby influence the rate and direction of succession. Most site modifications are, in principle, designed to accomplish one or both of the following: 1) creation of topoedaphic conditions conducive to the type of ecosystem ultimately desired; and 2) provision of initial climatic and topoedaphic conditions favorable to establishment and growth of biological organisms, after their introduction. With these goals in mind, specific site preparation practices can be divided into the following categories:

1) Grading to influence macrotopography,
2) Mechanical treatment, to provide microtopography and soil conditions conducive to stabilization, microclimatic modification and organism establishment,
3) Temporary direct climatic augmentation to relieve climatic constraints, and
4) Improvement of substrate for initial and ultimate support of the biological community.

It is beyond the scope of this paper to completely review practices within each of the above categories and their ecological effects. However, to illustrate the importance of site modification, we will briefly discuss the fourth concept of substrate improvement, and present results of selected recent research.

Edaphic conditions following drastic land disturbance often pose major challenges to establishment of organisms. Common problems in the western United States include excessive salt concentrations, acidity, inimical physical characteristics and low inherent fertility. Amelioration of such problems may be approached by: 1) amendments to correct the problem, or 2) isolation of the problem by application of better-quality soil material.

Various types of amendments have been studied for alleviation of edaphic problems. For example, soils may be amended with chemicals (e.g., gypsum, calcium chloride, etc.), water for leaching, or organic materials to correct salt-related problems (Malcolm 1982, Sandoval and Gould 1978), while application of lime may ameliorate acidic conditions (Mays and Bengtson 1978). Certain physical soil problems, such as high clay or sand content, may be overcome by organic amendments or mechanical treatments (Dollhopf et al. 1985, Kay 1978). If chemical or physical soil problems are overly severe, however, amendment techniques have sometimes yielded only ephemeral benefits (Doll et al. 1984, Farmer et al. 1976). In such cases, burial of problem material (i.e., the isolation principle) may prove the only viable long-term solution. The isolation principle is exemplified by topsoiling. However, use of topsoil does not necessarily eliminate the need for certain additional soil amendments. For example, the frequently poor nutrient status of topsoil in the West after salvage, storage and reapplication may sometimes necessitate supplemental fertilization. The following paragraphs will discuss

171

results of recent research illustrating ecological effects of topsoiling and fertilization as examples of manipulative practices.

Topsoiling--The influence of topsoiling on the reconstruction of drastically disturbed lands cannot be over-emphasized. This one activity may do more for restoring ecosystem function on disturbed lands than any other reclamation procedure. The application of topsoil over unweathered geologic material induces secondary rather than primary succession, and therefore accelerates the recovery process. Numerous benefits contribute to such acceleration.

Many drastic disturbances leave unweathered geologic material at the land surface. Such geologic material is usually less suitable than topsoil (A and B horizon material) for supporting vegetation (Hargis and Redente 1984). It is low in organic matter and usually is less favorable than topsoil with respect to structure, aeration and infiltration capacity. Geologic material often lacks important plant nutrients, or nutrients may be in forms unavailable to plants and microbes. Woodmansee et al. (1980) likened revegetation of unweathered overburden to primary succession, and estimated that it would take up to 2,160 years for the nitrogen (N) pool to increase sufficiently to support a stable plant-soil system.

Topsoil is also an important source of microorganisms that play essential roles in nutrient cycling, energy flow and soil structural development (Hargis and Redente 1984). Certain topsoil-introduced microbes may also form beneficial, sometimes obligatory symbioses with higher plants (Danielson 1985). In addition to providing micro-organisms, nutrients and a more favorable structural environment for plant growth, topsoil provides viable plant propagules for added diversity in the plant community (Howard and Samuel 1979). However, topsoil may also be a source of propagules of early successional species (lverson and Wali 1982b) that may actually slow the successional process.

Numerous studies have shown the benefits of topsoiling for plant community establishment on western disturbed lands (Barth 1984, McGinnies and Nicholas 1980, Redente et al. 1982, Schuman et al. 1985). However, most studies have reported only three to four years of data, therefore only providing information on early plant establishment and giving very little insight into long-term plant community dynamics. Hargis and Redente (1984) conducted an extensive review of topsoiling literature pertinent to western surface mine reclamation, and concluded that the present start-of-the-art in topsoil management is at the plant cover and biomass response level. Very little information exists on either short- or long-term ecosystem level responses.

A study by Biondini et al. (1985a, 1985b) addressed the effects of topsoiling on patterns of secondary succession and soil biological activity in Colorado. This study will be used as a test case for inferences on the effect of topsoiling on ecosystem development.

Treatments included the application of 30 cm of topsoil (A and B horizon material) over retorted oil shale and 60 cm of topsoil over a 30 cm rock capillary barrier over retorted shale. Both treatments were compared to a soil control with no retorted shale present in the profile. Mixtures of native or introduced plant species were seeded over all topsoil treatments. The study was conducted in northwest Colorado at a site with an elevation of 2,020 m and an average annual precipitation of 30 cm.

Vegetation measurements, consisting of plant canopy cover and aboveground biomass by species, were made annually for a five-year period. Measurements of soil organic matter, dehydrogenase and phosphatase enzymatic acitivty, and non-symbiotic N_2 fixation were used as indices of soil biological activity (Klein et al. 1982). Dehydrogenase enzymes can function in soils only in intact organisms, and are a reliable index of the capacity of the microflora to process carbon (Skujins 1978). The majority of phosphatase enzymes in the soil are also linked to microorganisms (Speir and Ross 1978). Phosphatase activity and non-symbiotic N_2 fixation are both related to soil heterotrophic microorganisms (Sorensen 1982, Speir and Ross 1978). These attributes can thus serve as indices of the activity levels of free soil microorganisms and, as such, potential general indicators of the availability of free carbon and nutrients in the soil. Organic matter was used as an indicator of potential soil carbon availibility.

The introduced species mixture consisted of a combination of grasses, forbs and shrubs potentially adaptable to the climatic and edaphic conditions of the study site. Ultimately dominant grass species included crested wheatgrass (<u>Agropyron desertorum</u>), intermediate wheatgrass (<u>A</u>. <u>intermedium</u>), and pubescent wheatgrass (<u>A</u>. <u>trichophorum</u>). One species, tall wheatgrass (<u>A</u>. <u>elongatum</u>) which was present during the first two years of plant community development, was completely excluded from the community after 3 years. Introduced shrub species, Siberian peashrub (<u>Caragana</u> <u>arborescens</u>) and Russian olive (<u>Elaeagnus</u> <u>angustifolia</u>), never established on the site.

During five years of plant community development, the composition of total perennial grasses was consistently lower in 30 cm of topsoil than in 60 cm of topsoil (Fig. 2). Conversely, forb composition was consistently higher in 30 cm topsoil. The leguminous forb alfalfa (<u>Medicago</u> <u>sativa</u>) was the dominant species on the 30 cm soil treatment after five years; its composition increased from 9% in year 2 to 51% in year 5. The composition of alfalfa in the 60 cm topsoil treatment never exceeded 8%.

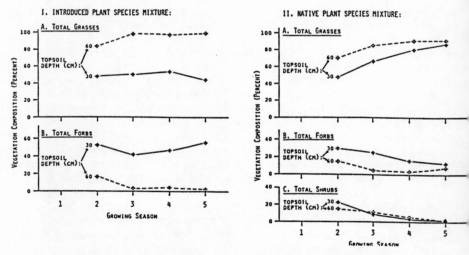

Fig. 2. Trends in plant community composition as influenced by varied topsoil thickness for spent oil shale sites seeded to mixture of: I. Introduced plant species, and II. Native plant species, Piceance Basin, Colorado. Derived from data of Biondini et al. (1985b).

174

The rate of successional change was calculated using changes in species composition over time. Results indicated that changes were more rapid on the shallowest than on thickest topsoil treatment. Deeper soils resulted in a rapid dominance by grasses, and as such slowed successional change.

Vegetation responses on sites seeded to the native mixture (grasses, forbs and shrubs) showed similarities to and differences from introduced mixture responses (Fig. 2). Grass composition was initially higher with 60 than with 30 cm of topsoil, but differences between topsoil depths diminished over time. Some grasses, bluebunch wheatgrass (Agropyron inerme) and big bluegrass (Poa ampla), increased in composition with time on both topsoil depths. In contrast, streambank wheatgrass (A. riparium) decreased in composition over time on the 60 cm but not on the 30 cm topsoil depth, and western wheatgrass (A. smithii) showed no changes over time in percent composition. Bluebunch wheatgrass exhibited highest composition on 60 cm topsoil, while big bluegrass was most abundant on 30 cm topsoil. Perennial forb composition declined over time, but the 30 cm topsoil depth tended to have the highest forb composition. Shrubs, primarily winterfat (Ceratoides lanata) and fourwing saltbush (Atriplex canescens), showed no clear response to topsoil depth treatments. No differences in calculated rate of successional change were detected between topsoil depths.

Relationships among topsoil depth, species composition and soil biological activity were determined for the site seeded to introduced species. Lower dehydrogenase activity was found in initial stages of succession with shallowest topsoil depth (Fig. 3). However, dehydrogenase activity generally increased with time for both topsoil thicknesses. A temporal increase in microbial activity, as suggested by the dehydrogenase data, may be related to an increase in rhizosphere activity as perennial species became more abundant and mature. However, topsoil depth did not appear to be a controlling factor of this process over time.

Phosphatase enzymatic activity was unrelated to vegetation changes but was affected by topsoil thickness (Fig. 3). Phosphatase activity was usually lowest in the 30 cm topsoil treatment and declined in both topsoil treatments over time. The latter relationship may

175

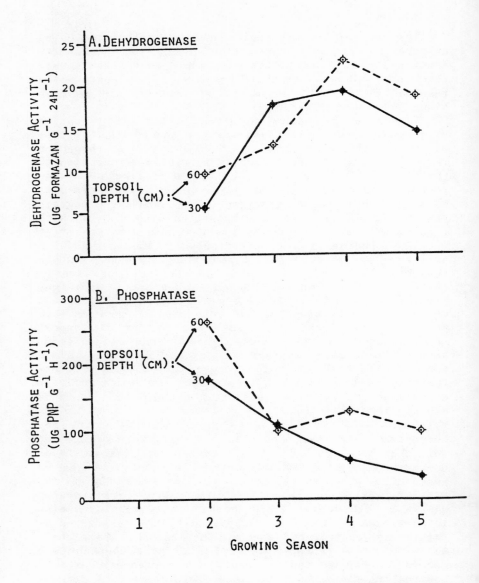

Fig. 3. Trends in soil dehydrogenase and phosphatase activity as influenced by topsoil depth on spent oil shale sites seeded to introduced plant species, Piceance Basin, Colorado. Derived from data of Biondini et al. (1985b).

176

reflect a shift in microflora from predominantly heterotrophic microbes that depend on free nutrients in the soil early in succession to plant-dependent microbes which function in the rhizosphere later in succession. Non-symbiotic N_2 fixation responded in a fashion similar to phosphatase activity, and the two soil measurements were linearly related. Organic matter levels were not related to vegetation parameters or to any other soil microbiological parameters measured.

Soil microbial responses on sites seeded to native species were quite similar to those on sites seeded to introduced species. Dehydrogenase activity increased with time and perennial species dominance, while phosphatase and non-symbiotic N_2 fixation were inversely related to topsoil depth and time since seeding.

This study provided evidence that different plant species will respond in different ways to topsoil thickness; and because of competitive interactions among species, species response will differ over time. Soil microbial activity can be variously linked to species composition, time and topsoil thickness. Such results are corroborated by other research on semiarid disturbed lands demonstrating varied responses of vegetation productivity, species composition and diversity to differences in depth and physiochemical attributes of topsoil (Pinchak et al. 1985, Redente et al. 1982, Stark and Redente 1985). The use of topsoil as a site modification practice on disturbed lands, therefore has value in influencing plant community composition and belowground processes over the short-term.

Fertilization--Ecological disturbances have frequently been noted to temporarily increase nutrient availability (Redente and Cook 1986), which subsequently declines as nutrient cycling becomes more closed with successional advancement (Vitousek 1985). Despite this, initial deficiencies in available nutrients still sometimes occur. Certain drastic disturbances may leave geologic material at or near the surface that is inherently less fertile than pre-disturbance soil. Even if topsoil is replaced, mixing during salvage and reapplication may dilute concentrations of nutrients. Losses of mobile nutrients "freed" by topsoil disturbance may be increased by the loss of soil structure and nutrient-cycling biota, or by topsoil storage prior to reapplication. Consequently, correcting nutrient deficiencies is sometimes important for improved plant establishment. The use of inorganic fertilizer is one of several approaches possible to accomplish this.

Considerable research on the use of fertilization has been conducted on disturbed lands in the West (Bauer et al. 1978). Plant and community responses to fertilization have proved quite variable (Berg 1980), leading to controversy over the value of the practice. Much of this controversy relates to lack of understanding of fertilization effects on ecosystem function over both the short and long-term, which are subjects little-emphasized in most research. Functional and temporal effects of fertilization are extremely important in the context of ecosystem reconstruction (Righetti 1982), and will be emphasized in our discussion of fertilization as a site modification practice.

Research on coal-mined lands in southeastern Montana provided a number of insights on the ecological effects of fertilization. Holechek et al. (1982) noted little effect of fertilization on first year establishment of perennials, but found a significant stimulation of perennial plant growth five years later. This would suggest that effects of initial nutrient additions may sometimes require time for full ecological expression. Work by Sindelar (1984) and DePuit et al. (1978) indicated that fertilization enhanced the growth and competitive ability of aggressive perennial species, but that over-fertilization was an important factor contributing to stand deterioration. With excessive fertilization, plant biomass was produced at levels exceeding the decompositional capacity of immature minesoils. This resulted in massive litter accumulations that altered microclimatic conditions, immobilized nutrients, and disrupted nutrient cycling--thus eventually reducing plant vigor. DePuit et al. (1978) and DePuit and Coenenberg (1979) also noted effects of fertilization on plant community composition and diversity. N and P fertilizer increased, to a point, total vegetation productivity primarily due to responses of a limited number of introduced perennial grass species, which competitively retarded less fertilizer-responsive species such as native grasses and legumes. Consequently, plant community diversity was usually reduced by increased or repeated fertilization.

Reclamation research in northwest Colorado (Redente et al. 1984) has shown that fertilization increases production of perennial grasses, decreases forb production because of increased competition from grasses, and has a variable effect on shrub production (Fig. 4). Effects of a one time application of N and P were still evident in increased perennial grass production five

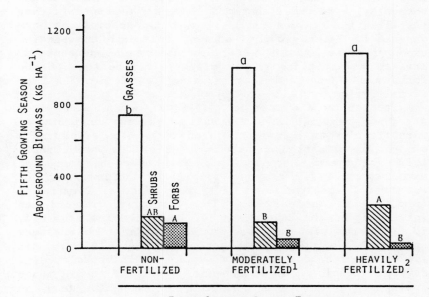

[1]N AND P AT 56 AND 28 KG HA^{-1}, RESPECTIVELY

[2]N AND P AT 112 AND 56 KG HA^{-1}, RESPECTIVELY

Fig. 4. Fifth growing season responses of perennial grass, shrub and forb biomass to variations in first year fertilization regime on topsoiled spent oil shale, Piceance Basin, Colorado. Biomass means within plant classes followed by different letters are significantly different at $P \leq 0.10$. Derived from data of Redente et al. (1984).

years after fertilizer application, again illustrating
the longer-term effects fertilization can have. In the
above study and additional studies by Stark and Redente
(1985) and Biondini and Redente (1986), it has been shown
that fertilization decreases species diversity for two
primary reasons. First, the application of N fertilizer
may reduce the N-fixing advantage held by legumes while
increasing growth rates of vigorous, N-responsive
grasses, allowing the latter to rapidly dominate the
community. Second, there is some evidence that
fertilization favors earlier growing species at the
expense of later growing species. Although the species
used in these studies were all cool season perennials,
grasses may initiate growth slightly before some of the
forbs and shrubs and thus receive greater benefit from
fertilization.

Studies by Klein et al. (1984) on the same sites
reported above have investigated the effect of
fertilization on belowground processes. The effect of N
and P fertilization can be seen on plots seven years
following treatment (Fig. 5). With added N, increased
ammonium ion and (not shown) nitrate oxidation potentials
were still observed, and decreases in hypal lengths of
fungi were evident. This suggests that with
fertilization the development of the microbial community
is being retarded, an observation also made by Fresquez
and Lindemann (1982). In the study by Klein et al.
(1984), decreased fungal development could be related to
several possible interactions. More N could have
influenced plant root exudation, or may have been an
indirect effect of shifted carbon:nitrogen ratios which
influenced the fungal-bacterial balance in decomposition.
Increased nutrient availability could also have led to
the functioning of a smaller, yet more active, fungal
population with a higher turnover rate.

Fertilization may also retard development of certain
components of the microbial community in other ways.
Range and disturbed land fertilization has frequently
been found to stimulate growth of weedy, pioneer species;
many such species are non-mycorrhizal (Allen and Allen
1984, Redente and Cook 1986). If pioneer species are
stimulated to the point of curtailing the growth of
perennial, mycorrhizal species, mycorrhizal colonization
could conceivably be retarded due to reduced host plant

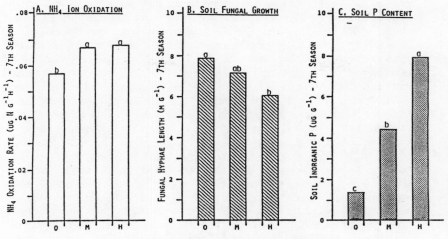

A. NH₄ ION OXIDATION

B. SOIL FUNGAL GROWTH

C. SOIL P CONTENT

FIRST GROWING SEASON FERTILIZATION TREATMENTS[1]

[1] O = NON-FERTILIZED
M = N AND P AT 56 AND 28 KG HA^{-1}, RESPECTIVELY
H = N AND P AT 112 AND 56 KG HA^{-1}, RESPECTIVELY

Fig. 5. Seventh growing season responses of NH_4 ion oxidation, soil fungal hyphae length and soil P content to variations in first year fertilization regime on topsoiled spent oil shale, Piceance Basin, Colorado. Means with different letters are significantly different at $P \leq 0.05$. Derived from data of Klein et al. (1984).

availability. There is also some evidence of reduced receptivity of plants to mycorrhizal infection under nutrient (i.e., P) enriched conditions (Ratnayake et al. 1978).

The study of Klein et al. (1984) noted an especially clear fertilizer effect for inorganic P, where a direct relationship between P added and seventh-year extractable P was evident (Fig. 5). These results again emphasize the longer term effects of initial fertilization in semiarid ecosystems.

These studies show that fertilization, as a site modification practice, ·can have specific effects on ecosystem structure and function. Newly developing plant communities on drastically disturbed lands in the semiarid West can be changed by altering nutrient availability. Primary production can be increased, at least initially, and species composition can be modified depending on the rate and frequency of fertilizer application. Certain life forms can be favored or inhibited through fertilization, which will influence species diversity. In addition, the use of fertilizer will have dramatic influence on belowground processes through direct and indirect effects on the microbial community.

   Implications of Initial Substrate Improvements--The above-reviewed research suggests that practices such as topsoiling and fertilization can be used to improve substrates, thereby both enhancing plant establishment and influencing plant-soil systems over the short term. The logical conclusion that such site modification practices therefore accelerate and direct succession, however, remains conjectural for several reasons. For example, specific topsoil depths and physiochemical characteristics favoring maximum plant establishment and growth have actually been shown to retard rates of successional change (Biondini et al. 1985a, 1985b). Further, site modification techniques that have increased plant growth (e.g., increasing tospoil thickness, and improving topsoil fertility or other physiochemical attributes) have usually decreased plant diversity (Biondini et al. 1985a, DePuit and Coenenberg 1979, Stark and Redente 1985). Biondini and Redente (1986) felt this commonly observed inverse relationship between plant productivity and diversity to be a result of increased expression of interspecific competition and consequent competitive exclusion under conditions more favorable to plant growth, in agreement with the postulates of Grime (1979) and Huston (1979). The case for successional acceleration by certain site modification techniques (e.g., fertilization) is also weakened by negative effects on specific soil microbiological functions (Fresquez and Lindemann 1982, Klein et al. 1984).
   In summary, while research has indeed demonstrated effects of initial substrate improvement practices on succession, such effects have been expressed variably-- from positive to negative--upon different components,

functions and characteristics of reclaimed ecosystems. Further, such effects have been observed only over the short-term. The long-term influence of topsoiling, fertilization and other initial site modification practices on the rate and direction of succession is consequently unknown under present knowledge.

Biotic Propagule Supply--The nature of propagule supply can influence both the rate and, at least over the short-term, direction of succession (Denslow 1985). Natural migration of propagules to disturbed sites in the semiarid West has often proven erratic or compositionally undesirable (Redente and Cook 1986). Consequently, natural migration is usually augmented by man through various propagule supply practices. In principle, such practices are applied to both hasten the establishment and influence the composition and function of initial biota, thereby affecting the subsequent processes of ecosystem reconstruction.

Biotic propagules may be introduced to disturbed sites in a number of ways. As noted previously, application of topsoil is a valuable means of supplying propagules of both plants and microorganisms. The nature and efficacy of topsoiling as a means of propagule introduction depend upon numerous factors, such as the storage interval prior to application, the method of application, and the species composition of propagules within the topsoil (DePuit 1984). In cases where the combined effects of such factors yield inadequate or undesirable propagule supply, other means of introduction are usually necessary.

As reviewed by DePuit (1986), the influence of anthropogenic plant propagule supply on succession depends upon both species introduced and methods of introduction. Results of a number of studies well illustrate short-term effects of variations in these factors on western disturbed lands.

The role of rapidly establishing, highly productive pioneer species in succession on disturbed sites has often been postulated (Allen and Knight 1984, Iverson and Wali 1982a). However, in certain instances such species have proven overly persistent on disturbed sites--to the detriment of accelerated succession (Wagner et al. 1978). Various approaches have been taken to address this problem. The introduction of pioneer species with known short persistence for equivalent ecological function is one such approach, with such species established either in advance of or concurrent with later seral species (DePuit et al. 1978, Schuman et al. 1980). Another approach relies upon introducing properly designed mixtures of later seral species to shorten the longevity of naturally colonizing pioneer species, thereby accelerating succession.

Smith et al. (1988) studied plant succession on a series of uneven-aged oil/gas drill sites within sagebrush-grassland and coniferous forest habitat types in western Wyoming. Recently abandoned sites had been seeded to mixtures of perennial grasses, while older sites had simply been abandoned without any reclamation treatment. All drill sites were compared to surrounding undisturbed plant communities for percent vegetation similarity (using the Spatz Index; Mueller-Dombois and Ellenberg 1974). Differences in percent similarity over time (years since abandonment) were then used as indicators of successional progression toward undisturbed conditions. Fig. 6 summarizes selected results of this study. Regression analysis indicated that seeding mixtures of grasses accelerated successional progression on drill sites within sagebrush-grassland plant communities; the slope of the similarity:time function was positive, and seeded drill sites were more similar to undisturbed vegetation than were non-seeded sites after 18 to 19 years of succession. In contrast, the practice of grass seeding had an apparently detrimental effect on successional development toward undisturbed conditions on drill sites located in coniferous forests, as indicated by a negatively sloping similarity: time function and little difference in similarity values between seeded and non-seeded drill sites after 21 to 22 years of succession. These relationships demonstrate the importance of proper cognizance of autecological, synecological and site-related factors in species mixture design if successional acceleration is desired. It is possible that the rate of succession might have been accelerated rather than retarded on coniferous forest drill sites if more properly designed mixtures of species (e.g., including species other than grasses alone) had been introduced.

Studies in the Northern Great Plains (DePuit et al. 1978, Schuman et al. 1982) have indicated the importance

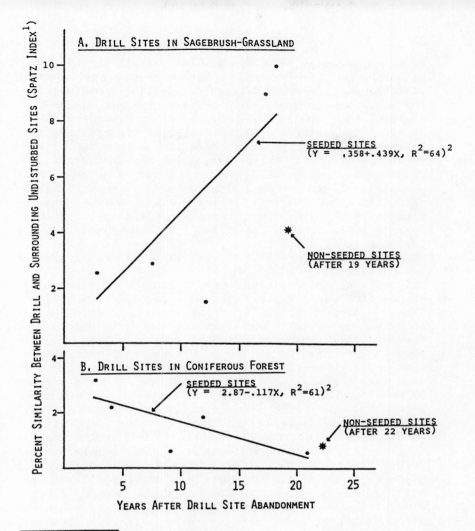

Fig. 6. Patterns of percent vegetation similarity between seeded/non-seeded petroleum drill sites and surrounding undisturbed sites over time (years after drill site abandonment) within sagebrush-grassland and coniferous forest habitat types in western Wyoming. Derived from data of Smith et al. (1988).

185

of mixture design both to adequate overall establishment of perennial species and to short-term achievement of plant communities with desired composition and diversity. For example, inclusion of overly vigorous species in mixtures has usually reduced vegetation diversity due to eventual competitive reduction of less vigorous species. DePuit (1982) suggested several approaches toward enhancing synecological compatibility within mixtures and consequent vegetation diversity, such as provision of phenological and morphological variety, properly varied proportionality among species and adequate species richness within mixtures. However, field application of such principles has sometimes yielded mixed results (Redente et al. 1984).

DePuit et al. (1980) investigated effects of several seed mixtures with varied species richness and proportional composition on vegetation productivity, composition and diversity on coal mined lands in Montana. Table 1 summarizes results from the two most disparate mixtures evaluated. Both mixtures contained only native species that had not proven overly competitive in previous studies in the area. Mixture A contained 18 species, and consisted of cool-season grasses, shrubs, warm-season grasses and forbs at 60, 24, 8 and 8 percent of the total seeding rate, respectively. Mixture B, although sown at the same total rate, differed in both richness (the 18 species of Mixture A plus 10 additional species) and proportionality (43, 16, 33 and 8 percent cool-season grasses, shrubs, warm-season grasses and forbs, respectively). After three growing seasons both mixtures produced nearly identical aboveground biomass. Both mixtures also yielded higher seeded species diversity index values than those in previous studies of other mixtures containing overly vigorous species. However, diversity was higher for the more floristically rich Mixture B than for Mixture A. Differences between mixtures in percent seed mix composition were only partially reflected in vegetation composition. Despite differences in proportionate seeding rates, both mixtures were similarly and largely dominated by cool-season perennial grasses the third growing season. A high shrub seeding rate in Mixture A did result in higher eventual shrub composition, although shrub composition in both mixtures was somewhat lower than seeding rate proportion. The composition of warm-season grasses and forbs was inconsequential and far lower than seeding rate proportions for both mixtures. Further, quadrupling warm-season grass seeding rates in Mixture B had no effect in increasing establishment of this class of species.

Results of the above study and similarly oriented research in Colorado (Doerr et al. 1983, Redente et al. 1984) indicate that attributes of reconstructed plant

Table 1. Attributes of two different seed mixtures and their influence on third growing season composition, richness, diversity and total aboveground biomass on coal mined lands in southeastern Montana. Third growing season means followed by different letters are significantly different at $P \leq 0.05$. Derived from data of DePuit et al. (1980).

	SEED MIXTURES		THIRD GROWING SEASON VEGETATION	
	Seed Mix A	Seed Mix B	Seed Mix A	Seed Mix B
A. COMPOSITION (percent)				
Cool-Season Grasses	60	42	74a	79a
Warm-Season Grasses	8	32	2a	3a
Shrubs	24	18	18a	13b
Forbs	8	8	2a	2a
B. RICHNESS (no. species)[1]				
Cool-Season Grasses	5	8	5	8
Warm-Season Grasses	1	5	1	4
Shrubs	3	6	1	3
Forbs	9	9	6	6
Total	18	28	13	21
C. SHANNON-WIENER DIVERSITY INDEX[1]	–	–	0.59	0.72
D. TOTAL ABOVEGROUND BIOMASS (kg ha^{-1})	–	–	1510a	1561a

[1]For seeded species

communities are only partially controlled by variations in plant species introduced. Clearly, a number of other factors exert influence, including the specific methods of plant introduction. For example, research in Montana has shown initial vegetation composition, diversity or productivity to respond differently to variations in seeding date (DePuit and Coenenberg 1979, Young and Rennick 1982). Other research in Montana (DePuit et al. 1980) and Colorado (Doerr et al. 1983) has indicated varied responses of vegetation composition and diversity to different seeding methods.

DePuit et al. (1980) found differences in total seeding rates to influence third year productivity and diversity. Both mechanical (i.e., drill) and broadcast seed application yielded third year plant communities dominated by perennial grasses, despite the fact that other species comprised nearly 30% of seeded mixtures. However, increasing seeding rates generally increased perennial grass productivity (Fig. 7) and composition, and this relationship was stronger under mechanical than under broadcast seeding. In contrast, vegetation diversity tended to decline at higher seeding rates under both seeding methods. These relationships suggest that expression of interspecific competition was greater under the high plant densities produced by higher seeding rates. If so, competitive exclusion of less vigorous species by increasingly dominant perennial grasses may have been the cause of reduced diversity at heavier seeding rates.

Despite such evidence for differential effects of varied plant propagule introduction on vegetation attributes, the persistence of such effects remains an open question in lack of longer-term data. Indeed, a number of the studies cited above (DePuit and Coenenberg 1979, DePuit et al. 1980, Redente et al. 1984) noted that differences in certain vegetation attributes among plant introduction treatments tended to diminish over time. It is therefore questionable whether the nature of initial propagule supply permanently influences the direction of succession; or whether such anthropogenic influence is confined to a temporary acceleration of revegetation. If the latter is true, the ultimate direction of succession may be controlled by factors other than initial propagule supply and vegetation composition.

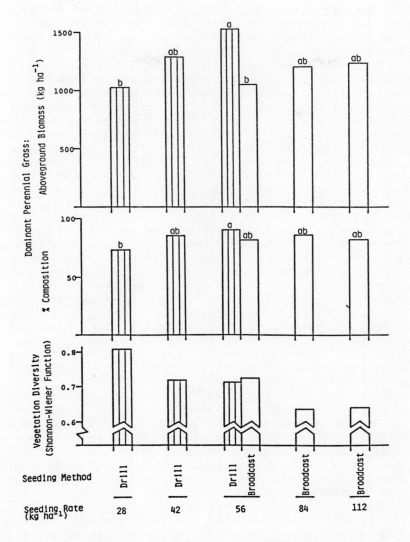

Fig. 7. Effects of varied seeding methods and rates on third year perennial grass aboveground biomass and plant community diversity on coal mined lands in southeastern Montana. Biomass means followed by different letters are significantly different at P $\leq$ 0.05. Derived from data of DePuit et al. (1980).

189

<u>Management</u>--The dynamics of reconstructed ecosystems may be influenced by application of various types of management following initial reconstruction inputs. While effects of initial manipulations of site and biotic factors may sometimes persist, such manipulations are applied only at the outset of the reconstruction process. In contrast, managerial manipulations may be applied repeatedly over time. Broad goals of management, therefore, are to further accelerate and direct ecosystem recovery following initially applied treatments.

Despite the recognized importance of management (Packer and Aldon 1978), relatively little research on the ecological effects of varied managerial practices has been conducted on disturbed lands in the semiarid West. Many potentially effective practices certainly exist (DePuit 1982, Kleinman 1983). For example, biotic processes such as plant species interactions and nutrient cycling may be influenced by the management practices of mowing, haying, prescribed burning or spraying with selective herbicides. Deferred interseeding or interplanting may be managerial approaches to induce plant species compositional changes after sites have undergone sufficient autogenic modification to allow establishment of later successional species. Again, the ecological effectiveness of these and other management practices remains largely unresearched on western disturbed lands.

Herbivory can have a major influence on the development, maintenance or retrogression of ecosystems. Consequently, a number of studies have been conducted on western disturbed lands to investigate varied livestock grazing systems in a managerial sense (Hofmann et al 1981, Laycock and McGinnies 1985, Schuman et al. 1984). These studies have emphasized not only the capability of reconstructed ecosystems to support livestock, but also the effects of varied grazing management on vegetation and soils.

Results of a coal mined land grazing study in Montana (DePuit and Coenenberg 1980) illustrate certain aspects of manipulation of reconstructed ecosystems through management. A program of cattle grazing was initiated on a series of mined land pastures during the fifth year after seeding. A second series of pastures was left ungrazed for comparative purposes. Pasture vegetation was dominated by a relatively simple mixture of introduced, cool-season grasses and legumes at the outset of grazing. Pastures were grazed for three years in succession in similar fashion (i.e., during the spring and fall at moderate to heavy intensity). Figs. 8 and 9 summarize especially important points from this study.

In 1975, the year prior to initiation of grazing, total live biomass was similar between pastures to be grazed and left ungrazed (Fig. 8). Both sets of pastures were also characterized by excessive accumulations of undecomposed plant litter, which raised concern over nutrient immobilization and eventual carbon:nitrogen imbalances in the soil. In 1978, after three years of grazing, total live biomass became significantly higher in grazed than in ungrazed pastures. Although plant litter accumulations declined in both sets of pastures, by 1978 litter was significantly lower in grazed than in ungrazed pastures. This was attributed both to removal of current year plant production by grazing cattle and to soil incorporation of past production through trampling. The latter was felt to be responsible for higher soil cation exchange capacity, organic matter and total nitrogen content, and lower soil carbon:nitrogen ratios in grazed pastures in 1978. These effects, in combination with probable direct physiologic stimulation of plant growth by grazing, were cited as reasons for the higher plant productivity achieved under grazing.

Indicators of vegetation diversity were also similar between pasture sets prior to initiation of grazing in 1975 (Fig. 8). In 1978, after three years of grazing, differences in diversity became apparent between pastures. Although diversity index (Shannon-Wiener function) values declined from 1975 to 1978 in both sets of pastures, index values where higher in grazed than in ungrazed pastures in 1978. Grazed pastures also contained greater numbers of species than ungrazed pastures in 1978. These differences, although of limited magnitude, suggest grazing to have benefited the equity and richness components of plant community diversity. Such effects of grazing were related to both of the following: 1) an opening of the community for invasion of new species or improved growth of subdominant species, and 2) differential grazing responses among species.

All major plant species exhibited similar composition between pastures prior to grazing in 1975. Compositions of crested wheatgrass (<u>Agropyron</u> <u>cristatum</u>) and alfalfa

191

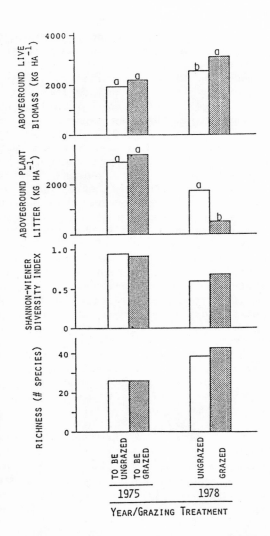

Fig. 8. Plant live biomass, ground litter, diversity, and species richness in ungrazed and grazed pastures prior to grazing initiation (1975) and after three consecutive years of grazing (1978) on coal mined lands in southeastern Montana. Within years, biomass means followed by different letters are significantly different at P ≤ 0.05. Derived from data of DePuit and Coenenberg (1980).

(Medicago sativa) remained similar between grazed and ungrazed pastures in 1978, after completion of the grazing program (Fig. 9). However, grazing had differential effects on other species. Tall wheatgrass (Agropyron elongatum) composition was significantly higher in grazed pastures in 1978, whereas smooth brome (Bromus inermis) composition was significantly reduced by grazing. Although aggregate composition of other, subdominant species was low and statistically similar between pasture sets in 1978, composition of such species in grazed pastures was nonetheless double that in ungrazed pastures.

These results, in brief, suggested a potential role for the management practice of grazing in ecosystem recovery. In this study, grazing improved overall plant community productivity, benefited the function of plant-soil systems, enhanced plant diversity, and induced plant compositional change over the short-term. To realize such benefits over longer time frames or on other sites, grazing must be properly designed; Ries and Hofmann (1984), for example, noted reductions in plant productivity and increases in erosional soil loss under overly heavy grazing on mined land pastures in North Dakota. The possibility of using varied grazing systems to induce accordingly varied ecosystem responses is being investigated by current research on Colorado mined lands (Laycock and McGinnies 1985).

CONCLUSIONS

Our understanding of shrub and grassland ecosystem reconstruction in the semiarid western United States has improved dramatically over the past two decades, most markedly in terms of short-term manipulation of the process. As illustrated by the selected research reviewed in this chapter, certain of the site and biotic factors governing ecosystem recovery can be altered anthropogenically, thereby influencing the initial rate and direction of succession.

Unfortunately, much of the research contributing to progress in western land reclamation has been limited in scope and duration. In addition, research has usually been empirical rather than functional, and in many cases

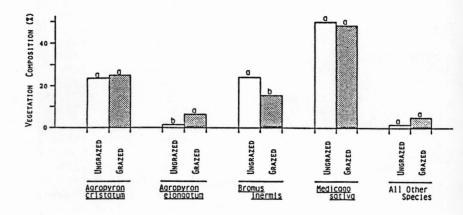

Fig. 9. Effects of three consecutive years of grazing vs. non-grazing on composition of dominant plant species on revegetated coal mined lands in southeastern Montana. Within species, means followed by different letters are significantly different at P ≤ 0.05. Derived from data of DePuit and Coenenberg (1980).

has been non-ecological in orientation. Consequently, our theoretical understanding of the ecosystem reconstruction process has evolved more slowly than knowledge of its technological manipulation. In short, while the initial effects of specific manipulations are becoming better defined, neither the causes, ecological ramifications nor persistence of such effects are well understood.

Maturation of ecosystem reconstruction as a field of applied ecology, in the semiarid West and elsewhere, will depend on overcoming the above shortcomings through maintained and properly directed ecological research. Such research must emphasize functional relationships in the reconstruction process, be of adequate breadth to address the wide array of interacting factors influencing ecosystem function, and be of sufficient duration to reflect long-term changes in ecosystems as they develop on disturbed lands. Only in this manner may progress toward theoretical understanding of reconstructed ecosystem dynamics be achieved. Without such understanding, technology for manipulation of the reconstruction process will remain incompletely based upon ecological principles and, therefore, of limited effectiveness.

LITERATURE CITED

Allen, E.B., and M.F. Allen. 1984. Competition between plants of different successional stages: mycorrhizae as regulators. Canadian Journal of Botany 62:2625-2629.

Allen, E.B., and D.H. Knight. 1984. The effects of introduced annuals on secondary succession in sagebrush grassland, Wyoming. Southwestern Naturalist 29:407-422.

Barbour, M.G., J.H. Burk, and W.D. Pitts. 1980. Terrestrial Plant Ecology. Benjamin Cummings Publishing Company, Menlo Park, California, USA.

Barth, R.C. 1984. Soil-depth requirements to re-establish perennial grasses on surface mined areas in the northern Great Plains. Colorado School of Mines, Mineral and Energy Resources 27(1).

Bauer, A., W.A. Berg, and W.L. Gould. 1978. Correction of nutrient deficiencies and toxicities in strip-mined lands of semiarid and arid regions. Pages 451-466 in F.W. Schaller and P. Sutton, editors. Reclamation of Drastically Disturbed Lands. American Society of Agronomy/Crop Science Society of America/Soil Science Society of America. Madison, Wisconsin, USA.

Berg, W.A. 1980. Nitrogen and phosphorus fertilization of mined lands. Pages 20(1)-20(8) in Proceedings: Symposium on Adequate Reclamation of Mined Lands, Soil Conservation Society of America and WRCC-21, Billings, Montana, USA.

Biondini, M.E., C.D. Bonham, and E.F. Redente. 1985a. Secondary successional patterns in a sagebrush community as they relate to soil disturbance and soil biological activity. Vegetatio 60:25-36.

Biondini, M.E., C.D. Bonham, and E.F. Redente. 1985b. Relationships between induced successional patterns and soil biological activity of reclaimed areas. Reclamation and Revegetation Research 3:323-342.

195

Biondini, M.E., and E.F. Redente. 1986. Interactive effect of stimulus and stress on plant community diversity in reclaimed lands. Reclamation and Revegetation Research 4:211-222.

Box, T.W. 1978. The significance and responsibility of rehabilitating drastically disturbed lands. Pages 1-10 in F.W. Schaller and P. Sutton, editors. Reclamation of Drastically Disturbed Lands. American Society of Agronomy/Soil Science Society of America/Crop Science Society of America. Madison, Wisconsin, USA.

Brisbin, I.L. 1982. The principles of ecology as a frame-work for a total ecosystem approach to high altitude revegetation research. Pages 1-11 in R.L. Cuany and J. Etra, editors. Proceedings: High Altitude Revegetation Workshop No. 5. Water Resources Research Institute Information Series No. 48. Colorado State University, Fort Collins, Colorado, USA.

Cundell, A.M. 1977. The role of microorganisms in the revegetation of strip-mined land in the western United States. Journal of Range Management 30:299-305.

Danielson, R.M. 1985. Mycorrhizae and reclamation of stressed terrestrial environments. Pages 173-201 in R.L. Tate and D.A. Klein, editors. Soil Reclamation Processes: Microbiological Analyses and Applications. Marcel Dekker, Inc., New York, New York, USA.

Denslow, J.S. 1985. Disturbance-mediated coexistence of species. Pages 307-323 in S.T.A. Pickett and P.S. White, editors. The Ecology of Natural Disturbance and Patch Dynamics. Academic Press, Orlando, Florida, USA.

DePuit, E.J. 1982. Cool-season perennial grass establishment on Northern Great Plains mined lands: status of current technology. Pages B1(1)-B1(24) in Proceedings: Symposium on Surface Coal Mining and Reclamation in the Northern Great Plains. Montana Agricultural Experiment Station Research Report 194. Bozeman, Montana, USA.

DePuit, E.J. 1984. Potential topsoiling strategies for enhancement of vegetation diversity on mined lands. Minerals and the Environment 6:115-120.

DePuit, E.J. 1985. An ecologist's perspectives on reclamation success. Invited Paper at Second Annual Meeting, American Society for Surface Mining and Reclamation, Denver, Colorado, USA.

DePuit, E.J. 1986. Western revegetation in perspective: past progress, present status and future needs. Pages 6-34 in M.A. Schuster and R.H. Zuck, editors. Proceedings: Seventh High Altitude Revegetation Workshop. Colorado State University, Fort Collins, Colorado, USA.

DePuit, E.J., and J.G. Coenenberg. 1979. Responses of revegetated coal strip mine spoils to variable fertilization rates, longevity of fertilization program and season of seeding. Montana Agricultural Experiment Station Research Report 150. Bozeman, Montana, USA.

DePuit, E.J., and J.G. Coenenberg. 1980. Plant response and forage quality for controlled grazing on coal mine spoil pastures. Montana Agricultural Experiment Station Project Final Report to U.S. Environmental Protection Agency, Cincinnati, Ohio, USA.

DePuit, E.J., J.G. Coenenberg, and C.L. Skilbred. 1980. Establishment of diverse native plant communities on coal surface mined lands in Montana as influenced by seeding method, mixture and rate. Montana Agricultural Experiment Station Research Report 163. Bozeman, Montana, USA.

DePuit, E.J., J.G. Coenenberg, and W.H. Willmuth. 1978. Research on revegetation of surface mined lands at Colstrip, Montana: progress report 1975-1977. Montana Agricultural Experiment Research Report 127. Bozeman, Montana, USA.

Doerr, T.B., E.F. Redente, and T.E. Sievers. 1983. Effect of cultural practices on seeded plant communities on intensively disturbed soils. Journal of Range Management 36:423-428.

Doll, E.C., S.D. Merrill, and G.A. Halvorsen. 1984. Soil replacement for reclamation of stripmined lands in North Dakota. North Dakota Agricultural Experiment Station Bulletin 514. Fargo, North Dakota, USA.

Dollhopf, D.J., D.W. Hedberg, S.A. Young, J.D. Goering, W.M. Schafer, and C.J. Levine. 1985. Effects of surface manipulation on mined land reclamation. Montana Agricultural Experiment Station Special Report 18. Bozeman, Montana, USA.

Farmer, E.E., B.Z. Richardson, and R.W. Brown. 1976. Revegetation of acid mining wastes in central Idaho. U.S. Department of Agriculture Forest Service Research Paper INT-178, Ogden, Utah, USA.

Fresquez, P.R., and W.C. Lindemann. 1982. Soil and rhizosphere microorganisms in amended mine spoils. Soil Science Society of America Journal 46:751-755.

Grime, J.P. 1979. Plant Strategies and Vegetation Processes. John Wiley and Sons, New York, New York, USA. Hargis, N.E., and E.F. Redente. 1984. Soil handling for surface mine reclamation. Journal of Soil and Water Conservation 39:300-305.

Hintgen, T.M., and W.R. Clark. 1984. Impact of small mammals on the vegetation of reclaimed land in the Northern Great Plains. Journal of Range Management 37:438-441.

Hofmann, L., R.E. Ries, and R.J. Lorenz. 1981. Livestock and vegetative performance on reclaimed and non-mined rangelands in North Dakota. Journal of Soil and Water Conservation 36:41-44.

Holechek, J.L., E.J. DePuit, J. Coenenberg, and R. Valdez. 1982. Long-term plant establishment on mined lands in southeastern Montana. Journal of Range Management 35:522-525.

Howard, G.S., and M.J. Samuel. 1979. The value of fresh stripped topsoil as a seed source of useful plants for surface mine revegetation. Journal of Range Management 32:76-77.

Huston, M. 1979. A general hypothesis of species diversity. American Naturalist 113:81-101.

Iverson, L.R., and M.K. Wali. 1982a. Reclamation of coal mined lands: the role of Kochia scoparia and other pioneers in early succession. Reclamation and Revegetation Research 1:123-160.

Iverson, L.R., and M.K. Wali. 1982b. Buried viable seeds and their relation to revegetation after surface mining. Journal of Range Management 35:648-652.

Kay, B.L. 1978. Mulch and chemical stabilizers for land reclamation in dry regions. Pages 467-484 in F.W. Schaller and P. Sutton, editors. Reclamation of Drastically Disturbed Lands. American Society of Agronomy/ Crop Science Society of America/Soil Science Society of America, Madison, Wisconsin, USA.

Klein, D.A., W. Metzger, and B. Crews. 1984. Soil microorganisms and plant community development in disturbed ecosystems. Pages 37-50 in E.F. Redente and C.W. Cook, editors. Ecological Studies of Natural and Established Ecosystems in Energy Related Disturbances in Colorado. Department of Range Science, Colorado State University, Fort Collins, Colorado, USA.

Klein, D.A., D.L. Sorensen, and W. Metzger. 1982. Soil microorganisms and management of retorted oil shale reclamation. Pages 27-44 in E.F. Redente and C.W. Cook, editors. Revegetation Studies on Oil Shale Related Disturbances in Colorado. Department of Range Science, Colorado State University, Fort Collins, Colorado, USA.

Kleinman, L.H. 1983. Levels of management for reclaimed lands. Pages 105-107 in Proceedings: Symposium on Western Coal Mining Regulatory Issues-Land-Use, Revegetation and Management. Science Series No. 35, Range Science Department, Colorado State University, Fort Collins, Colorado, USA.

Laycock, W.A., and W.J. McGinnies. 1985. Reclamation and grazing management on a surface coal mine in northwestern Colorado. Pages 73-76 in Proceedings, Second Annual Meeting, American Society for Surface Mining and Reclamation, Denver, Colorado, USA.

Mackey, C.V., and E.J. DePuit. 1985. Natural revegetation of surface-deposited spent oil shale in Colorado. Reclamation and Revegetation Research 4:1-16.

Malcolm, C.V. 1982. Wheatbelt salinity: a review of the salt land problem in southwestern Australia. Western Australia Department of Agriculture Technical Bulletin No. 52, Perth, Australia.

Majer, J.D. 1984. The influence of ants on seeding operations in northern Australian mined areas. Reclamation and Revegetation Research 2:299-313.

Majer, J.D., J.E. Day, E.D. Kabay, and W.S. Perriman. 1984. Recolonization by ants in bauxite mines rehabilitated by a number of methods. Journal of Applied Ecology 21:355-375.

Mays, D.A., and S.W. Bengtson. 1978. Lime and fertilizer use in land reclamation. Pages 307-328 in F.W. Schaller and P. Sutton, editors. Reclamation of Drastically Disturbed Lands. American Society of Agronomy/Crop Science Society of America/Soil Science Society of America. Madison, Wisconsin, USA.

McGinnies, W.J., and P. Nicholas. 1980. Effects of topsoil thickness and nitrogen fertilizer on the revegetation of coal mine spoils. Journal of Environmental Quality 9:681-685.

Moore, R.T., S.L. Ellis, and D.R. Duba. 1977. Advantages of natural successional processes on western reclaimed lands. Pages 274-282 in Proceedings: Fifth Symposium on Surface Mining and Reclamation. National Coal Association, Louisville, Kentucky, USA.

Mueller-Dombois, D., and H. Ellenburg.1974. Aims and Methods of Vegetation Ecology. John Wiley and Sons, New York, New York, USA.

Nielsen, R.F., and H.B. Peterson. 1972. Treatment of mine tailings to promote vegetative stabilization. Utah Agricultural Experiment Station Bulletin 485. Utah State University, Logan, Utah, USA.

Packer, P.E., and E.F. Aldon. 1978. Revegetation techniques for dry regions. Pages 425-450 in F.W. Schaller and P. Sutton, editors. Reclamation of Drastically Disturbed Lands. American Society of Agronomy/Crop Science Society of America/Soil Science Society of America. Madison, Wisconsin, USA.

Pickett, S.T.A., and P.S. White. 1985. Patch dynamics: a synthesis. Pages 371-384 in S.T.A. Pickett and P.S. White, editors. The Ecology of Natural Disturbance and Patch Dynamics. Academic Press, Orlando, Florida, USA.

Pinchak, B.A., G.E. Schuman, and E.J. DePuit. 1985. Topsoil and mulch effects on plant species and community responses of revegetated mined land. Journal of Range Management 38:258-261.

Ratnayake, M.R., R.T. Leonard, and J.A. Menge. 1978. Root exudation in relation to supply of phosphorus and its possible relevance to mycorrhizal formation. New Phytologist 81:543-552.

Redente, E.F., and C.W. Cook. 1986. Structural and functional changes in early successional stages of a semiarid ecosystem. Colorado State University Research Report to U.S. Department of Energy, DOE/EV/04018-9, Fort Collins, Colorado, USA.

Redente, E.F., T.B. Doerr, C.E. Grygiel, and M.E. Biondini. 1984. Vegetation establishment and succession on disturbed soils in northwest Colorado. Reclamation and Revegetation Research 3:153-166.

Redente, E.F., C.B. Mount, and W.J. Ruzzo. 1982. Vegetation composition and production as affected by soil thickness over retorted oil shale. Reclamation and Revegetation Research 1:109-122.

Ries, R.E., and L. Hofmann. 1984. Pasture and hayland: measures of reclamation success. Pages 307-317 in F.F. Munshower and S.E. Fisher, editors. Proceedings: Third Biennial Symposium on Surface Coal Mine Reclamation on the Great Plains. Billings, Montana, USA.

Righetti, T.L. 1982. Importance of soil nitrogen and phosphorus in semiarid reclamation. Pages 80-86 in E.F. Aldon and W.R. Oaks, editors. Proceedings: Symposium on Reclamation of Mined Lands in the Southwest. Soil Conservation Society of America, Albuquerque, New Mexico, USA.

Sandoval, F.M., and W. Gould. 1978. Improvement of saline and sodium-affected disturbed lands. Pages 485-504 in F.W. Schaller and P. Sutton, editors. Reclamation of Drastically Disturbed Lands. American Society of Agronomy/Crop Science Society of America/Soil Science of America. Madison, Wisconsin, USA.

Schafer, W.M. 1984. Minesoil restoration and maturity: a guide for managing minesoil development. Pages 172-185 in Proceedings: Symposium on Surface Coal Mining and Reclamation in the Great Plains. Montana State University, Bozeman, Montana, USA.

Schafer, W.M., and G.A. Nielsen. 1978. Soil development and plant succession on 1 to 50 year old strip mine spoils in southeastern Montana. Pages 541-549 in M.K. Wali, editor. Ecology and Coal Resource Development. Pergamon Press, New York, New York, USA.

Schafer, W.M., G.A. Nielsen, D.J. Dollhopf, and K. Temple. 1979. Soil Genesis, hydrological properties, root characteristics, and microbial activity of 1 to 50 year old stripmine spoils. U.S. Environmental Protection Agency, EPA-600/7-79-253. Cincinnati, Ohio, USA.

Schuman, G.E., D.T. Booth, J.W. Waggoner, and F. Rauzi. 1984. The effect of grazing reclaimed mined lands on forage production and composition. In Working Papers, Second International Rangeland Congress, Adelaide, Australia.

Schuman, G.E., F. Rauzi, and D.T. Booth. 1982. Production and competition of crested wheatgrass-native grass mixtures. Agronomy Journal 74:23-26.

Schuman, G.E., E.M. Taylor, F. Rauzi, and G.S. Howard. 1980. Standing stubble vs. crimped straw mulch for establishing grass on mined lands. Journal of Soil and Water Conservation 35:25-27.

Schuman, G.E., E.M. Taylor, F. Rauzi, and B.A. Pinchak. 1985. Revegetation of mined land: influence of topsoil depth and mulching method. Journal of Soil and Water Conservation 40:249-251.

Sindelar, B.W. 1984. Vegetation development on surface mined lands in eastern Montana. Pages 6/1-30 in Ecological Studies of Disturbed Landscapes. U.S. Department of Energy, Washington, D.C., USA.

Skujins, J. 1978. History of abiotic soil enzyme research. Pages 1-49 in R.G. Burns, editor. Soil Enzymes. Academic Press, London, England.

Smith, C.P., E.J. DePuit, and B.Z. Richardson. 1988. Plant community development on petroleum drill sites in northwestern Wyoming. Journal of Range Management 41 (in press).

Sorensen, D.L. 1982. Biochemical activities in soil over-laying Paraho processed oil shale. Ph.D. Dissertation, Colorado State University, Fort Collins, Colorado, USA.

Speir, T.W., and D.J. Ross. 1978. Soil phosphates and sulfatase. Pages 197-250 in R.G. Burns, editor. Soil Enzymes. Academic Press, London, England.

Stark, J.M., and E.F. Redente. 1985. Soil-plant diversity relationships on a disturbed site in northwestern Colorado. Soil Science Society of America Journal 49:1028-1033.

Stiller, D.M., G.L. Zimpfer, and M. Bishop. 1980. Application of geomorphic principles to surface mined land reclamation in the semiarid West. Journal of Soil and Water Conservation 35:274-277.

Tate, R.L., and D.A. Klein, editors. 1985. Soil Reclamation Processes: Microbiological Analyses and Applications. Marcel Dekker, Inc., New York, New York, USA.

Toy, T.J. 1984. Geomorphology of surface mined lands in the Western United States. Pages 133-170 in J.E. Costa and P.J. Fleischer, editors. Developments and Applications of Geomorphology. Springer-Verlag, Berlin, West Germany.

Vitousek, P.M. 1985. Community turnover and ecosystem nutrient dynamics. Pages 325-333 in S.T.A. Pickett and P.S. White, editors. The Ecology of Natural Disturbance and Patch Dynamics. Academic Press, Orlando, Florida, USA.

Wagner, W.L., W.C. Martin, and E.F. Aldon. 1978. Natural succession on strip-mined lands in northwestern New Mexico. Reclamation Review 1:67-73.

Wali, M.K. 1975. The problem of land reclamation viewed in a systems context. Pages 1-17 in M.K. Wali, editor. Practices and Problems of Land Reclamation in Western North America. University of North Dakota Press, Grand Forks, North Dakota, USA.

White, P.S. 1979. Pattern, process and natural disturbance in vegetation. Botannical Review 45:229-299.

Whitford, W.G., and N.Z. Elkins. 1986. The importance of soil ecology and the ecosystem perspective in surface mine reclamation. Pages 151-187 in C.C. Reith and L.D. Potter, editors. Principles and Methods of Reclamation Science. University of New Mexico Press, Albuquerque, New Mexico, USA.

Williams, S.E., and M.F. Allen, editors. 1984. VA mycorrhizae and reclamation of arid and semiarid lands. Wyoming Agricultural Experiment Station Science Report No. SA 1261. Laramie, Wyoming, USA.

Wollenhaupt, N.C., and J.L. Richardson. 1982. The role of topography in revegetation of disturbed lands. Pages C2(1)-C2(11) in Prodeedings: Symposium on Surface Coal Mining and Reclamation in the Northern Great Plains. Montana Agricultural Experiment Station Research Report 194. Bozeman, Montana, USA.

Woodmansee, R.G., J.D. Reeder, and W.A. Berg. 1980. Nitrogen in drastically disturbed lands. Pages 376-392 in C.T. Youngberg, editor. Forest Soils and Land Use. Colorado State University, Fort Collins, Colorado, USA.

Young, S.A., and R.B. Rennick. 1982. Establishment of seeded species on coal minesoils following temporary irrigation. Montana Agricultural Experiment Station Research Report 200. Bozeman, Montana, USA.

9. The Hydrologic Role of Vegetation in the Development and Reclamation of Dryland Salinity

ABSTRACT

The globally widespread phenomenon called dryland salinity occurs where there is the combination of a store of salt in the soil and a rising water table. The rising water mobilizes the stored salt upwards and also down slope where it may form salt seeps and enter streams.

Water tables rise when a greater proportion of the rainfall than before enters the soil. Such increase in recharge to the water table occurs when vegetation becomes more sparse, due, for instance, to overgrazing or to clearing of deep-rooted perennial forests or woodlands for agriculture. The reason why shallow-rooted, sparse or short vegetation increases recharge is that the shallower roots harvest less water, the smaller leaf area permits less transpiration and together with reduced leaf area, less interception of rainfall (evaporation from wet leaves) occurs.

To reclaim dryland salinity, a revegetation strategy is required that will discharge sufficiently more water to lower the water table to a safe level. Several major issues in forming such a strategy are addressed. The quantity of water which needs to be discharged to lower the water table to a required level must be estimated, and the combined evaporative discharge from transpiration and rainfall interception must be measured using candidate species. Of similar importance are location of vegetation in the landscape and choice of species. Extent of revegetation, cost of revegetation, and lead time to reclamation need to be determined. Several examples of successful reclamation are given.

INTRODUCTION

Every reader of this chapter is likely to know that reduction in vegetative cover may lead to such degradation as soil erosion. The connection is obvious both to the eye and the mind and it has been widely publicized. But it is not obvious, nor is it well known, that reduction of vegetative cover, particularly in low-rainfall regions, may lead to dryland salinity. Yet dryland salinity occurs in every continent except Antarctica (Dudal and Purnell 1986, Barrett-Lennard et al. 1985).

Until recently, management of dryland salinity has been restricted almost entirely to salt-tolerant vegetation established for grazing on the affected areas. International experience with that approach has been edited by Barrett-Lennard et al. (1985). Now it is becoming more widely known that vegetation managed in one way may cause dryland salinity yet when managed in another may lead to its reclamation. What is the causal connection between vegetation management and dryland salinity which allows such an apparent paradox? For until that is clear it is not possible to develop a rational or effective strategy either for prevention or reclamation.

Salinity is largely a groundwater problem. For salinity suddenly to develop at the surface of apparently non-saline land there has to be first, a store of salt somewhere in the subsoil, second, a source of water and third, some mechanism which brings groundwater into contact with the stored salt and transports it to the surface. All of these factors are invisible from the surface but sensitive to changes in vegetation in low rainfall regions.

The objective of this chapter is to alert managers of vegetation and land to the mechanism of this insidious problem, to suggest predictive or preventive methods and to outline strategies for successful reclamation projects.

206

VEGETATION AND THE CYCLES OF SALT AND WATER

The low rainfall and high potential evaporation in semiarid regions ensures that, where pristine vegetation exists, most of the rain is evaporated by transpiration and canopy interception. Therefore only a small proportion of rain may drain below the root zone to the water table. Of course other factors influence drainage such as infiltration rate of the soil type and the intensity and distribution of rainfall. However, since water is the primary agent of salt movement, it is the high ratio of rain evaporated to drainage which provides the conditions for salt to accumulate in the subsoil and persist. Where does this salt come from in the first place?

Rain contains small quantities of cyclic salt derived from the ocean. For example salt from the Indian Ocean travels long distances inland over Western Australia (Fig. 1, Hingston and Gailitis 1976). Some of the salt which falls in the rain and enters the root zone will be taken up in the transpiration stream. Some is excluded by the roots and so accumulates in the root zone (many species of eucalypts, and perhaps other types of vegetation, have the ability to exclude some of the salt in the soil solution from the transpiration stream).

Under high rainfall (e.g., >900 mm), the salt concentrating process is matched by leaching which flushes the salt to the groundwater where eventually it will discharge into the drainage system and eventually the ocean. In contrast, in low-rainfall regions, salinity can reach high levels in the root zone (Dimmock et al. 1974). In soils under native forest in Western Australia the soil solution may have a salt concentration higher than that of the ocean. The mass of salt may exceed 9.5×10^5 kg ha^{-1}. Yet Figure 2 demonstrates that such highly saline soils have a negligible concentration of salt at the surface. Such soils thus fulfill the first of the two requirements for the development of dryland salinity. Drilling used to be required to delineate the salt store (Dimmock et al. 1974). Recently,

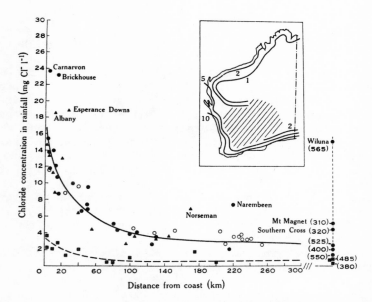

Fig. 1. Decrease in concentration of chloride (mg Cl⁻ 1⁻¹) in rainfall with shortest distance from the coast. ■ North-west centers (north of 24°S latitude). ● South-west centers, distances from the west coast. ▲ South-west centers, distances from the south coast. O Previous data (Hingston 1958). Inset: Map of chloride concentrations in rainwater. Hatched area indicates the region of variable values (2-10 mg Cl⁻ 1⁻¹). From Hingston and Gailitis (1976). Reprinted with permission.

electromagnetic induction (Williams and Hoey 1987, Engel et al. 1987) have made that task easier.

Suppose now that a certain change to the vegetation occurs such that LAI (= leaf area index) is reduced. For example, the native herbaceous vegetation is overgrazed, or the native forest is cleared for dryland agriculture, wood chipping or strip mining or harvested for fuel and building material. What will be the effect on the salt cycle? First, transpiration will be less and this will tend to slow down the accumulation of salt. Of more importance, the extra throughfall of rain through the thinner canopy will increase recharge to the watertable causing it to rise into the stored salt. That is, though the annual input of cyclic salt will not change, the stored salt will begin to move into the stream lines.

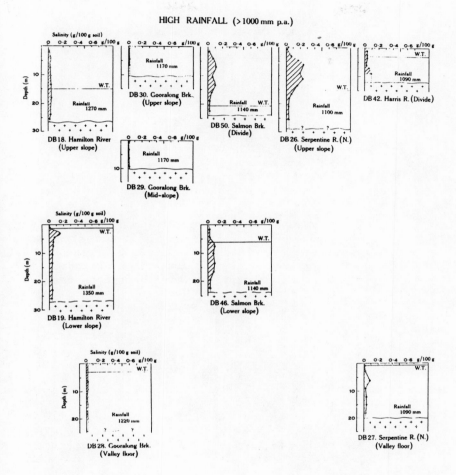

HIGH RAINFALL (>1000 mm p.a.)

Fig. 2. Salinity profiles (as g/100 g) for bores in the catchments of the Serpentine, Collie and Williams Rivers, arranged vertically according to position on slope and horizontally in order of decreasing annual rainfall (in mm). +++: Hard rock; 'W.T.': position of water table at time of boring. After Dimmock et al. (1974). Reprinted with permission.

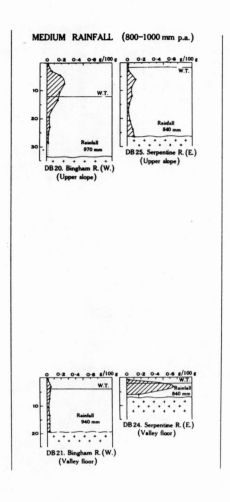

Fig. 2 (continued).

LOW RAINFALL (<800 mm p.a.)

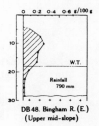

DB 48. Bingham R. (E.)
(Upper mid-slope)

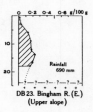

DB 23. Bingham R. (E.)
(Upper slope)

DB 49. Bingham R. (E.)
(Lower mid-slope)

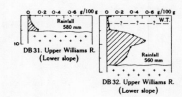

DB 31. Upper Williams R.
(Lower slope)

DB 32. Upper Williams R.
(Lower slope)

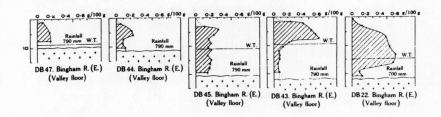

DB 47. Bingham R. (E.)
(Valley floor)

DB 44. Bingham R. (E.)
(Valley floor)

DB 45. Bingham R. (E.)
(Valley floor)

DB 43. Bingham R. (E.)
(Valley floor)

DB 22. Bingham R. (E.)
(Valley floor)

Fig. 2. (continued).

211

Alternatively, LAI may increase, say by growing crops instead of grazed pasture (defoliation reduces leaf area and root growth and therefore transpiration) or by re-aforestation or agroforestry. Under such treatments leaching will tend to decline, resulting in a net increment of stored salt.

Recent work in a farm catchment (750 mm yr^{-1}) illustrates the speed and direction of change in salt storage (Fig. 3). There were three types of vegetation-relict eucalypt forest, grazed annual pasture and cereal crops established on cleared forest land and eucalypt plantations established on that farm land. These plantations had very high transpiration rates (Greenwood et al. 1985). Salt storage was greatest under relict forest. On land cleared for farming, salt storage had declined progressively, being less after 18 than after 10 years. Storage had increased after only eight years of plantation.

In southern Australia it can be generalized that salt storage is least in regions of high rainfall and highest in semiarid regions. This is because the dominant process determining the storage of salt is not the quantity of the rainfall but the extent of flushing.

There is no clearer demonstration of the effect of change in vegetation on salt storage than the data of Peck and Hurle (Peck and Hurle 1973). They measured salt input from rain and salt discharge on fifteen catchments (Table 1). In the mainly forested catchments, salt flow and salt fall were nearly balanced, whereas clearing resulted in salt flow greatly exceeding the salt fall.

Hydrologists make much use of the concept of water balance or budget. That is, rainfall may be partitioned into its various pathways - evaporation, runoff, seepage, soil-water storage, and drainage to one or more aquifers. The sum of all these quantities must account for all of the rainfall. In practice, accurate measurement of water balance is extraordinarily difficult and is rarely successful. But the concept is helpful to make a simple statement about the hydrologic role of vegetation with respect to dryland salinity. In the case of pristine vegetation I assume there to be equilibrium in the hydrologic cycle. There will be variation in each of the components of water balance in any one year because of the erratic rainfall, particularly in low rainfall

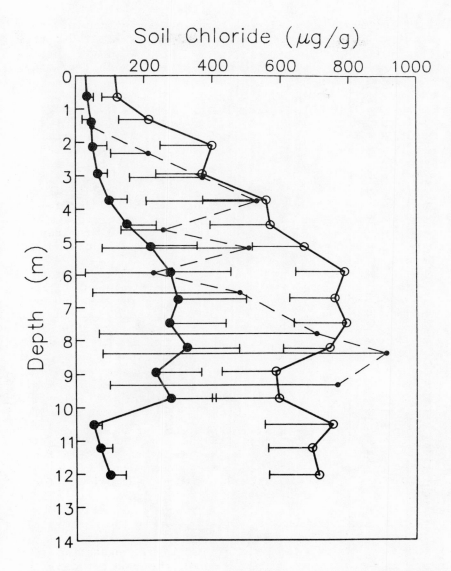

Fig. 3.   Profiles of mean soil chloride levels beneath grazed annual pasture (●——), relict <u>Eucalypt</u> forest (O——), and pasture before any trees were planted (·---)   Bar shows standard error.   Greenwood et al. unpublished.

Table 1. Salt (chloride) balances of uncleared and cleared catchments.

Catchment	Salt Fall, kg/ha yr	Salt Flow, kg/ha yr	Salt Flow less Salt Fall, kg/ha yr	Salt Flow/Salt Fall
Predominantly Forested Catchments				
Julimar	53	78	25	1.5
Seldom Seen	118	163	45	1.4
More Seldom Seen	116	137	21	1.2
Waterfall Gully	109	178	69	1.6
North Dandalup	133	175	42	1.3
Davies	126	135	9	1.1
Yarragil	97	130	33	1.3
Harris	84	131	47	1.6
Catchments with Substantial Areas of Cleared Farmland				
Brockman	80	342	260	4.3
Wooroloo	78	420	340	5.4
Dale	24	460	440	19
Hotham	48	369	320	7.7
Williams	31	650	620	21
Collie East	50	740	690	15
Brunswick	111	346	240	3.1

After Peck and Hurle (1973). Reprinted with permission.

regions. But, in general, the mean annual level of the watertable will be fairly constant.

Suppose that the LAI of pristine vegetation is substantially reduced. Rainfall will not be affected, but the reduction in leaf area will reduce interception and transpiration, with a balancing increase in throughfall, run off, infiltration, soil water storage and drainage to the groundwater. Permanent water tables will rise and perched or seasonal water tables may form or persist longer. There is now convincing documentation of the rise in water tables following a reduction in vegetative cover. Figure 4 is an example from southwestern Australia (Sharma and Williamson 1984). It shows the matching groundwater levels in a paired catchment study in a native forest and the immediate and continued rise in water table after clearing for agriculture.

It is not difficult to imagine the effect which a rising water table may have on the salinity of

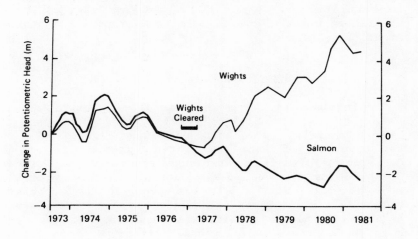

Fig. 4. Change in groundwater level for the deep aquifer in a forested (Salmon) and cleared (Wights) catchment pair. From Sharma and Williamson (1984). Reprinted with permission.

215

groundwater (e.g., Fig. 2). In the pristine state the water table and salt profile will presumably have been in broad equilibrium for centuries. The small annual increment of salt store has been matched by a similar discharge of salt in the groundwater. Salt concentrations at the zone of the yearly fluctuation of the water table are low. Suppose the annual rise of the water table following the reduction of LAI is 0.5 m per year. Each year, as the water table ascends, the salinity of the groundwater will increase. Since the groundwater is not a pond but a slow flowing aquifer, the dissolved salt will begin to move laterally. And as the water table rises hillside seeps will form and land will become saturated with saline water.

Thus it is the process of salt exclusion by vegetation which causes the store of cyclic salt to develop, and it is increased throughfall brought about mainly by a lower LAI which provides the extra water to mobilize that store and distribute it unfavorably in the landscape. We are led inevitably to the proposition that if one kind of vegetation (mis)management can induce salinity, another revegetation management might be able to control or reclaim it by reducing the amount of mobilizing water. How good is that proposition and how might it be tested?

VEGETATION AND SALINITY CONTROL

Unfortunately, the successful demonstration of salinity control by vegetation is rare and circumstantial. The best documented example is the replacement of shallow-rooted grasses with the deep-rooted alfalfa on recharge areas of the Northern Great Plains of the U.S.A. (Doering and Sandoval 1976, Brown et al. 1983). It was economically successful because a careful revegetation strategy had been planned. An economic plant, alfalfa was chosen and it was grown only where it was hydrologically effective - the uplands which had been identified as the main recharge area for the rising water table. The remaining portion of the farm was untreated. The necessary increase in evaporation was thus achieved without greatly disrupting farm operations. It follows that the control of dryland salinity by vegetation requires a species that has a high

216

water use and ideally, is economically productive and does not greatly disrupt land-use operations.

VEGETATION STRATEGY

Vegetation has four extremely useful attributes that can be applied to the management of dryland salinity. Some of these attributes are obvious, but it is worth stating them lest they be overlooked. First, it is accessible on the land surface, can be assessed by eye (as distinct from groundwater and salt stores in the soil), and it can be modified with relative ease. Second, rigorously designed plots can be established for preliminary feasibility studies for ranking species on the basis of water-use (Greenwood et al. 1985, Greenwood and Beresford 1979, 1980, Greenwood et al. 1981, 1982, 1985). Third, vegetation can be distributed in the landscape in such a way as to take full advantage of atmospheric advection ("clothes line" effect). A small plantation of trees can use several times the annual value of rainfall falling on it (Greenwood et al. 1985). Such a vegetation treatment can be extraordinarily efficient as a groundwater pump. Fourth, there is a wide range in annual total evaporation rate across vegetation types and species from which to select candidates for revegetation e.g., grazed annual or perennial pasture crops and trees (Table 2). The term total evaporation is the sum of evaporation from the surfaces of soil and wet leaves (interception) and from transpiration. It is a more precise term than the more usual term evapotranspiration.

Broadly, for a given climate, the magnitude of annual evaporation depends on rooting depth (Brown et al. 1983), depth to water table, salinity ((Hylckama 1974), oxygenation of the groundwater for root growth, LAI, and the advective aerodynamic energy around each leaf.

With the above in mind, you may ask - why is so little use made of vegetation for the reclamation of dryland salinity? One reason has been the difficulty of measuring evaporation by vegetation treatments accurately. How can one rate, or even rank, species for annual evaporation without being able to measure evaporation directly? You may argue that water use by vegetation has been measured for decades with the neutron

Table 2. Annual rates of evaporation (E) from ventilated chambers, throughfall (T), stem flow (S) and interception (I).

Site	Vegetation	E	T	S	I
Upslope	Pasture	370 ± 50			
	E. cladocalyx	2,660 ± 140	304 ± 3	11 ± 3	184 ± 6
	E. globulus	2,690 ± 40	387 ± 18	6 ± 2	106 ± 19
	E. maculata	2,330 ± 329	371 ± 2	9 ± 1	119 ± 1
Midslope	Pasture	410 ± 30			
	E. globulus	2,210 ± 360	515 ± 30	4 ± 1	104 ± 25
	E. leucoxylon	1,840 ± 390	373 ± 24	4 ± 1	123 ± 25
	E. wandoo	1,620 ± 190	407 ± 18	12 ± 1	81 ± 18

E was measured from November 1981 to November 1982 (684 mm rainfall); T, S and I ran from February 1982 to February 1983 (499 mm rainfall); all values in mm yr. -1. After Greenwood et al. (1985a).

probe and in some situations that may be sufficient. However, where substantial uptake of water also occurs at the phreatic (saturated) zone then the neutron probe alone will be misleading.

Historically, vegetation has been used to manipulate groundwater in such crude projects as the draining of malarial swamps and the clearing of riparian vegetation to conserve water for rural water supply (Gatewood et al. 1950). The most thoroughly researched, precise and successful example of the use of revegetation to reclaim saline farm land is the establishment of the deep-rooted alfalfa on recharge in the Northern Great Plains in USA referred to earlier (Brown et al. 1983).

In any new salinity project, how does one develop a rationale for reclamation? What are the essential questions to be asked? What information is required before undertaking a reclamation project? The following sections outline generalized answers to these questions.

QUANTITY OF GROUNDWATER TO BE DISCHARGED

First priority in planning a reclamation strategy is to estimate how much extra water reaches the water table since the new vegetation regime began. What practicable methods are available for estimating this increased recharge accurately enough for reclamation purposes? Hydrologists have used the response of groundwater level, the water budget method and tracer techniques to estimate increase in recharge following a change in vegetation.

If the annual rise in water table elevation and volume of water per unit of rise are known, then the increased quantity of groundwater can be estimated. However it is difficult to obtain reliable values if the aquifer medium is variable. The water budget approach is a cumbersome procedure with, often, uncertain results. A third approach to measuring recharge which shows great promise is the use of tracers. These may be dyes, natural tracers such as chloride ion, or isotopes. These alternatives have been briefly reviewed by Nulsen (1986).

Another approach is to measure annual evaporation from remnants of the pre-salinity vegetation in the landscape. Concurrent measurement of evaporation from pre- and post- salinity vegetation will provide an estimate of increased recharge to the water table though changes in runoff need also to be measured. Appropriate methods for measuring evaporation are described in a later section.

LOCATION OF VEGETATION IN THE LANDSCAPE

When planning the reclamation of dryland salinity it is useful to divide the landscape of the catchment into two elements. One is the recharge area where the cause of salinization lies; the other is the discharge area where the effects are evident. The reason for separating these two elements is that they require quite different treatment. There has been controversy as to which element should be given priority in reclamation. I believe both should be treated but that for the recharge area is mandatory.

There are two approaches to reclamation treatment of recharge areas. One is to use a species whose annual evaporation is only a little greater than the one to be replaced. It would need to be established over most of the recharge area to be effective. On the other hand, if the treatment vegetation has a much higher rate of evaporation than the original it may not be needed over the entire area of recharge.

The recharge area is important for reclamation. It is at the seat of the problem and the vegetation performs better because of the lower salinity, and deeper rooting there. Where vegetation with higher evaporation is established it follows that there will be less drainage to the watertable. It would be especially effective if such treatment vegetation was capable of sending roots down to the phreatic, or saturated, zone of the soil (phreatophytes) because of the permanent supply of water. It frequently occurs that upslope the aquifers are unconfined (the watertable is free to rise and fall), whereas downslope impermeable or semi-permeable hard pans (aquitards) may occur which tend to prevent the aquifer from forming a free watertable. Leaks in such confining layers are the route by which the saline aquifer discharges to the surface under pressure where evaporation concentrates the salt to form the bare, highly erodible hillside seep.

The presence of aquitards in the discharge area also affects the biology of reclamation. Roots cannot

220

penetrate the confining layer (Fig. 5), and even if they could, they encounter groundwater which may be both saline and anoxic. In contrast, vegetation growing over the recharge area can use water from seasonal perched aquifers as well as the permanent saline aquifer, and there is a potential for deep rooting systems to develop. In other words conditions are good for optimizing water uptake.

However not all seeps develop over confined aquifers and Malcolm and co-workers (Malcolm 1982, Malcolm 1986, Runciman 1986) have developed productive halophytic pastures on saline discharge areas where a watertable is near the surface. Such land management might be considered simply as a means to produce an income from land otherwise devastated by salinity. But such plants also help to lower the saline watertable (Greenwood and Beresford 1980) and to that extent they must also be considered as assisting reclamation as well as producing income. However, halophytes have a limited ability to use water for two reasons. One is that they are heavily defoliated by economic grazing and so possess a small evaporating surface. The second is that high salt concentrations inhibit water uptake (Hylckama 1974).

How can we apply the above ideas to the location of high-evaporation vegetation in the landscape? First it must be decided, if possible, which of the two aquifers (permanent or seasonal - perched) is responsible for the formation of dryland salinity. Let us take two examples of successful reclamation viz. Brown et al. (1983) who reclaimed saline discharge areas by growing alfalfa on the recharge areas already cited and Biddiscombe and co-workers in Australia (Biddescombe et al. 1981, 1985a, 1985b, Rogers 1985) who used high-evaporation eucalypt plantations. They established two multi-species eucalypt plantations, each 1.5 ha, in a 26 ha catchment in 1976. One catchment was upslope and over an unconfined, permanent, saline aquifer with a watertable some 5-8 m deep. The other plantation was midslope where the permanent aquifer was partly confined except, supposedly, where it leaked to form a saline seep. The plantation was established around, and partly in, the seepage area. By 1986 the seepage area had been reclaimed in that it no longer discharged in the six-month dry season and the salt-sensitive <u>Trifolium subterraneum</u> pasture, formerly present, had re-established. This was in contrast to

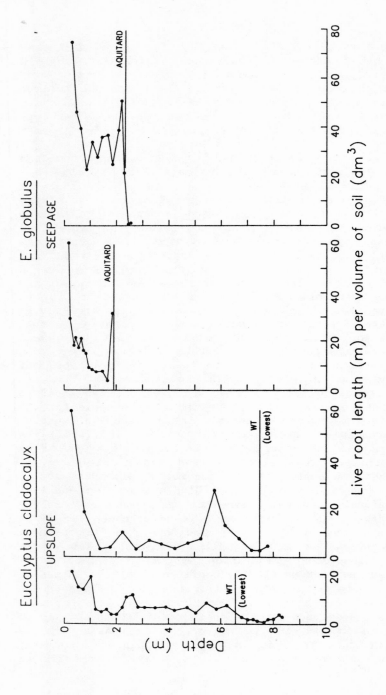

Fig. 5. Live root length vs. depth of two Eucalyptus species in upslope and seepage areas. WT = water table. Greenwood et al. unpublished.

222

similar untreated seepage areas on the farm. What was the contribution of each of these strategically placed plantations to that reclamation?

Annual evaporation, measured from the three best species in each plantation, was very high in both plantations, averaging about three times the rainfall upslope and 2.5 times midslope near the seep by the seventh year. It can be seen in Table 2 that rainfall interception, though large, was not the major source of evaporation. This implies that very large quantities of water were discharged by transpiration.

One statement can be made with some certainty on the basis of the root profiles from these plantations (Fig. 5). The roots of the plantation by the seep must have drawn heavily on the perched seasonal aquifer since they did not penetrate the confining layer. It was also found that the salinity of the perched aquifer increased from 200 mg 1^{-1} above the plantation to 2000 mg 1^{-1} at the lower edge of it. This concentration may have been the combined result of salt exclusion discussed in an earlier section and the leaking deeper groundwater.

The large source of water transpired by the upslope plantation would come from the deep unsaturated zone of the soil and the perched and permanent aquifers. The proportion of annual transpiration which came from each of the two aquifers cannot be established with certainty since the levels of watertables in both systems had still not fallen by the time the seep had been reclaimed.

You may be disappointed that I chose such a complex and inconclusive, albeit successful, example of reclamation. Two points are made in explanation. First, there are very few well documented cases from which to select. Second, it is extremely difficult to draw confident conclusions from the evidence of measured hydrologic parameters because of the immense sampling problems. The comment applies to both examples in this section. Indeed, in some dryland salinity systems the vegetative cause may extend back 100 km from the salt-affected land (Jenkin 1981). In such cases, landscapes have to be treated on a regional and even sometimes on a continental scale.

Given that the appropriate part of the catchment on which to plant high-evaporation vegetation has been decided, there are several ways in which it might be distributed. These include one large plantation, several smaller plantations, the wide rows of agroforestry or a maximum-dispersion grid or simply, "park land" spacing.

On purely hydrologic grounds, and assuming roots are at or near the watertable the factor most limiting evaporation will be atmospheric energy. On those grounds, maximum dispersion would be the most effective distribution. But problems of land use may override these considerations and one of these factors may be the management of the plants themselves. Some of the other factors will emerge in later sections.

CHOICE OF SPECIES

The selection of the treatment vegetation is complicated by several conflicting constraints - climate, soils, marketable products, technology, economics and traditions. This section is confined to the criteria for selection for the hydrologic task of reducing the recharge of groundwater. The underlying requirement therefore is to choose species with superior water harvesting and evaporating surfaces. Plants with shallow roots transpire less than plants with deeper roots. The data of Brown et al. (1983) show that, over a wide range of crop and grassland species, water use is proportional to root depth. Grazed annual pastures evaporate less than annual crops because leaf area is kept low by grazing. Defoliation also reduces root growth (Greenwood et al. 1974) and presumably, root depth. Annuals tend to evaporate less than perennials because annuals tend to have a shorter leaf area index duration and shallower roots. Ground vegetation evaporates less than trees. The elevated canopy of trees can make better use of advective energy of the atmosphere, which leads to greater evaporation from wet leaves (rainfall interception) and to higher vapour pressure deficits (evaporative demand). Deciduous trees may evaporate less than evergreens because, like annual herbs, they have a shorter leaf area duration. This applies especially to trees at a low altitude and in a climate with wet winters. Non-phreatophytes transpire less than phreatophytes because of a more limited water supply. This may be modified if the salinity of the saturated zone is high or if the depth to the phreatic surface is great (Hylckama 1974), or if the oxygen content is low.

224

It follows that, in general, the most effective type of vegetation hydrologically for recharge areas would be a phreatophytic, evergreen tree of high leaf area index, assuming adequate groundwater in the long term. Halophytes are essential for discharge areas. There is a wide range among halophytes to use groundwater as judged by canopy density. However, it seems from Malcolm (1982) that there has been no study of comparative water use in halophytic shrubs.

EXTENT OF REVEGETATION

The extent of revegetation required will differ between the discharge and the recharge areas. It is axiomatic that the whole of the salt-affected area should be revegetated if a productive (of income) halophyte can be established. Ideally, on-seep revegetation maximizes income, improves appearance (property value), minimizes soil erosion from continuous waterlogging and contributes to the reduction of saline outflow into the regional drainage system. The ultimate success of the total reclamation treatment would be that eventually the halophytes could be replaced by more valuable salt-sensitive species.

For the recharge component of the landscape there are two options. It can be devoted entirely to broad-scale crops or forages which have higher water use than the current vegetation. Alternatively high water-use vegetation can be interspersed with the current species as discussed in the previous section. In that case, three items of information are required to estimate the extent of treatment. These are: the expected annual rate of evaporation by that vegetation, the quantity of groundwater to be removed, and the size of the recharge area.

It is obvious then that a rational strategy for reclamation is impossible without the ability to measure each of the above quantities.

MEASUREMENT OF EVAPORATION

The first step in measuring evaporation is to decide which technique to use, since there are several quite

225

different methods. The main considerations are those of scale of operation, accuracy, practicability and cost.

The scale of operation can be as small as a few square centimetres if a leaf porometer is used; it can be a square kilometre for aerodynamic methods. Eventually one might expect of remote sensing that it will use sensors which scan whole regions for evaporation. So the first decision to make is the scale best suited to the particular exercise in salinity reclamation.

At first it may seem reasonable to call for a fairly large scale to cope with the areas which are sometimes involved with salinity, but that can be avoided in practice. For the scale of measurement is only one of several decisions to be made early in planning vegetation strategy, in particular, the choice of species and the part of the landscape to be treated. So it is not necessarily large areas, but rather trial plots of candidate species in several locations that may well be the initial scale of operations. Thus the scale may be that of agronomy or arboretum plots ranging say from 0.1 to 10 ha.

The method best suited to small plots is the ventilated chamber (Greenwood et al. 1985, Reicosky and Peters 1977, Dunin and Greenwood, 1986). For the larger scale, provided the terrain is subdued, the Bowen ratio and associated energy balance equipment is the most appropriate method (McIlroy 1980, McIlroy and Dunin 1982). A third method, applicable to trees of all ages is the recently improved thermo-electric heat pulse device (Cohen et al. 1981, Edwards and Warwick 1984). While the ventilated chamber and Bowen ratio methods measure total evaporation (from soil surface, wet foliage and transpiration) the heat pulse measures transpiration only as it passes through the sapwood in the tree trunk.

References to other methods of measuring evaporation from vegetation have been collated (Greenwood 1986).

COST OF REVEGETATION

It is generally thought that revegetation is costly, particularly in countries where the cost of labor is high. This is no longer true. Revegetation projects which have been abandoned because the cost could not be recovered should be re-examined.

226

The main costs of establishing trees and shrubs have been seedling production in nurseries, labor for planting, fencing for the exclusion of livestock and lost or deferred economic return. It is often unnecessary to establish shrubs and trees as seedlings, as many species also establish as well, or better, from seed. Research in Australia, often initiated and promoted by farmers themselves, indicates that highly effective establishment can be achieved through the minor modification of conventional crop-sowing equipment. But each species of seed and each type of soil may need individual investigation. The reward for such research is great. For large-scale reclamation, an infrastructure needs to be established either commercially or by government in order to bring together sources of seed, sowing equipment and expertise. A special case is the development of seed production and contract sowing equipment for halophytes which has the potential to transform large areas of arid and semiarid saline waste land in Australia (Malcolm 1986, Malcolm and Allen 1981).

The above developments have almost eliminated the labour content of revegetation. This may be irrelevant for countries with abundant labor for early feasibility studies. But once a regional scheme of revegetation has been justified then manual methods may prove to be too slow.

LEAD TIME TO RECLAMATION AND LIKELIHOOD OF SUCCESS

When forests are felled, the full hydrologic effect commences in the first year as seen in Fig. 4 (Sharma and Williamson, 1984). In the reverse process of reclamation it may take several years for trees to reach their full capability (Greenwood and Beresford, 1979). Crops, on the other hand may reach their full potential in the first year of sowing.

Even when full evaporation capability has been developed, evidence of the reclamation process may not be visible for several years. Two processes must take their full course before saline areas may again support salt-sensitive vegetation. First, the rising saline water table must be checked and eventually begin to fall below the current level of the salt store in the soil profile. The second process is the leaching of salt from

227

the soil surface by rain for perhaps several years after the saline water table has retracted to a safe level. Reclamation can be expedited by increasing evaporation and one way of doing this is to increase the proportion of land treated. The work of (Loh 1985) illustrates this point clearly (Table 3).

Is it possible to estimate in advance the degree to which a proposed strategy of reclamation will be physically successful? The estimation success is dependent on the initial hydrogeologic and vegetative investigations. Such studies are costly and may take several years. Against this must be placed the urgency for reclamation and the potential resistance to the proposals by the land users. Thus there may arise for the land manager the multiple dilemma of the delay, cost and uncertainty of, and resistance to, reclamation strategy and the possibility of devastation if nothing is attempted.

CONCLUSIONS

Procedures which enhance the likelihood of success of revegetation of dryland salinity fall into two categories - those which define the problem and those which deal with the logistics of resolving the problems. Not all salinity problems require formidable treatment. The occurrence of hillside saline seeps at certain points in the landscape may need minimal research for their treatment. I recommend that researchers and managers concentrate initially on hydrology and geophysics. The next steps are to locate the recharge area of the rising saline aquifer and measure its base-flow rate, locate the store of salt by electromagnetic induction, and measure water use (including rainfall interception by trees and shrubs). A multi-disciplinary approach is important.

Table 3. Reductions in groundwater levels for different degrees of reforestation.

Portion Replanted	Stem Density		Reduction in Annual Minimum Levels (meters)	Species Planted	Stand Age (years)
	Initial (stems/ha)	June 84 (stems/ha)			
80%	1200	1200	2.2	E. camaldulensis E. wandoo	6
50-60%	900	600-900	1.3	E. camaldulensis E. wandoo	6
31%	625	625	0.6	E. wandoo E. rudis	5
42-55%	900	150-300	0.5	E. camaldulensis	6
6-20%	667	667	0.3	E. wandoo E. camaldulensis P. radiata P. pinaster	7

After Loh (1985). Reprinted with permission.

229

LITERATURE CITED

Barrett-Lennard, E.G., C.V. Malcolm, W.R. Stern, and S.M. Wilkins, editors. 1985. Forage and fuel production from salt-affected wasteland. Reclamation and Revegetation Research 5:1-3.

Biddescombe, E.F., A.L. Rogers and E.A.N. Greenwood. 1981. Establishment and early growth of species in farm plantations near salt seeps. Australian Journal of Ecology. 6:383-389.

Biddescombe, E.F., A.L. Rogers, E.A.N. Greenwood and E.S. De Boer. 1985a. Growth of tree species near salt seeps, as estimated by leaf area, crown volume and height. Australian Forest Research 15:141-154.

Biddescombe, E.F., A.L. Rogers, H. Allison and R. Litchfield. 1985b. Response of groundwater levels to rainfall and to leaf growth of farm plantations near salt seeps. Journal of Hydrology. 78:19-34.

Brown, P.L., A.D. Halvorson, F.H. Siddoway, H.F. Mayland and M.R. Miller. 1983. Saline-seep diagnosis, control and reclamation. United States Department of Agriculture, Agricultural Research Service. Conservation Research Report No. 30.

Cohen, Y., M. Fuchs and G.C. Green. 1981. Improvement of the heat pulse method for determining sap flow in trees. Plant and Cell Environment 4:391-397.

Dimmock, G.M., E. Bettenay and M.J. Mulcahy. 1974. Salt content of lateritic profiles in the Darling Range, Western Australia. Australian Journal of Soil Research. 12:63-69.

Doering, E.J. and F.M. Sandoval. 1976. Hydrology of saline seeps in the Northern Great Plains. Transactions of the American Social Agricultural Engineering. 19:856-865.

Dudal, R. and M.F. Purnell. 1986. Land resources: salt affected soils. Reclamation and Revegetation Research. 5:1-9.

Dunin, F.X. and E.A.N. Greenwood. 1986. Evaluation of the ventilated chamber for measuring evaporation from a forest. Journal of Hydrological Processes 1. in press.

Edwards, W.R.N. and N.W.M. Warwick. 1984. Transpiration from a kiwifruit vine as estimated by the heat pulse technique and the Penman-Monteith equation. New Zealand Journal of Agricultural Research. 27:537-543.

Engel R., D.J. McFarlane and A.J. Street (in press). Using geophysics to define recharge and discharge areas associated with saline seeps in South-Western Australia. In: M.L. Sharma, editor. Groundwater Recharge Estimation. July 1986. A. Balkema Publishing Co., Amsterdam.

Gatewood, H.S., T.W. Robinson, B.R. Colby, J.D. Hem and L.C. Halfpenny. 1950. Use of water by bottom land vegetation in the lower Safford Valley of Arizona. Water Supply Paper 1103. U.S. Geological Survey, Washington, D.C.

Greenwood, E.A.N. 1986. Water use by trees and shrubs for lowering saline groundwater. Reclamation and Revegetation Research 5:423-434.

Greenwood, E.A.N. and J.D. Beresford. 1979. Evaporation from vegetation in landscapes developing secondary salinity using the ventilated-chamber technique. I. Comparative transpiration from juvenile Eucalyptus above saline groundwater seeps. Journal of Hydrology 42:369-382.

Greenwood E.A.N., and J.D. Beresford. 1980. Evaporation from vegetation in landscapes developing secondary salinity using the ventilated-chamber technique. II. Evaporation from Atriplex planatations over a shallow saline water table. Journal of Hydrology 45:313-319.

Greenwood, E.A.N., Z.V. Titmanis and N.A. Campbell. 1974. The effects of defoliation on emergent annual grass swards under simulated grazing. Journal of the British Grassland Society 29:37-45.

Greenwood, E.A.N., J.D. Beresford and J.R. Bartle. 1981. Evaporation from vegetation in landscapes developing secondary salinity using the ventilated-chamber technique. III. Evaporation from a Pinus radiata tree and the surrounding pasture in an agroforestry plantation. Journal of Hydrology 50:155-166.

Greenwood, E.A.N., J.D. Beresford, J.R. Bartle and R.J.W. Barron. 1982. Evaporation from vegetation in landscapes developing secondary salinity using the ventilated-chamber technique. IV. Evaporation from a regenerating forest of Eucalyptus wandoo on land formerly cleared for agriculture. Journal of Hydrology 58:357-366.

Greenwood, E.A.N., L. Klein, J.D. Beresford and G.D. Watson. 1985a. Differences in annual evaporation between grazed pasture and Eucalpytus species in plantations on a saline farm catchment. Journal of Hydrology 78:261-278.

Greenwood, E.A.N., L. Klein, J.D. Beresford, G.D. Watson and K.D. Wright. 1985b. Evaporation from the understorey in the jarrah (Eucalyptus marginata Don ex Sm.) forest in Southwestern Australia. Journal of Hydrology 80:337-349.

Hingston, F.J., and V. Gailitis. 1976. The geographic variation of salt precipitated over Western Australia. Australian Journal of Soil Research 14:319-335.

Hylckama, T.E.A. van. 1974. Water use by salt cedar as measured by the water budget method. Professional paper 491E, US Geological Survey, Washington, D.C.

Jenkin, J.J. 1981. Terrain, groundwater and secondary salinity in Victoria, Australia. Agricultural Water Management 4:143-171.

Loh, I.C. 1985. Stream salinity control by increased transpiration of vegetation. Water authority of Western Australia. Internal Report.

Malcolm, C.V. 1982. Wheatbelt salinity. A review of the salt land problem in South Western Australia. Western Australian Department of Agricultural Technical Bulletin. No. 52. pp. 1-65.

Malcolm, C.V. 1986. Production from salt affected soils. Reclamation and Revegetation Research 5:343-361.

Malcolm, C.V. and R.J. Allen. 1981. The mallen niche seeder for plant establishment on difficult sites. Australian Rangelands Journal 3:106-109.

McIlroy, I.C. 1980. Routine measurement of evaporation from land surfaces. Pages 88-95: in hydrology and water resources symposium. Institution of Engineers, Australia Conference, Adelaide.

McIlroy, I.C. and F.X. Dunin. 1982. A forest evaporation technique comparison experiment. Pages 12-17. in the first national symposium on forest hydrology. Institution of Engineers, Australia Conference, Melbourne.

Nulsen, R.A. 1986. Management to improve production from salt affected soils. Reclamation and Revegetation Research 5:197-209.

Peck, A.J. and D.H. Hurle. 1973. Chloride balance of some farmed and forested catchments in southwestern Australia. Water Resources Research 9:643-657.

Reickosky, D.C. and D.B. Peters. 1977. A portable chamber for rapid evapotranspiration measurements on field plots. Journal of Agronomy 69:729-732.

Rogers, A.L. 1985. Foliar salt in Eucalyptus species. Australian Forest Research 15:9-16.

Runciman, H.V. 1986. Forage production from salt affected wasteland in Australia. Reclamation and Revegetation Research 5:17-29.

Sharma, M.L. and D.R. Williamson. 1984. Secondary salinization of water resources in Southern Australia. Pages 571-580 in R.H. French, editor. Salinity in Watercourses and Reservoirs. Butterworth Publishers, Stoneham, Massachusetts, U.S.A.

Swanson, R.H. and D.W.A. Whitfield. 1981. A numerical analysis of heat pulse velocity theory and practice. Journal of Experimental Botany 32:221-239.

Williams, B.A. and D. Hoey 1987. The use of electromagnetic induction to detect the spatial variability of the salt and clay contents of soils. Australian Journal of Soil Research 25:21-27.

10. Multifactorial Reconstruction of Semiarid Mediterranean Landscapes for Multipurpose Land Uses

ABSTRACT

The complex landscape mosaics of semiarid Mediterranean uplands have been shaped by closely interwoven natural and cultural processes as multivariate anthropogenic functions. In these, agro-pastoral land-use impacts were major driving forces. The harsher and more fragile the independent state factors of soil parent material, relief, climate, hydrology and biota, the more far-reaching was the human impact on dependent vegetation, soil and functional/structural ecotype variables. In most landscapes a long-term homeorhetic flow equilibrium has been established between regeneration and degradation processes, leading to unique spatio-temporal dynamics and heterogeneity and ensuring evolutionary metastability and resilience. With present accelerating anthropogenic degradation, the removal of inherent natural and cultural negative feedbacks is leading to total landscape desertification. Therefore, such destroyed ecosystems cannot be restored anymore, but can be rehabilitated by multifactorial state factor modification to ensure the optimization of multi-beneficial production, regulation and carrier functions for multiple land uses. This interdisciplinary and multidimensional nature of conservation and reconstruction research and their implementation requires a holistic landscape ecological approach.

INTRODUCTION

Throughout its history from the Pleistocene until present times the Mediterranean Basin has endured long-lasting and intensive human impacts. In no other region - and especially in its drier parts - has the unfortunate combination of a vulnerable environment and a long history of man's misuse of the land caused so far-reaching and severe soil erosion, landscape desiccation and desertification. Nowhere else are the dangers of the combined traditional and modern technological pressures by accelerating populations, tourists and urban-industrial developments more threatening than in semiarid uplands.

But, at the same time, because of these long lasting and severe human pressures, nowhere else - at least in comparable climatic and ecological conditions - can the striking resilience, regeneration powers and soil-building and protecting capacities of the native vegetation be demonstrated better than on the denuded Mediterranean uplands.

This chapter attempts to show how an integrated landscape ecological approach should be applied to the reconstruction of these deteriorating uplands. For this purpose neither the restoration of a non-existing natural pristine state nor of an illusionary climax can serve as models. But they could be reclaimed or rehabilitated, according to Bradshaw and Chadwick (1980) by activities which seek to bring them back into beneficial use, by rehabilitating biological potential. In these uplands rehabilitation should be reconciled with the socio-economic advancement of their populations by incorporating multipurpose land uses.

For this purpose I shall first outline briefly some of the major holistic paradigms of landscape ecology on which this reconstruction should be based.

LANDSCAPE ECOLOGY - THE SCIENTIFIC BASIS FOR LAND RECONSTRUCTION

Landscape ecology emerged after World War II in Central and Eastern Europe as an interdisciplinary branch of contemporary ecology and geography. It can be regarded as a significant attempt of academic and professional ecologists, geographers, planners, agronomists, foresters, conservationists, landscape architects and other land managers to replace the narrow discipline-oriented and reductionistic tendencies in their professions by integrative, holistic approaches. During the last twenty years in Eastern and Central Europe landscape ecology became the major unifying force for landscape appraisal, planning, management, conservation and restoration. It is already taught in many universities and practiced in governmental and other institutes.

By dealing with landscapes in their totality as ecological and cultural entities, landscape ecology has transcended the purely natural realm of classical biology and ecology. It is becoming more and more a global, transdisciplinary human ecosystem science (Naveh 1982). At the same time, with the growing involvement of scientists from North America and other countries, it is broadening its conceptual and methodological scope for coping with the complex spatio-temporal heterogeneity. This includes both functional and structural landscape heterogeneity and flows between elements of the landscape (Forman and Godron 1986).

The _ecotope_ is an efficient conceptual and methodological tool for landscape ecological research which bridges the gap between natural, agricultural and urban systems. It is used by European landscape ecologist as the smallest holistic landscape entity (Zonneveld 1972). Naveh and Lieberman (1984) have further defined the ecotope as the smallest space-time defined _concrete ecosystem_. In the classification of ecosystems, of which the ecotopes are their study sites, they distinguished between _bio-ecosystems_ and _techno-ecosystems_. The former are driven by biological conversion of solar energy by autotrophic organisms and self-regulated by biological and physico-chemical information. But the latter are man-made urban-industrial systems, driven by technological conversion of fossil and nuclear energy and their positive feedback loops with human scientific, technological, socio-economical and political information. They are, therefore, growing exponentially on account of the bio-ecosystems. The _biosphere_ can be considered as the largest, global bio-ecosystem, and the _technosphere_ as the largest, global landscape and concrete system of the

Total Human Ecosystem. However, presently, on a global scale the biosphere as a whole and its cybernetic feedback systems with the geosphere, and especially the atmosphere, are threatened by the expansion of the technosphere and its unrecycled waste products.

In Figure 1 a simple model of the ecosphere landscapes of our Total Human Ecosystem is presented. It shows the missing feedback loops of the technosphere with the biosphere and the geosphere and its one-sided impacts on both.

Man, as a biological creature, is dependent for his existence on the viability of natural and agricultural ecosystems and their life supporting, protective and regulative functions. Therefore, the uncontrolled, exponential growth of the technosphere and its outputs is endangering our global survival (Odum 1971, Ehrlich and Ehrlich 1981, Vester 1976). Landscape ecology can contribute to the urgently needed full integration of the biosphere and technosphere by providing these missing regulative feedbacks through science and education. These should lead to holistic land appraisal and study, planning and management, conservation, and reconstruction.

The reconstruction of ecotopes of degraded and disturbed bio-ecosystems and their life-supporting functions should be considered as a vital part of our attempts to ensure the sustain ability of our Total Human Ecosystem ecosphere. In a broader, philosophical sense of environmental ethics, landscape reconstruction can contribute to the urgently needed reconciliation between society and nature at the critical interface of land use.

ECOLOGICAL CHARACTERISTICS OF SEMIARID
MEDITERRANEAN UPLANDS

Great parts of the mountainous and hilly uplands around the Mediterranean Basin, especially in the coastal foothills and lower mountains can be considered semiarid. These generally receive between 400-600 mm precipitation with great intra- and interseasonal variability. Rainfall occurs mainly between October and April with tendencies of violent autumn and winter rainstorms after the long summer drought, creating severe erosion on bare and denuded slopes. This is also the typical

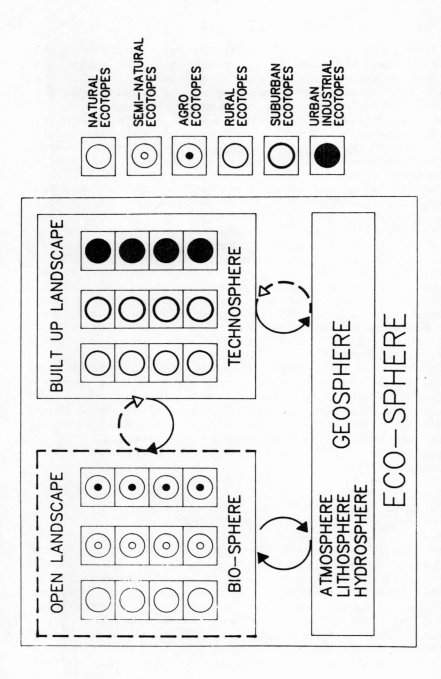

Fig. 1. Biocybernetic regulation of the Total Human Ecosystem landscapes.

"Mediterranean fire-bioclimate" in which great acute fire hazards prevails during 150-200 days (Naveh 1986a and Oechel, this volume).

Mediterranean landscapes gained their present high, sharp folded and faulted geomorphological forms of mountain and hills, often rising close to the coast, by violent uplifting in the late Tertiary and early Quaternary periods. Sedimentary limestones of varying hardness predominate the geological base of the region. Being highly dissected and complex, with many steep slopes and shallow and rocky soils, they are very vulnerable to sheet and gully erosion if their protective natural canopy is denuded and their shallow soil mantle is exposed to desiccation in the dry summer and to torrential rains in winter (Bradbury 1973).

Natural vegetation has remained only on non-tillable uplands, too steep and too rocky for cultivation, and makes up 50-80% of the total area in most Mediterranean countries. The soils are highly complex and varying in depth, but most are shallow and heavily eroded, especially those which were terraced, cultivated and later on neglected (Naveh and Dan 1973). Of these, most abundant are rather fertile and well-structured terra rossa soils, derived from hard limestone and dolomite of Upper Cretaceous and Tertiary rocks and rendzinas, derived from soft limestone with hard calcareous Nari crusts. Much poorer are the highly calcareous pale rendzinas derived from soft limestone, chalk and Eocenic marls, which are abundant in the East Mediterranean, as well as non-calcareous brown soils derived from granitic rock, sandstone and metamorphic rocks which are abundant in the West Mediterranean.

These Mediterranean uplands are part of the so-called Sclerophyll Forest Zone, in which broadleaved and chiefly evergreen trees and shrubs with thick but mostly leathery leaves ("sclerophylls") reach their optimum development and distribution. Their closest ecological counterparts outside the Mediterranean are the broadleaved sclerophyll shrublands and woodlands in central and southern California and in similar bioclimatic regions in central Chile. Although of low economic value, these shrublands and woodlands have great ecological importance for environmental and watershed protection of the densely populated valleys and coastal regions. They are dominated by Quercus calliprinos ("Kermes oak") in the eastern Mediterranean and by Q. coccifera in the western Mediterranean. Here, in the most favorable conditions well developed sclerophyll forests dominated by Q. ilex can be found.

Most of these sclerophyll trees and shrubs are distinguished by dual root systems spreading both horizontally and penetrating deep into rock cracks, and by resprouting after fire, grazing or cutting, they also respond favorably to pruning and coppicing on one stem. If resprouting from suckers is prevented by recutting or browsing, they soon attain the stature of small trees. Thereby, closed one-layered, very fire-prone and unproductive shrub thickets can be converted into rich, multilayered park-like groves and woodlands. This, apparently, was the way sacred oak groves have been created in cemeteries, which have mistakenly been regarded as remnants of "climax oak communities".

In the coastal foothills and lower mountain elevations in the slightly drier and warmer region the natural potential vegetation has a park-like nature, dominated by scattered Ceratonia siliqua, the highly valuable carob tree or by Olivea europea, the native olive tree, with a rich shrub and grass understory, dominated by Pistacia lentiscus, the eumediterranean "mastic". This evergreen shrub combines low palatability and great drought resistance and limestone tolerance with vigorous regeneration powers after fire and cutting and serves us as an ecological and bio-engineering model for rehabilitation and slope stabilization (Yogev and Naveh 1986). It is one of the last shrubs to survive over large areas of overgrazed, depleted, mosaic-like shrub-grassland with low or non-palatable early maturing annuals (Whittaker and Naveh 1979). However, if these pressures are released, a striking vegetative recovery of woody plants occurs, together with a very species-rich productive grass cover.

Another important formation in drier parts consists of deciduous oak woodlands of Quercus ithaburense in Israel and Q. macrolepi in Turkey, very much resembling the Blue oak (Q. douglasii) woodlands in California. Here, a very species-rich, productive grass and legume understory can be maintained under moderate grazing pressures. However, by overgrazing or by too light grazing or prolonged, full protection, species diversity is reduced, and tall, aggressive grasses and perennial thistles take over (Naveh and Whittaker 1979).

Most productive herbaceous, natural pastures can be found in even drier submediterranean conditions on fertile rendzinas and basaltic soils, rich in phosphate and therefore conducive to vigorous growth of many valuable pasture plants. The highly calcareous pale rendzinas, as well as the poor brown soils from granitic rocks, sandstone and metamorphic rocks are much lower in fertility and highly erodible. On these, the herbaceous plants are dominated by xerophytic phanerophytes and chamephytes, including many unpalatable, aromatic Labiatae and also Cistus species (called "Batha" in Israel and "Phrygana" in Greece). Being favored by frequent burning and heavy grazing, these occupy large areas in many Mediterranean countries. Their conversion into more productive ecosystems should be considered, therefore, as a major rehabilitation challenge.

THE EVOLUTION OF THE SEMI-NATURAL AND AGRO-PASTORAL MEDITERRANEAN LANDSCAPE

Full comprehension of the nature of present Mediterranean landscapes and their restoration can be attained only by understanding their evolution and dynamics as an integral part of the Mediterranean Total Human Ecosystem. This evolution coincided with the major phases of cultural transition of primitive man from hunting and food-gathering Homo erectus to intensive food collecting Homo sapiens and finally to food producing Homo sapiens from the Middle Pleistocene onwards. As a closely coupled dynamic process of physical, geomorphological, biological and cultural evolution it lead first to the creation of semi-natural landscape ecotopes and then, with accelerating speed to semi-agricultural and agro-pastoral ones. This process can therefore, rightly, be called after Di Castri (1981) "the co-evolution between Mediterranean man and landscape".

The Mediterranean geoflora evolved since Cretaceous times in the borderlines between temperate and tropical floras and as a mixture of both predecessors. The sclerophyll woody species were apparently best preadapted to the new climatic patterns of increasing drought and lowering winter temperatures that developed during the

Pleistocene. Most herbaceous species evolved in this period, now constituting up to 50% of all species (Pignatti 1978).

The shaping of these landscapes took place in the Quarternary in highly dynamic situations of climatic fluctuations, tectonic and volcanic activities with increasing diversification of local site conditions. Raging fires, heavy ungulate and other herbivore grazing pressures and increasing human modifications played, most probably, an important evolutionary role as selection forces. As described in detail for Mt. Carmel in Israel (Naveh 1984b), fire was used not only for heating and cooking, but also for food collecting and hunting in order to open dense forests and shrublands and for the creation of more accessible and richer ecotopes for man and his game (Perles 1977).

The final stages of this "co-evolution" started several thousand years later from the neolithic period onwards. By domestication of crops, livestock, and fruit trees, and from the Iron Age onward also by terracing and cultivation of the upland slopes, man modified the semi-natural landscapes and converted them into man-dominated, intensively utilized agro-pastoral ones.

According to recent palynological findings (Bottema and van Zeist 1981), the landscape desiccation in the early Holocene was caused chiefly by these increasing agro-pastoral land pressures. The use of fire for slash-burn cultivation of the lowland forests and for the improvement of upland pastures, combined with grazing, cutting, and coppicing, continued and further intensified the Pleistocene defoliation pressures and encouraged further interspecific variation and the invasion of more xeric elements of herbaceous and woody colonizers, best adapted to these combined natural and cultural perturbations.

At the same time, the natural woody vegetation was apparently left for soil protection along terrace walls. These and the scattered favorable microsites between rock outcrops were planted with fruit trees, and protected from grazing animals by thorn and stone fences. As we can learn from biblical and talmudic Hebrew sources and from historical Greek and Roman sources, very intensive, multiple, and mostly conservative use could be made of the rough terrain.

But, on the other hand, catastrophic soil erosion, flooding and siltation, leading to badlands and swamp formation, occurred as the result of the abandonment and neglect of the terrace walls and the disintegration of their local base levels in periods of political upheaval, warfare and depopulation. This was the case during the decline of the Roman Empire and again after the downfall of the Byzantine Empire during many centuries, especially in the Levant (Reifenberg 1951, Vita-Finzi 1969, Naveh 1986a, Thirgood 1984, Baruch 1983).

Recent palynological findings in both Israel (Baruch 1983) and in the western Mediterranean (Pons 1981) indicate that during periods of intensive agricultural activities and land use pressures by dense populations, the natural woody vegetation receded with the extension of cultivated crops, especially olives. But it increased again during periods of instability, and agricultural and population decay, such as the last period of the Ottoman Empire until World War I.

THE DYNAMIC AGRO-PASTORAL FLOW EQUILIBRIUM AND ITS PRESENT DISTORTION

Throughout the long history of agro-pastoral utilization, the semi-natural and pastoral ecotopes of open forests, shrublands, woodlands, and grasslands, and the agricultural ecotopes of terraces, patch- and hand-cultivated rock polycultures, became closely interwoven dynamic landscape mosaics. The transfer of fertility (through grazing) and of seeds (through grazing, wild herbivores and insects), created ideal conditions for introgression and spontaneous hybridization of wild and cultivated plants and biotypes, as well as for the evolution of genotypes with high adaptation to this man-modified habitat (Zohary 1969). Selection pressure most probably favored the survival of species and ecotypes with the highest resilience to the combined impact of environmental rigor and defoliation pressures by maximizing their adaptive feedback responses (Naveh 1974, Naveh 1984b).

Two main factors contributed to the global stability and persistence of these ecotopes, even under heavy human pressures, the great variation in space and time (namely microsite and floristic diversity), and the short-term, mostly cyclic, seasonal and annual climatic fluctuations.

In the traditional Mediterranean pastoral systems, great seasonal and annual fluctuations in productivity (Naveh 1982b) apparently prevented overgrazing. The numbers of livestock which could be supported during critical periods of low food availability in early winter and in drought years were not sufficient to overgraze pastures during the spring flux of growth and seed setting and in wet years. This can be compared to the self-regulation of natural wildlife populations, depending in their food supply solely on the natural vegetation. At the same time, over-cutting and over-burning were prevented by burning and coppicing rotations necessary to ensure sustained productivity and sufficient recovery.

In those upland ecotopes that were neither over- nor under-used, these regular grazing, burning and coppicing regimes led to the establishment of a man-maintained dynamic flow equilibrium (sensu Waddington (1975), and explained below) of regeneration and degradation patterns between the woody and herbaceous components (Naveh and Dan 1973). Superimposed on the great macro- and micro-site heterogeneity of the rocky and rough terrain it induced the floristically and structurally very rich and metastable patch dynamics in space and time, which contributed much to the striking biological and ecological diversity and attractiveness of the open Mediterranean landscapes and became their most important asset for recreation and tourism (Di Castri 1981).

These landscapes resemble in many aspects the shifting mosaic landscape dynamics, recently described by Forman and Godron (1986), for systems exhibiting a pattern of long-term change (in our case changes of land-use patterns during historical times) and along with short-term, internal spatial conversion (in our case climatic fluctuations and cultural rotational cycles).

The closely interwoven environmental and cultural processes which shaped Mediterranean landscapes for many thousands of years can be best described as multivariate anthropogenic functions. These have created the above mentioned, complex and highly dynamic degradation and regeneration patterns which do not fit any of the deterministic successional models. Contrary to the classical "facilitation model" (Connell and Slatyer 1977), most secondary successions after abandonment of cultivation on uplands are arrested at early grass or dwarf shrub stages. By contrast, the regeneration of the "climax" sclerophylls is chiefly an auto-successional process by vegetative resprouting from stunted or burned plants. It may occur also by direct invasion of abandoned orchards, vineyards and pine groves and it is facilitated by birds and rodents and the shade of these trees. But it is evidently not preceded by "seral" stages of dwarf and tall shrubs (Debussche et al. 1982, Naveh 1986b).

During historical times, these multivariate anthropogenic functions became a series of man-driven degradation and regeneration cycles, each lasting for several hundred years, according to the duration of the historical land use periods. But presently urban-industrial, recreational and other neo-technological impacts, combined with either the intensification of agro-pastoral land uses or with their complete cessation through abandonment or replacement by pine or eucalyptus afforestation, have disrupted this dynamic equilibrium of the recent, traditional agro-pastoral functions. Their inherent natural and cultural regulative feedbacks have been replaced by accelerating degradation functions which endanger the future of the open Mediterranean landscape (Ambio 1977, Di Castri 1981, Naveh 1986a).

A DYNAMIC, MULTI-FACTORIAL APPROACH TO MEDITERRANEAN LANDSCAPE DYNAMICS AND RECONSTRUCTION

Following Vogl (1980), semiarid Mediterranean shrubland and grassland ecotopes can be defined as semi-natural perturbation dependent-systems. In these ecotopes natural and human caused perturbations may help to ensure stability and increase structural and floristic diversity. If they are regularly but not catastrophically disturbed by man, his livestock and ax, they do not progress in deterministic, successional stages, toward a homeostatic stationary climax but maintain a dynamic flow process or "homeorhesis" (from the Greek, for "preserving the flow"). This term was coined by the eminent geneticist and science philosopher Waddington (1975) for multifactorial, evolving systems to denote evolutionary stability, or the preservation of the flow process of the evolutionary pathway of change through time. This stability is not concerned with preserving the measure of some system components at a constant value, as in homeostatic systems, but it acts to ensure that the system goes on altering in the same way that it has been altering in the past.

Waddington (1975,1977) used topological models of attractor surfaces with three dimensions as applied in catastrophe theory. These present multidimensional space, occupied by the innumerable variables simultaneously controlling these dynamic processes. Their surfaces have the shape of valleys with stabilized streams as canalized pathways of changes, or "chreods" (from the Greek for "necessary path"). The diversification processes through time are simulated by the branching of the single first valley into several smaller streams, thereby creating the "epigenetic landscape" of a river plan, shown in Figure 2. The points of measurement of the component at any given time are symbolized by little balls rolling on the valley bottom. The change going on through time in the system, controlling the development, can be presented as a "catastrophe" by bending the attractor surface, thereby displacing the ball and letting it fall either into a lower chreod or out of the chreod. Thus, the broadness of these chreod valleys describes the response of the developing system to fluctuation, affecting it - or in other words, the local stability. In Fig. 2b the ball was displaced from A to A' and first attracted back to the attractor surface, hitting the hillsite somewhere up the side up the valley (B). Running down the valley bottom, it will have some momentum to continue in this direction. It will, therefore, not run straight down the hillside to the nearest place on the valley bottom, but will run down at a slant, reaching the bottom (C) somewhere ahead of where it started.

Mediterranean bio-ecosystems and their concrete landscape ecotopes apparently meandered in a very broad chreod river plain, as long as their developmental dynamics were governed by the traditional agro-pastoral biofunction. But with the disruption of this homeorhetic flow equilibrium they are presently pushed out of the chreod over the watershed by accelerating neo-technological degradation functions. The disruptions include also abandonment and protection, causing the decline of biological diversity, productivity and global stability.

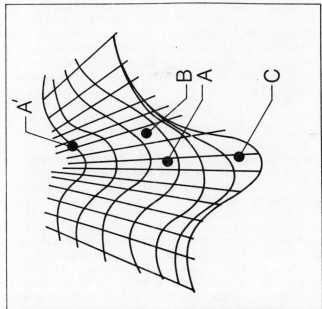

B

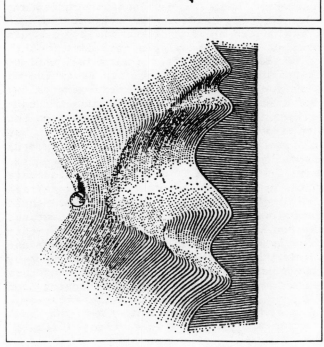

A

Fig. 2. Topological models of homeorethic flow equilibrium along stable pathways of chance ("chreods") in epigenetic landscape. For an explanation for 2B see text (After Waddington, 1975, 1977).

The harsher and/or more fragile are the independent state factors of soil parent material, relief, climate, hydrology and biota, the more severe and far reaching are these human impacts on dependent functional and structural ecotope variables. Therefore, the farther they are pushed away from their chreods, the sooner total landscape desertification will be reached.

CONCLUSIONS

Relating these findings to the practical problems of landscape restoration, it is obvious that our main challenge lays in the re-establishment of the multifactorial flow process that ensured the metastability and resilience values of these Mediterranean upland ecotopes.

But at the same time, rehabilitation should also be considered within the broader context of the complex problems of Mediterranean upland utilization. For this reason it must become an integral part of comprehensive regional and national landscape development masterplans based on interdisciplinary landscape ecological research and management, which are still in their infancy in this region. Restoration and rehabilitation projects will be most successful if they are coordinated with legislative, administrative, political and - above all - educational efforts to overcome the severe socio-economical constraints and the indifference, shortsightedness, ignorance and greed at all levels of decision making.

In order to reconcile the conflicting demands of nature conservation with the aspirations of local populations and regional and national interests, restoration should be aimed at maximum attainable ecological, social and economic benefit by optimization of "hard" and "soft" landscape values and their production, protection, regulation and carrier functions (Naveh and Lieberman 1984).

This multifactorial, holistic approach to landscape restoration can be illustrated in a semi-formal way by following the functional-factorial approach introduced by Jenny (1980) as a generalized ecotope restoration equation, $E_{s, v, \ldots} = f\ H_{re}(P,R,C,O,T\ldots)$, where $E_{s, v,}$ are the dependent ecotope variables of soil (fertility, structure etc.), vegetation (biomass, diversity, vitality etc.) as a function of H_{re}, namely, human restoration activities as the dominant driving force. H_{re} is modified by all other physical and biotic ecotope state factors, such as the initial physical state factors of soil parent material (P) and relief (R) (by terracing, fertilizing, mulching), the driving fluxes of climate (C) and organisms (O) (by irrigation, mulching and by seeding and planting, inoculation with mycorrhiza and rhizobia, restocking with browsing ungulates etc.). T is the time or duration of this restoration function, according to site conditions and intensity of modification, and the ellipsis points (...) represent other undefined dependent variables and state factors.

In multifactorial restoration of degraded landscapes of <u>nature</u> <u>reserves</u> <u>and</u> <u>parks</u>, the prevention of destructive processes caused by mass recreation pressures and accumulation of large amounts of highly inflammable fuel, should be combined with the restoration of ecological processes, ensuring protection, regulation and carrier functions and maximum attainable ecological diversity (Ricklefs et al. 1984). This will require the controlled manipulation of the plant-animal complex by optimum defoliation pressures of grazing, cutting, and burning.

However, in <u>highly</u> <u>disturbed</u> <u>ecotyopes</u> such as denuded slopes of roadsides or camping and picnic grounds we can no longer rely on natural regeneration processes and our main concern is to achieve rapid and efficient environmental rehabilitation and stabilization by the multifactorial reclamation of ecotope state factors. Here, our aim should be to establish semi-natural, multistructured and stable plant communities, resembling as far as possible their less disturbed counterparts in similar sites.

For this purpose a process of condensed natural succession that contains two strategies can be simulated: 1) the establishment of rapidly spreading and low resource demanding, indigenous "pioneer" grasses, legumes and low cover shrubs with dense foliage canopies for rapid soil protection and erosion control, and 2) the simultaneous planting of taller, but slower growing and more demanding but persistent, deep rooting shrubs and trees with maximum soil ameliorating effects. Wherever feasible and necessary, agro-technical and biological means, such as fertilizer, mulching, inoculation with mycorrhiza and rhizobia, etc., should be applied.

For the rehabilitation of degraded ecotopes in the open landscape, for multi-purpose agro-pastoral and sylvicultural land uses, additional means can be applied to raise the biological and economical production potentials by reseeding, fertilizing, selective weed control and agro-forestry. In the latter case, the aim should be to create semi-natural, multi-layered park-like forests. These should resemble the richest Mediterranean semi-open forests and woodlands in structure, diversity and stability, but have greater social and economical values and greater fire hazard resistance.

Our studies in the last 15 years showed that this can be achieved by replacing inferior indigenous plants by more valuable and similarly hardy drought and limestone tolerant, introduced shrubs and trees (Naveh 1975, Naveh 1978, Naveh and Lieberman 1984).

In highly disturbed, devastated and derelict areas, such as denuded slopes of quarries, and roadsides outside nature reserves, exotic plants could be used, if they fulfill the following conditions: 1) they should be superior in their multi-beneficial ecological, bio-engineering and ornamental values to indigenous plants, and 2) they should be able to thrive, like the hardiest native plants with minimum horticultural care and irrigation. At the same time, however, great care has to be taken to avoid the use of local as well as exotic plants which can become troublesome weeds. This was the case with Spartium junceum, an attractive indigenous flowering legume shrub, which initially showed much promise because of its rapid establishment in harsh sites (Naveh 1975). But after a couple of years, it started to spread from volunteering seedlings and to encroach on all other trees and shrubs. At the same time, the older shrubs became senescent, infested with smuts and highly inflammable.

In revegetation trials in the foothills of the Lower Galillee we used methods similar to those for the establishment and maintenance of pine forests in Israel. But instead of planting such highly inflammable, monospecific pine forests, we attempted to convert degraded rocky slopes into multiple use recreation and fodder forests with the help of plants from three major ecological groups:

250

(1)   Fast growing, soil protecting low cover
subshrubs which can replace and compete successfully with
dwarfshrubs like _Sarcopoterium spinosum_ and herbaceous
weeds in the drier, rockiest and/or highly calcareous
micro-sites. Among these are _Rosmarin officinalis_, a
highly ornamental and valuable honey plant from the West
Mediterranean; _Myoporum mulyiglotum_, a very prostrate,
highly ornamental and fire resistant cover plant from
Australia, and _Atriplex glauca_, a valuable fodder shrub
from Australia.

(2)   Deep-rooted, evergreen or summergreen, taller
shrubs for slightly more favorable micro-sites. These
are faster growing, more palatable and productive and
have higher ornamental and multipurpose values but
similar drought and limestone tolerance, regeneration
capacities after fire and grazing and soil amelioration
properties, like the indigenous sclerophylls. Most
promising among these are _Cotoneaster franchetti_ and _C._
pannosa, ornamental shrubs from China, which proved
themselves as highly palatable and productive fodder
shrubs; _Atriplex nummularia_, one of the most valuable
limestone-tolerant fodder shrubs from Australia which
also competes successfully with _Sarcopoterium spinosum_
under heavy goat grazing on highly calcareous, poor
rendzinas, and several promising _Acacia_ species from
Australia, combining fodder value with wood and
ornamental values.

(3)   Slower growing but peristent tall shrubs and
trees for the most favorable micro-sites which have high
fodder and/or forest and ornamental potentials and can
serve also as shade trees in recreation forests. Here,
local trees, like _Ceratonia siliqua_ (Carob tree),
Quercus calliprinos, _Q. ithaburensis_, _Pistacia atlantica_,
Cercis siliquastrum and several Australian _Acacia_ trees
show great promise.

In order to ensure the greatest possible overall
benefit from these often clashing land use demands,
flexible multi-purpose strategies should be applied
according to site potentials and local and national
requirements. This could be realized in practice by the
creation of closely interwoven networks of multiple land
use patterns. For this purpose, flow charts of
management strategies and cybernetic models of the mutual
impacts of these options and their production, protection

and regulation functions and environmental variables should be prepared.

From such models and a preliminary balance sheet of cost/benefit it already became apparent that the highest overall multiple use benefits can be expected for environmental and watershed protection, fire hazard resistance, biotic diversity and wildlife, recreation amenity, forest production, and water yields for aquifers from semi-natural, multi-layered park-forests. Because of their overwhelming impact, managerial interests in maximal forestry and livestock production should be weighed carefully against interests in all other expected benefits. On the other hand, increase in water yields from aquifers can hardly be regarded as a principal managerial goal of land use: it should be viewed only as a desirable by-product in certain types of land use. Recreation, because of its potentially negative impacts on vegetation and on soil, should be handled with care. Excessive recreation pressures will conflict not only with forestry and livestock production, but also with certain protective functions to which highest priority should be given in any Mediterranean restoration, rehabilitation and landscape development scheme.

Some of the most promising local and introduced plants for these purposes, which have proved themselves in our previous studies, are already used in afforestation and reclamation projects in Israel, but we are still far from large-scale application of these principles in Israel or elsewhere in the Mediterranean. For this purpose, Multiple-Use Management Areas or Managed Resource Areas (IUCN 1978) in Biosphere Reserves are especially suitable. Such a combined conservation and reconstruction strategy should be promoted both on the international and national level, as a major vehicle for inducing lasting and far-reaching, desirable changes in Mediterranean upland use, especially if they will be combined with demonstration, research and training in MAB projects.

In conclusion, the complex multifactorial nature of Mediterranean upland reconstruction requires an innovative, holistic approach. This should embrace all ecological, socio-economical and cultural aspects on a multidimensional scale from the smallest ecotope to the largest total human ecosystem landscape unit.

ACKNOWLEDGMENT

This study was supported by the Fund for Promotion of Research of the Technion.

LITERATURE CITED

Ambio. 1977. The Mediterranean (Special Issue) 6.

Baruch, V. 1983. The Palynology of Late Holocene Cores from Lake Kinnereth. Hebrew University, Jerusalem, Dept. Archeology (Hebrew).

Bottema, S. and W. van Zeist. 1981. Palynological History of the Near East. Pages 11-123 in J. Cauvin, and P. Sanlaville, editors. Prehistoire du Levant. CNRS, Paris.

Bradbury, D.E. 1981. The Physical Geography of the Mediterranean Lands. Pages 53-67 in F. di Castri, W. Goodall and R.L. Specht, editors. Ecosystems of the World II. Mediterranean-type Shrublands. Elsevier Scientific Publishing Company, Amsterdam, Oxford, New York.

Bradshaw, A.D., and M.J. Chadwick. 1980. The Restoration of Land. Blackwell Scientific Publication, Oxford.

Connell, J.H. and R.O. Slatyer. 1977. Mechanisms of succession in natural communities and their role in community stability and organization. The American Naturalist 111:1119-1144.

Debussche, M., J. Escarre and J. Lepart. 1982. Ornithochory and plant succession in Mediterranean abandonded orchards. Vegetatio 48:255-266.

di Castri F. 1981. Mediterranean-type Shrublands of the World. Pages 1-52 in Ecosystems of the World II-Mediterranean-type Shrublands, F. di Castri, F., W. Goodall and R.L. Specht editors. Elsevier Scientific Publishing Company, Amsterdam, Oxford, New York.

Ehrlich, P. and A. Ehrlich. 1981. Extinction. Ballantine Books, New York.

Forman, R.T.T., and M. Godron. 1986. Landscape Ecology John Wiley and Sons, New York, Chichester.

Jenny, H. 1980. The Soil Resources, Origin and Behaviour. Springer Verlag, New York.

International Unit for Conservation of Nature and Natural
Resources. 1978. Categories, objectives and criteria
for protected areas. Commission on National Parks and
Protected Areas. International Unit for Conservation
of Nature and Natural Resources, Gland Switzerland.

Naveh, Z. 1973. The ecology of fire. Pages 131-170 in
R. Kommarek, editor. Proceedings 13th Tall Timbers
Fire Ecology Conference, Tallahassee Florida March
1973.

Naveh, Z. 1974. The evolutionary significance of fire
in the Mediterranean region. Vegetatio 29:199-208.

Naveh, Z. 1975. The degradation of Mediterranean
landscapes and their restoration with drought resistant
plants Journal of Landscape Planning 2:139-146.

Naveh, Z. 1978. A model of multi-purpose ecosystem
management for degraded Mediterranean uplands.
Environmental Management 6:57-64.

Naveh, Z. 1982a. Landscape ecology as an emerging
branch of human ecosystem science. Advances in
Ecological Research 12:189-237.

Naveh, Z. 1982b. The dependence of the productivity of
a semi-arid Mediterranean hill pasture ecosystem on
climatic fluctuations. Agriculture and Environment
7:47-61.

Naveh, Z. 1984a. Resilience and homeorhesis of
Mediterranean shrublands. In 4th International
Conference on Mediterranean Ecosystems (MEDECOS).
Perth, Australia. (Unpublished manuscript)

Naveh, Z. 1984b. The vegetation of the Carmel and Nahal
Sefunim and the evolution of the culture landscape.
Pages 23-63 in A. Ronen, editor. The Sefunim Cave on
Mt. Carmel and its Archeological Findings. B.A.R.,
Oxford.

Naveh, Z. 1986a. Pasture and Forest Management in the
Mediterranean Uplands. Pages 55-73 in H. Finkel,
editor. Semi-arid Soil and Water Conservation. CRC
Press, Inc. Boca Raton, Florida.

Naveh, Z. 1986b. A Critical Appraisal of the Climax-
Succession Theory in the Mediterranean, Unpublished
Manuscript.

Naveh, Z. and J. Dan. 1973. The Human Degradation of
Mediterranean Ecosystems. Pages 320-390 in F. di
Castri and H.A. Mooney, editors. Mediterranean Type
Ecosystems, Origin and Structure. Springer Verlag,
Berlin.

Naveh, Z. and R.H. Whittaker. 1979. Structural and floristic diversity of shrublands and woodlands in Northern Israel and other Mediterranean areas. Vegetatio 41:171-190.

Naveh, Z. and A.S. Lieberman. 1984. Landscape Ecology-Theory and Applications. Springer Verlag, New York.

Odum, E.H. 1971. Fundamentals of Ecology. Third Edition, W.B. Saunders Company, Philadelphia.

Perles, C. 1977. Prehistoire du Feu. Masson, Paris.

Pignatti, S. 1978. Evolutionary trends in Mediterranean flora and vegetation. Vegetatio 37:175-185.

Pons, A. 1981. The History of the Mediterranean Shrublands. Pages 131-138 in F. di Castri, F., W. Goodall and R. L. Specht, editors. Ecosystems of the World II, Mediterranean-type Shrublands. Elsevier Scientific Publishing Company, Amsterdam.

Reifenberg, A.N. 1955. The Struggle between the Desert and the Sown. The Rise and Fall of the Levant. The Jewish Agency, Publication Department, Jerusalem.

Ricklefs, R.E., Z. Naveh, and R.E. Turner. 1984. Conservation of Ecological Processes. Commission of Ecology Paper 8, International Unit for Conservation of Nature and Natural Resources, The Environmentalist 4, Supplement No. 8.

Thirgood, J.V. 1981. Man and the Mediterranean Forest. Academic Press, London.

Vita-Finzi, C. 1969. The Mediterranean Valleys. Geological Changes in Historical Times. Cambridge Press, Cambridge.

Vester, F. 1976. Urban Systems in Crisis. Understanding and Planning of Human Living Space; The Biocybernetic Approach. Deutscher Verlag, Stuttgart.

Vogl, R.J. 1980. The Ecological Factors that Produce Perturbation-dependent Ecosystems. Pages 63-94 in J. Cairns Jr., editor. The Recovery Process in Damaged Ecosystems, Ann Arbor Science Publishers, Ann Arbor, Michigan.

Waddington, C.H. 1975. The Evolution of an Evolutionist. Cornell University Press, Ithaca, New York.

Waddington, C.H. 1977. Tools for Thought. Paladin Granada Publication, Frogmore, England.

Whittaker, R.H., and Z. Naveh. 1979. Analysis of Two-Phase Patterns in Plant Communities. Pages 21-47 _in_ G.P. Patil and M.L. Rosenzweig, editors. Statistical Ecology Series, Vol 12. International Publishing House.

Yogev, I., and Z. Naveh. 1986. The effect of fertilizing and mulching on the establishment of _Pistacia lentiscus_ in limestone debris. Pages 403-412 _in_ Proceedings, Third International Conference of the Israel Society for Ecology and Environmental Quality Sciences. Jerusalem, 1-4 June 1986.

Zohary, D. 1969. The progenitors of wheat and barley in relation to domestication and agricultural dispersal in the old world. Pages 42-66 _in_ J. Ucko and G.W. Dimple, editors. The Domestication and Exploitation of Plants and Animals. Aldine, Chicago.

Zonneveld, I.S. 1972. Textbook of Photo-Interpretation. Vol. 7, Chapter 7. International Institute for Aerial Survey and Earth Sciences (ITC), Enschede, Netherlands.

11. Ecological Approaches in Theory and Practice: To What Degree Is Reconstruction Possible?

This volume is meant to offer new insights to both practitioners and theorists of ecological land reconstruction, but in many instances the meeting point between theory and practice is not defined. Some of the chapters contain information that can immediately be used by practicing reclamationists, while others present concepts that must be further tested before they will be readily accepted, or before the technology or reclamation machinery is developed to apply them. This concluding chapter will review the potential for application of some of the ecological approaches, and discuss the degree to which ecological reconstruction is possible.

The practical is emphasized in the chapter by DePuit and Redente, which examines the effects of different cultural practices and site preparation on ecosystem development. Many of these practices (e.g., topsoiling, fertilization) are already well known and widely used, but their effects on succession are only beginning to be understood. Greenwood also takes a practical approach in suggesting that the high transpiration rates of native vegetation, especially phreatophytes, can be used to advantage in reclaiming salinized soils with high water tables. He admits that there is little empirical evidence that this will always succeed, so further research and field trials are important in the application of this technique.

Prairie restoration provides examples of the oldest man-made natural vegetation in the United States, some more than 50 years old (Burton et al.). The authors relate a number of case studies and techniques used to

recreate prairie ecosystems. At the same time they
discuss some of the basic ecological tenets, such as
niche partitioning, which restorationists need to
understand to recreate diverse plant communities. This
basic understanding is important in all aspects of the
restoration process, from choosing co-adapted species to
planting in the proper sequence.

The chapters by Bell and Oechel cover some basic
processes related to seed reserves and seedling
establishment that are important to reconstruction.
Bell's research has immediate application for the
reclamationist who wishes to increase species diversity
by taking advantage of natural seed reserves and the seed
rain. The low seedling water potentials that Oechel
found in the chaparral point to the need for further
research on seedling water relations. How much to
irrigate, if at all, is always a concern of the
reclamationist. Knowledge of the minimum critical soil
moisture level required for seedling establishment would
help determine irrigation levels. Where irrigation is
not possible, this information would assist in species
selection and in predicting the success of seedling
establishment during years of variable precipitation.

At the opposite end of the scale from individual
plant establishment is landscape reconstruction. A
central theme of Naveh is that ecosystem reconstruction
should be suited to the ability of a site to support a
vegetation type, a point which is echoed by Burton et al.
and Greenwood. There is a tendency in reclamation to use
a uniform seed mixture across slopes and soil types
because of perceived economic constraints or lack of data
on appropriate seed mixtures which are adapted to certain
sites. Inappropriately chosen seed mixtures will
decrease productivity and stability across a landscape.

Whitford gives an example of current reclamation
practices that do not result in successful reclamation.
The low diversity grass stand, which was planted in dense
rows using a seed drill, declined in productivity,
decomposition rates, and key microorganisms. He suggests
that we must manage for appropriate microorganisms, as
the reclamation species that are chosen may not have the
same associated microbial species as vegetation that may
be present on the site. The need to manage
microorganisms is echoed by E. Allen, who demonstrated
that inoculation with mycorrhizal fungi will alter the

outcome of succession. The study and management of soil microorganisms still constitutes one of largest gaps in our knowledge of disturbed land reconstruction.

An innovative approach to the reestablishment of microorganisms and natural levels of soil fertility in arid land is taken by M. Allen. Plants in arid lands are more widely dispersed than in mesic lands, and form natural "islands of fertility." Nutrients, organic matter, microorganisms, and animals tend to accumulate in these islands. Current reclamation practices do not attempt to simulate this dispersed pattern, but rather, as in the study by Whitford, use row plantings that may be too dense for arid lands. Allen maintains that long-term stability and productivity are dependent on reconstructing these islands of fertility. Dispersed plantings of arid land shrubs are done mainly to attract wildlife in the western United States, but these are considered small scale, expensive restoration practices. Successful field experiments of dispersed plantings are the first step in demonstrating to practicing reclamationists that such an approach is necessary in arid lands. Hand planting of shrubs in dispersed patterns is still expensive, so appropriate techniques or machinery will need to be developed.

While even the most theoretically based chapters lend themselves to some immediately practical ecological approaches, they also have another feature in common. To some extent each author discusses the question, to what degree can arid lands be reconstructed? As defined in the introductory chapter, the goal of reconstruction varies from restoration of the original ecosystem to a similar (reclamation) or different, but useful (rehabilitation) ecosystem. The problem of an appropriate reference area as a guideline to assess a restored or reclaimed ecosystem is discussed (Burton et al., Naveh). The choice of reference area remains a central problem for restoration of ecosystems that have largely disappeared due to overuse, and also for reclamation of mined lands that are subject to reclamation legislation. In many cases the original native ecosystems have been disturbed to such an extent that the small remnant patches probably do not represent undisturbed vegetation. According to Naveh, pristine vegetation is nonexistent. Therefore, managers will necessarily make somewhat arbitrary decisions as to what constitutes "restoration."

Reconstruction efforts may result in ecosystems that are similar or dissimilar to the predisturbance site, depending on the degree of disturbance (E. Allen). No reconstruction efforts are required at all in relatively mild disturbances such as fire, where natural succession occurs rapidly (Oechel). True restoration requires intensive inputs of time and money (Burton et al.). In the opposite extreme, DePuit and Redent present case studies of severely disturbed lands that can be neither restored or reclaimed, but they also show examples of practices that promote rehabilitation. It is no longer possible to restore severely desertified Mediterranean lands, but rehabilitation to some useful state is possible (Naveh). The inability to reclaim or restore lands may be related to changes in microorganisms that we currently cannot control (Whitford, M. Allen). An inability to produce commercially available propagules of all desired plant species also reduces the ability to restore land. Even the utilization of residual or colonizing propagules does not assure restoration of the full complement of species (Bell). The notion of restoring the function of arid lands without necessarily using the same plant species appears throughout the book. This is ideally the goal of reclamation. For instance, the large-scale hydrologic function may be restored by choosing appropriate phreatophytes (Greenwood). Below ground functioning may be restored by choosing plant species that encourage the establishment of desirable microorganisms, e.g., nitrogen fixers (Whitford). Natural levels of fertility as well as microorganisms may be restored in an arid system by planting species with appropriate root arditectunes in appropriate spatial patterns (M. Allen). Field demonstrations using structurally similar species to restore function are underway by these authors. In summary, the authors agree that some degree of reconstruction is possible, and that rehabilitation or reclamation are feasible, but economic and ecological factors limit the ability to restore ecosystems.

The optimistic outlook of each of these authors, plus numerous other published and unpublished successful reconstruction attempts, is a reversal of early predictions of the difficulties of arid land

260

reconstruction. Lands that receive fewer than 240 mm precipitation were once considered impossible to reclaim (NAS 1974). Many of the general concepts presented are applicable to mesic as well as arid lands (e.g., a landscape approach, use of residual propagules and natural succession). These, coupled with others that are specific to arid lands (e.g., moisture requirements of seedlings, simulating natural dispersion of arid land plants) are presented here to help form a basis for economic reconstruction of even the most arid of disturbed lands.

LITERATURE CITED

Natural Academy of Sciences. 1974. Rehabilitation Potential of Western Coal Lands. Ballinger Publ. Co. Cambridge, Massachusetts.

About the Contributors

Edith B. Allen is adjunct professor in the Department of Biology and the Systems Ecology Research Group at San Diego State University. Previously, she was research assistant professor in the Department of Range Science and director of the Institute for Land Rehabilitation at Utah State University. Her major research interests include plant community and physiological ecology; succession; plant competition, water relations, and nutrient uptake; and restoration of disturbed arid lands. She has received a number of research grants and served as officer for various professional groups. She has written numerous papers on plant interactions and succession, mycorrhizae and arid lands, and ecological restoration. She received a B.A. magna cum laude in Biology and German from Tufts University, a M.S. in Botany from Rutgers University, and a Ph.D. in Botany from the University of Wyoming.

Michael F. Allen is associate professor in the Department of Biology and the Systems Ecology Research Group at San Diego State University. His area of major research interest is fungal ecology, particularly the spatial and temporal dispersion of fungi and their relationship to nutrient dynamics during succession. He has presented and published many papers on mycorrhizae, disturbed ecosystems, arid lands, and plant succession. He has received a number of grants to study plant-microbial interactions in grasslands; reconstruction of arid ecosystems; and the role of mycorrhizae in competition, succession, and reversing desertification. He has been active in various professional societies, and he has been awarded several academic honors. He received a B.S. in Biology from Southwestern College in Kansas, and he received M.S. and Ph.D. degrees in Botany from the University of Wyoming.

David T. Bell is senior lecturer in plant ecology in the Department of Botany at the University of Western Australia, Nedlands, Western Australia. His major activities include research, teaching, and consulting in the areas of plant ecology, plant taxonomy, and plant physiology. He is a certified professional ecologist and belongs to several botanical and ecological societies. He has been elected to the Royal Society of Western Australia Council since 1980, and he has received substantial government and private research support. He has lectured and published extensively on plant ecology and the impact of man and of environmental stress on plant systems. He received B.A. and Ph.D. degrees from the University of California at Santa Barbara.

Philip J. Burton is research associate in the Department of Environmental Sciences at the University of Virginia. Previously, he was technical research biologist for the Illinois Natural History Survey, Section of Botany and Plant Pathology. His specific areas of interest are vegetation dynamics, community organization, forest regeneration, and predicting vegetation change. Work that he performed on coal mine reclamation planning and monitoring in western Canada involved monitoring the productivity of range and forage lands. He has conducted research and presented and published a number of papers on land reclamation and plant succession. He has received various academic honors and belongs to several professional groups. He received a B.Sc. from the University of Saskatchewan, a M.S. from the University of Hawaii, and a Ph.D. from the University of Illinois.

Edward J. Depuit is associate professor in the Department of Range Management at the University of Wyoming. His major fields of research and teaching interest are the applied revegetation, management, and reclamation of disturbed lands; range plant synecology and autecology; and range improvements. He has provided consulting services for various corporations and government agencies, and he has served on a number of academic and professional committees. He has received substantial government, academic, and corporate support to study range ecosystems, hydrology, and reclamation and revegetation of arid and mined lands. He has written and edited numerous publications and presented papers on arid range, mined, and disturbed land reclamation and revegetation. He received a B.S. with honors from Michigan Technological University, and M.S. and Ph.D. degrees from Utah State University.

Eric A.N. Greenwood is a senior principal research scientist in the Commonwealth Scientific and Industrial Research Organisation (CSIRO) Division of Groundwater Research, in Perth, Western Australia. After work at Virginia Polytechnic Institute, he became the leader of the crop physiology and the vegetation and water balance groups at CSIRO. In recent years he has specialized in developing methods for measuring evaporation from vegetation and in research on vegetation strategy for salinity reclamation and groundwater conservation. He received a B.Agr.Sc. from Melbourne University, Australia, and a Ph.D. from Nottingham University, United Kingdom.

Louis R. Iverson is terrestrial plant ecologist for the Illinois Natural History Survey, Section of Botany and Plant Pathology. His field of special interest is the reclamation of disturbed ecosystems and use of remote sensing and geographic information systems in ecological research. He has studied reclamation sites in western North Dakota, Illinois, and Britain. He has published articles in several professional journals as well as the volume Management for Rehabilitation and Enhancement of Ecosystems (CRC Press, Boca Raton, FL, 1988). He is a member of several professional societies and was a Fulbright-Hays scholar to the United Kingdom. He received a Ph.D. degree from the University of North Dakota.

Zev Naveh is professor on the Lowdermilk Faculty of Agricultural Engineering at Technion-Israel Institute of Technology in Haifa, Israel, teaching courses in general ecology and landscape ecology. He also conducts research in agroforestry, quantitative vegetation ecology, and use of plants as indicators of air pollutants. He has served as a consultant and advisor on U.N. and government projects relating to pasture improvement and uplands development. He is curator of the Ecological Garden, and he has served on environmental committees and as ecological advisor to government agencies and professional societies. He has participated in a number of international meetings and has been awarded several honors for distinguished research. He has written and edited numerous papers, articles, chapters, and volumes on the ecosystems of arid range, pasture, and grasslands, as well as shrublands, woodlands, and uplands. He received M.Sc.Agr. and Ph.D. degrees from Hebrew University in Jerusalem.

Walter C. Oechel is professor in the Department of Biology at San Diego State University. He has conducted research for government and private foundations on the dynamics of plant ecology, including arctic, subarctic, tundra, and chaparral ecosystems. He has presented and published numerous papers and reports on such topics as carbon dioxide exchange patterns, climate factors in photosynthesis, moss production, and plant adaptation. He is a member of several professional organizations. He received an A.B. degree from San Diego State University and a Ph.D. from the University of California at Riverside.

Edward F. Redente is professor of range science at Colorado State University. He specializes in the study of restoration of disturbed lands, plant-soil interrelationships, and plant community succession. He has written numerous journal articles on reclamation and has contributed chapters to several volumes on reclamation of drastically disturbed lands. He belongs to several professional and honorary societies, and he has been awarded significant government support to conduct reclamation related research. He received a B.A. in Geography and Biology from Western Michigan University, and M.S. and Ph.D. degrees in Range Science from Colorado State Univesity.

Paul G. Risser is Vice President for Research at the University of New Mexico. He specializes in plant ecology and natural resource management. He has written journal articles on prairies and holistic management, and

he contributed a chapter on grasslands to the volume
Biodiversity (National Academy of Sciences Press,
Washington, DC, 1988). He has held office as president
of both the Southwestern Association of Naturalists and
the Ecological Society of America, and as Chairman of the
U.S. National Committee for SCOPE. He has served also on
the National Academy of Sciences Committee on Global
Change and Board on Environmental Science and Technology.
He received a B.A. degree from Grinnell College, and M.S.
and Ph.D. degrees from the University of Wisconsin.

Kenneth R. Robertson is botanist and curator of the
Herbarium for the Illinois Natural History Survey;
affiliate appointment with the Department of Plant
Biology at the University of Illinois; and a member of
the graduate faculty. His area of research
specialization includes the systematic study of vascular
plants, specifically the Rosaceae, Convolvulaceae, and
Amaranthaceae; and floristics of the southeastern United
States and Illinois. He has written many papers and
reports on these topics and on endangered and threatened
plant species, vegetation preservation and management,
and erosion. He has received an award from American Men
of Science and a number of research grants. He has been
active in various professional groups and committees. He
received B.A. and M.A. degrees in Botany from the
University of Kansas, and a Ph.D. in Botany from
Washington University.

Walter G. Whitford is professor of biology at New Mexico
State University. He has presented work at invited
seminars and symposia on various aspects of arid
ecosystem dynamics and the physiology and ecology of
various fauna. He has fulfilled a number of government
and corporate consulting contracts on environmental
impact assessment, most recently relating to the dynamics
of desert soil, soil organisms in decomposition, and
nutrient cycling. He has published widely on topics
relating to animal physiology, community dynamics, and
arid ecosystems. He is active in a number of
ecological, zoological, and other scientific societies,
and he has received several professional honors. He
received B.A. and Ph.D. degrees from the University of
Rhode Island.